The Law Of Attraction & Advanced Manifestation Techniques (2 in 1): 50+ Meditations, Hypnosis, Affirmations & Strategies To Fulfil Your Desires- Money, Love, Abundance, Weight Loss

By Spiritual Awakening Academy

The Law of Attraction& Manifestations for Happiness Love& Money

33+ Guided Meditations, Hypnosis, Affirmations- Manifesting Desires- Health, Wealth& Abundance Even During Deep Sleep

Table of Contents

Introduction

We believe in the law of gravity because we see it in action every day. We recognize the laws of physics because we can measure and test them. We understand that two like magnets repel each other while two opposite magnets attract each other. In all honesty, nature has a lot of laws; some we see in action every day and some we barely know about. However, all of nature's laws have one thing in common, they work perfectly every time.

The law of attraction is a law of nature and just like every other law of the universe, it works perfectly every time. So why do we not see people receiving their desires each day? How come people struggle every day to reach their goals and experience their life's desires? Well, the answer is simple. The law of attraction is not driven by our thoughts or utterances. The law of attraction is influenced by the powerful subconscious energy that exists beneath the surface of our conscious awareness. Even if all you ever have are positive thoughts, if your subconscious energy is not aligned with the things you want to manifest, the law of attraction cannot work for you.

So what is the answer to tapping into this infinite wealth of energy to manifest abundance, wealth, and even the love of your life? The key is to tap into your subconscious energy and reset it to reflect the things you want to manifest. You must think and believe that you are wealthy to manifest wealth. You must think and believe you are worthy of love to receive love. Everything you want to manifest must come from the belief you hold in your subconscious, become entrenched in your mind before it can manifest into reality.

If you have been looking for a way to use the powerful law of attraction to manifest wealth, abundance, good health and your desires, the insights in this book are meant for you. In the following chapters, we explore how you can use meditation to tap into the powerful energy of the universe to manifest your desires. In the first part of the book, we will show you how to tap into your subconscious energy to create the positivity you need to attract positive outcomes.

This book is for anyone who is struggling to manifest their goals, achieve abundance or secure their financial future. With the law of attraction, anyone with the desire and commitment to the process can uncover the infinite power of the law of attraction. Whether you are a novice to mediation or experienced in mindfulness, the techniques described in this book are easy to perform, straightforward forward and effective.

All you need to do to start manifesting wealth, abundance and healthy relationships is delve with us deep into relaxing guided meditation to activate the law of attraction. Happy listening!

Chapter 1: The Power of Energy

What if you could have everything you ever wanted? The love that you have always desired, good health, wealth and peace of mind. All these things are well within your reach but it takes a lot more than the desire to have the things you want. Manifesting your dreams and deepest desires starts with understanding the nature of what you constantly give life to with your thoughts and words.

Just below the surface of your conscious mind is a powerful energy that comes from your subconscious mind. Your subconscious mind acts as the filter for your memories, beliefs and experiences. This filter determines what makes it to the surface and what does not. This means that to control your conscious mind you must first be aware of your subconscious filter and the kind of energy it is projecting. When you think of manifesting the things you want, it starts with tapping into the deepest layer of your mind which is the subconscious.

The thoughts on the surface, or the ones you are consciously aware of, are only a product of the subconscious mind that you may not always be aware of. Think of your subconscious as your MacBook's RAM. This RAM quietly runs hundreds of background processes while on your screen you may only be browsing Facebook. The heavy work is taking part in the background and what appears on the surface is only a small fraction of what is going on in your mind.

Once you understand that your subconscious mind is the store of your life's energy then you can utilize the power of meditation to manifest all your dreams and goals. It is not enough to just have positive thoughts but you must delve deeper into the subconscious and change the energy that directs your thoughts. All your deep-seated emotions, habits, experiences and beliefs are stored in your subconscious. Meditation allows you to get into these deeper layers and change your thoughts and energy from the inside out.

As we begin our meditations, realize that it is through the mindfulness of meditation that you can train your mind to focus on the things you want to manifest. The things you are able to bring forth into your life are the ones that you give the most focus to. When you tap deep into your subconscious mind you can train your mind to focus on the things you want to manifest. If most of your subconscious energy is dedicated to your fears, self-limiting beliefs or the things you do not want, then it is not possible to attract the things that you want.

Use meditation as the tool to take charge of your subconscious energy and harness this energy to attract all the things you have ever wanted. Meditation will help you to dig down into the depths of your subconscious and access your mind power in all its fullness. Session by session your level of consciousness and awareness will increase making it easier to direct your energy to manifesting your desires. Naturally, we will start this session with meditations that allow you to delve deep into your subconscious.

Meditation for Tapping Your Subconscious Mind - 25 minutes

This meditation will help you to release subconscious blockages and overcome negative mind blocks.

Duration – 25 minutes

Please start by sitting in a comfortable position in a quiet room free of distractions.

Close your eyes and turn your mind inwards. Shut down all external input. Focus your mind and all your awareness on your breathing.

Feel the breath entering then living your body. Inhale deeply and exhale slowly.

As you continue with the deep breathing, feel your whole body. Start from the top of your head and work your downwards.

Feel the arch of your spine, the curves of your hips all the way down to your toes.

Continue with the deep breathing as you become aware of every part of your body. Inhale deeply and exhale slowly.

As you continue with deep breathing let everything you are feeling rise to the surface. Allow the feelings that reflect what is going on in your life at the moment to rise to the surface. Allow yourself to feel these feelings and thoughts without judgement.

Feel the innermost fears that you are too afraid to voice. Feel the hurts that you keep holding back. Open your mind completely to everything that you keep buried under the surface. Let it all come to the surface.

Acknowledge these feelings and let them wash over you.

Now take a deep breath in through the nose to a count of 6. Hold the breath and then exhale slowly through your mouth.

Take another deep breath in through your nose to a count of 6. Hold the breath and exhale slowly through your mouth.

As you exhale, feel the negative emotions start to leave your body. Release them with every breath you exhale.

Release the fear, the anger, the hurt, the regret, and all the other negative emotions weighing you down.

Feel yourself getting lighter with every negative emotion or thought that you cut loose.

Keep breathing in deeply and exhaling slowly as you free yourself from all the negative thoughts and emotions. Let them all out. Feel yourself getting lighter and more grounded with every exhale.

Allow everything that is weighing you down to leave your body with every exhale. The worries, the regrets, the hurt, the self-doubt; feel them leave your body and see them floating away from you.

Visualize and start to feel the warm rays of the sun on your face every time you exhale and release negative emotions. Feel the warmth of the sun on your face and a soft breeze gently caressing your skin.

Lean into this light and feel yourself become bathed in it.

Gradually allow your breathing to return to its natural rhythm. As you do so keep feeling the warm rays of the sun bathing you in golden light and a fresh breeze caressing your face.

Now take your right hand and place it above your chest.

Repeat this mantra:

I am enough. Today I am happy. Today I am capable. Today I am worthy.

As you say these words visualize the golden light above your head. Feel this light bathing every part of your body from your head to your toes. Give yourself up to the golden light and bask in it.

Repeat the mantra:

I am enough. Today I am happy. Today I am capable. Today I am worthy.

Now visualize your body bathed in the golden light and feel the light start to permeate your being. Let the light in and feel it spread throughout your being. Revel in it and open yourself up to it completely.

Repeat the mantra:

I am enough. Today I am happy. Today I am capable. Today I am worthy.

Now visualize your body as the source of the radiant golden light. Let this light surround you and form an aura of protection all around you.

Breathe in deeply and exhale slowly. Allow yourself to luxuriate in the light, feel it inside you and see it all around you.

You are radiating the light from deep within. Become one with the light.

Repeat the mantra

I am enough. Today I am happy. Today I am capable. Today I am worthy.

Take a deep breath. Hold it and then exhale slowly. Slowly bring your awareness back to the present. When you feel ready you can open your eyes.

This guided meditation is now complete.

Meditation to Let the Universe Guide You - 25 minutes

This meditation is to help you let the universe guide you. It will help you trust your journey and free yourself from constant worry and fear. One of the biggest blocks that keep us away from the things that we want to manifest is the constant need for control. When you are not one with the universe, you will always feel like you are rowing uphill.

If you can let go of the constant stress and worry, the universe will guide you to the things you really want. This state of being is trust and surrender in the purest form. You can repeat this meditation every time you start to feel overwhelmed, doubtful, or disconnected from the present.

So let us get into the meditation.

Duration: 25 minutes

Find a quiet space with minimal distractions for this meditation. You can do it outdoors if possible in a nice quiet spot or indoors.

We will be doing this meditation barefoot so start by taking off your shoes.

Now stand in a comfortable position with your legs and arms in a relaxed stance.

Gently close your eyes and as you do that shut everything else but the awareness of your breathing.

Inhale deeply through your nose then exhale slowly through your mouth.

As you continue to take deep breaths, focus on the feeling of the ground beneath your feet. Bring your awareness to the ground beneath your feet. Focus on feeling grounded and connected to the earth beneath your feet.

Continue with the deep breathing with your mind and awareness focused on the connection between your feet and the ground beneath.

Feel the energy rising up from the ground into your body. Continue to breathe in deeply as you focus on feeling more grounded and connected to the earth through the ground that you are standing on.

Breathe in and feel your body relax, knowing that there is something beneath you holding you up. Feel the connection between your feet and the ground.

Keep taking deep breaths and exhaling slowly allowing your body to sink more and more into a relaxed state.

Now put your hands gently over your heart and take another deep breath in followed by a slow exhale.

Slowly bring your awareness to the top of your head. As you focus your awareness on this part of your body, visualize a warm glow on your forehead. Visualize this glow as a ray that is bathing you in its light and energy.

As the glow lights up your forehead, you start to feel lighter and more relaxed. Now slowly move your awareness down to your cheeks and your neck. As your awareness shifts downwards, let the glow follow suit.

Visualize the ray of light traveling down your body slowly. From the top of your head, down to your chest, your abdomen, your hips, your legs and finally your feet.

Visualize this ray loosening up every part of your body as it travels down. Your head feels lighter, your neck and shoulders are more relaxed.

Let the light relax all your muscles and feel the clean and invigorating energy emanating from the ray of light.

Bask in its glow and feel the heaviness slowly leave your body bit by bit.

You are lighter now, nothing is weighing you down and you are keenly aware of the ground beneath your feet.

You are present in the moment and all that matters is the here and now. Everything that you do not serve you is leaving your body and you feel lighter and lighter.

As you visualize the ray of light traveling all the way down to your feet, take a deep breath and slowly exhale.

Bring your awareness to your right foot and then the left feet that are now bathed in a warm glowing light.

Feel your feet get lighter as negative energy is released from your body to the ground beneath you.

Visualize the fears, the worries, the regrets all flowing out of you and being soaked up into the ground beneath you.

Start to feel lighter as all the negative energy drains downwards into the ground. You are now fully bathed in the warm glow of the ray of light. It is surrounding you and you feel relaxed and at peace.

In this moment, think of your happy place. See it in vivid detail. Feel yourself in this place where nothing and no one can hurt you. Look around you, listen to the sounds and immerse yourself in the experience. You feel at home here, you are safe, you are happy, you are at peace.

Breathe in deeply and feel connected to everything you see around you. Notice the sensations that you are feeling now, look around and observe the things that are surrounding you. This is where you belong, your inner sanctuary.

Visualize yourself walking around in this happy place. Your step is confident and you feel calm and at peace with yourself. Immerse yourself fully in this vision. You see everything that you want and everything that you need. It's all there for you.

As you let yourself soak everything in, repeat this mantra:

Everything I want is within my reach. I already have everything I need. I am one with the universe.

Take a deep breath and again savor your sanctuary and let yourself feel the freedom and peace of having all the things you ever wanted.

Repeat the mantra:

Everything I want is within my reach. I already have everything I need. I am one with the universe.

Inhale deeply and exhale slowly.

Now slowly start to bring your awareness back to the present. Lower your arms from your heart and let them fall back gently to your sides.

Take a deep breath in then gradually allow your breathing to return to normal.

Slowly open your eyes.

This meditation is now complete.

Shifting Consciousness -15 minutes

For most people, the problem is not in not knowing what they want but rather in not knowing how to shift focus from what they do not want. The law of attraction helps you manifest the things that you focus on most. So if you constantly focus on the things you do not want, you will keep manifesting them. The trick, therefore, is to learn to shift your consciousness from what you are trying to avoid or get away from to what you want. It is more important to know what you want rather than what you do not want.

So, if you struggle with keeping your mind on the things that you should be focusing on. This meditation will help you in shifting consciousness to the things you want to manifest.

Let us start the meditation

Duration:15 minutes

Settle into a comfortable position, you can choose to sit or lie down in a quiet room free of distractions.

Eyes closed, place your right hand over your diaphragm, or the area above your navel. Allow yourself to relax and empty your mind of all thoughts.

Now inhale deeply through your nose and exhale slowly through your mouth. Bring your awareness to the rising and falling of your diaphragm as you breathe in and out.

Feel your chest rise as you inhale and feel it fall as you exhale.

Allow yourself to sink deeper into relaxation as you continue to inhale deeply and exhale slowly.

Feel the heaviness of your body begin to lift and feel yourself start to connect deeply with your emotions.

Think of the things that you are grateful for on this day. Your life, your health, your family and all the other things that make your life worth living.

Focus only on the things that make you happy and express gratitude for them.

Repeat this mantra slowly:

I am grateful for my life. I am grateful for everything in my life. I am grateful for this moment.

Continue to take deep breaths while keeping your focus on all the things that you have in your life.

Repeat the mantra:

I am grateful for my life. I am grateful for everything in my life. I am grateful for this moment.

See everything that you are grateful for clearly in your mind. If it is your spouse or your children, see their faces clearly in your mind as you voice your gratitude for them.

If you are grateful for your job see it vividly as you express your gratitude. Everything that you are grateful for, see it, feel it and allow yourself to be connected to all your blessings.

Repeat the mantra:

I am grateful for my life. I am grateful for everything in my life. I am grateful for this moment.

Continue to take deep breaths and feel the air as it enters your body when you inhale and feel it leave your body as you exhale.

With every exhale you feel lighter and more at ease with yourself.

As you continue to ease yourself into deep relaxation, repeat this affirmation:

I will step forward with love and confidence. I am moving forward with courage and grace.

Take a deep breath and exhale slowly through your mouth. Repeat the affirmation:

I will step forward with love and confidence. I am moving forward with courage and grace

As you say this affirmation feel yourself get a fresh burst of confidence as you breathe in. Let this positive energy infuse you from your head to your toe.

Feel it all over you like a soft warm blanket shielding you from the cold.

Repeat the affirmation:

I will step forward with love and confidence. I am moving forward with courage and grace.

Breathe in deeply and again feel the positive energy all around you.

Slowly open your eyes and allow your breathing to go back to normal.

This meditation is now complete.

The Science of a Positive Attitude – 15 minutes

Manifestation relies on your own thoughts and beliefs to bring into reality the things you desire the most. In this way, your thoughts become self-fulfilling prophecies that create the blueprint from which your outcomes are drawn. That is why cultivating positivity is an intrinsic part of the law of attraction and manifesting your desires.

Positive thoughts create the positive energy that you need to attract positive things into your life. That is why it is crucial to bring more awareness into the kind of energy you are putting out into the world. This is the energy that shapes your reality. To help you harness the power of positivity to manifest your desires, this guided meditation will help you train your mind to embrace positivity.

Let us start the meditation.

Duration 15 minutes

Start by finding a comfortable sitting position.

Close your eyes and let your mind and body relax. Shut out all external input and bring your awareness to your inner self.

Take deep breaths and focus on being present in the moment.

Take your time to become aware of every part of your body. Start from the top of your head and work your way down to the tips of your toes.

Take a deep breath to a count of 6, then exhale slowly through your mouth

Bring your awareness to what you are feeling and thinking in the moment. Become aware of your emotions and open yourself up to them.

Continue to take deep breaths, followed by a slow exhale through your mouth.

Now just focus on the rise and fall of your chest

Keeping your eyes closed, listen to my voice as I start to count down from ten to one.

Continue to breathe deeply in that relaxed state

When I say the number 10 I want you to visualize yourself at the top of a small staircase.

As you stand at the top, you can see the bottom of the staircase, where you can see the

most comfortable bed you have ever seen.

The bed looks fresh and inviting with fluffy pillows just waiting for you to get on the bed

As I begin to count down, take a step down the staircase to the divine bed that is waiting for you at the bottom.

With each step that you take, you will feel more relaxed and with each step, you will enter a deeper level of relaxation.

10. You are at the top of the staircase. Now take one step down and feel yourself sink deeper into relaxation. Breathe in slowly and exhale slowly

9. Take the next step down and as you do see the bed at the bottom get even closer.

8. Another step, you are becoming more limp and loose.

7. Your eyes are getting heavier and heavier.

6. Your whole body is relaxed and the bed is so close now.

5. All the tension in your muscles is slowly easing up.

4. The bottom of the staircase is even closer and you are completely relaxed now.

3. Only two more steps to go now.

2. Take a deep breath and slowly exhale through your mouth.

1. Take the last step and feel yourself sinking into that comfortable bed. Feel the soft covers caress your skin as you lay down on the bed. Feel the comfort of the fluffy pillows underneath your head.

Relax completely and continue to take deep breaths and exhale slowly through your mouth

Now open your mind up completely and see all the things you want to attract and manifest in your life.

See the career that you want, see yourself sitting in that corner office and being the best version of yourself possible.

Visualize yourself sitting behind your desk doing exactly what you have always wanted to do. You are there in that moment, feel it. Look around you. Immerse yourself in it.

Take a deep breath and exhale slowly

Now you can see the family or partner that you have always wanted. See yourself in this role, surrounded by the people you love. Hear their laughter, see their smiles, feel their touch. Immerse yourself in the moment. Reach out and touch. Feel it

Take a deep breath and exhale slowly

Visualize yourself in the prime of health, with the body you have always wanted, in great health and feeling great. Feel the energy in your body, giving you the strength to face anything.

Take a deep breath and exhale slowly

At this point visualize anything else that you want to manifest in yourself. Do not just think about it. Feel it, touch it, immerse yourself in the experience.

Take a deep breath and exhale slowly

As you continue to lie on the divine bed keep bringing to the surface all the things that you want. Feel yourself moving toward them.

Now you can remain in this mindful state of relaxation for as long as you want.

Slowly open your eyes and bring your awareness back to the present.

This meditation is now complete.

Chapter 2: Attract Happiness

Stress and worry are usually a sign that you are not in vibrational alignment with what you would like to manifest. When you are constantly weighed down by negative energy you keep attracting the very things that you worry about. That is why a positive mindset is one of the core elements for manifesting the things you want. If you put out positive energy into the world you will attract joy and abundance.

When you want happiness and abundance you have to actively choose positivity over negativity. You cannot wait until everything works out to be happy. In fact, happiness and living your life in joy and gratitude is what will make it possible for things to work out. However, being positive and finding joy in your life are things you have to actively cultivate. This means using meditation to reset your energy every time you feel weighed down by stress and anxiety.
So, for these next sessions, we will go through meditations to help you find your joy in any circumstances. This will help you align your inner energy with the things you want to manifest. Think of the universe as a kind of mirror that is simply reflecting back what you are putting out. This way you can be more aware of your energy and make a conscious effort to choose joy.

Free Yourself from Anxiety, Stress, and Worry – 20 minutes

This meditation will help you calm an overactive mind and shift your energy from negative emotions and thoughts to a feeling of inner peace and calmness.

Let's get started.

Duration 20 mins

I invite you to make yourself comfortable. You can sit or lie down in a quiet room free of distractions.

We will start this meditation with your eyes open. With a soft gaze focus your line of vision on one point in front of you. This can be a spot on the floor or the wall in front of you. Just find something that draws your attention.

Focus all your attention on this single spot and allow everything else to fade into the background.

Take everything in from this single spot. Notice the color, the textures and notice every single detail about it. Take your time and simply examine this spot.

Now slowly broaden your focus from that single point and expand your focus outward like a camera lens widening.

Again with relaxed awareness, notice every little detail in your expanded view. Notice the color, the texture, and anything else that falls within your line of vision. Take in the details slowly.

Now slowly narrow your vision back down to the original point you had focused on earlier. At this point, as you narrow down your line of vision you are letting everything else fade into the background.

As your focus continues to narrow down, keep making the point of focus smaller and smaller until you gradually close your eyes.

With your eyes closed now, allow your awareness and focus to turn inward.

As you begin to look inside and settle physically, start with three deep breaths in through your nose and followed by a slow exhale through your mouth.

Embrace the feeling of calmness that engulfs you as you continue to take deep breaths.

Now begin to count to 5 as you breathe in then as you breathe out count to 6. With every exhale release any emotional stress and tension in your body. Feel it leave your body as you exhale.

Repeat this breathing cycle five times, each time focusing on releasing anything that is weighing you down. Let it go, and feel the calmness enter your body with every breath you inhale.

Become aware of your physical experience as you continue deep breathing. Notice first the palms of your hands and focus on the energy there. Perhaps you feel this as a warmth or tingling sensation.

Notice how by simply moving your awareness to this part of your body you also feel the energy go where your focus is.

You have the ability to move energy and move a positive sensation within you similar to broadening your visual focus from a single point.

Begin to widen the experience of your sensations by moving your awareness from the palms of your hands to your entire body. Feel your body awaken as you move your consciousness from one part of your body to the rest of your body. Your arms, your legs, your face, your feet.

Feel the energy moving within and you let your attention drift through the sensations in your body without directing it and without judging what you find. Simply allow your focus to tune into the sensations of your body right in this moment.

You are in the present and living in the space between your thoughts when your mind is. You are fully attentive to the sensations of your body.

Between your thoughts, in this space is where you can experience peace and calm

As I mention each part of your body, let your focus and awareness move to that part releasing any tension you feel in that area.

Become aware of your feet. Focus on them and simply relax this part of your body. Slowly move your awareness from your feet and up into your lower legs. Release any tightness in this area and allow it to relax completely as you continue to raise your awareness to your thighs.

Find a sense of ease in your thighs and hips as you let go completely. Then gradually bring your awareness up feeling the arch of your spine your abdomen and your chest. Take a deep breath and allow your upper body to relax completely.

Moving your attention upward feel any tension from your neck relax. Feel any tightness in your jaw and allow it to unclench as every part of your body eases deeper into relaxation.

Feel the small muscles of your cheeks eyes and forehead soften. Now your whole body feels light and relaxed and you feel grounded in the present.

Let your mind and body go deeper into this relaxed state

Now that you are fully relaxed you can begin the inward inquiry process by becoming aware of your emotions.

Experience all your emotions in this present moment without trying to change anything. Let your thoughts come and go. There is no need to attach to them or follow them.

Imagine your thoughts and feelings are flowing like a river and as they leave, you release them and allow fresh clean water to come in.

If you find your mind attaching to a negative thought or emotion, guide yourself back to the present by bringing your awareness back to your body, your breathing, and the sensations in your body.

Begin to deepen your breathing once more and embrace the inner peace and feeling of being present in the moment.

Slowly start to reactivate each part of your body from its relaxed state and feel gentle calming energy flowing into you as you ease yourself back to your normal breathing rhythm.

Now open your eyes slowly and take this calm energy with you as you go on with your day.

This guided meditation is now complete.

Happiness Visualization Technique – 10 minutes

This happiness visualization technique is meant to help you consciously shift your thoughts to a place of happiness and safety whenever you start to feel overwhelmed.

Let us get started.

Duration 10 minutes

Make sure that you are in a quiet space sitting comfortably or lying down

Focus on how you are feeling right now both physically and mentally.

Take a deep breath and repeat quietly in your mind:

I am ready to relax. I am ready to still my mind.

Now take another deep breath nice and slow. Feel your lungs expand and your chest rise.

Pull your breath right down into your belly and then exhale slowly.

You are safe, you are comfortable, you are beginning to relax.

I want you to focus your mind on your heart and imagine a ball of bright green light in the center of your chest

With every breath you take, this ball of light shines brighter and grows bigger

Take another deep breath make sure that you fill your lungs completely.

Repeat quietly in your mind:

I am strong and confident. I am loved just as I am. I am safe.

Continue to breathe slowly and deeply. Feel the flow of air as it moves gently through your body.

Every time you exhale feel any pent-up emotions, stress or anxiety leave your body.

You are safe, you are comfortable, you are relaxed.

Now, I want you to focus your mind on your solar plexus, the area just below your ribs and imagine a ball of bright yellow light in this area.

With every deep breath you take, the light grows bigger and brighter opening your solar plexus chakra to receive more light and love.

You feel strong and confident.

Now take another deep breath and pull the air right down into your solar plexus repeat as you repeat quietly in your mind:

I am strong and confident. I am loved just as I am. I am safe.

Breathe in deeply and with every breath feel your body get filled with confidence and strength. Repeat quietly in your mind:

I am strong and confident. I am loved just as I am. I am safe.

Allow your muscles to ease and soften. Relax your entire body and feel your shoulders and back lose any tension in the muscles.

As your body sinks deeper into relaxation your heart is being filled with a warm loving glow.

Continuing to take deep breaths, repeat quietly in your mind:

I am strong and confident. I am loved just as I am. I am safe.

You can feel a healing warmth spread slowly through your heart. Your mind and body feel lighter your emotions feel lighter you feel lighter.

Now gently stretch your arms and legs. Lift your arms above your head and gently stretch your back.

Take as much time as you need in this relaxed pose and just know that when you open your eyes you will feel refreshed, strong and confident.

Open your eyes when you are ready and slowly bring your awareness back to the present.

This visualization technique is now complete.

Confidence & Self-Esteem Meditation – 20 minutes

When you are full of self-doubt and limiting beliefs, you can only manifest your deepest fears. In times when your thoughts are clouded with self-judgment, the path to things you want to attract becomes blurred. It is only when you can reset your subconscious to have self-belief and self-love that you can truly begin to attract all the things that you deserve.

In this session, I want to guide you on how to bring back your thoughts to a place of self-love and confidence. This will help you in consciously creating the positive vibrational energy that you need to keep attracting happiness and abundance.

Let's get started.

Duration 20 minutes

Make yourself comfortable in a quiet room that is free of distractions. You can sit or lie down for this meditation.

Close your eyes if you like and gradually settle into a relaxed state with your mind only focused on your breathing and the feel of every breath as it enters and leaves your body.

Place your hands over your chest to bring your awareness to your heart and make the physical connection inward.

As you breathe in, imagine that you are breathing in light, love and peace into your heart.

In your mind see it as a bright glowing light that fills your heart and spreads warmth throughout your body.

As you continue to relax deeper and deeper, set the intention to open your heart today and to welcome in love and light.

With every breath in, open yourself up to receiving the loving energy of the world around you and with every breath out radiate that love outward.

See and feel this warm glowing energy entering your body and filling it up and then radiating that energy outward all around you.

Allow this light of love to ground your energy and protect you. Let go of resistance, let go of the tendency to force outcomes, let go of the need for control. Surrender yourself to this new healing and protective energy.

Feel yourself soften and let go with a relaxed awareness as you continue to feel the light radiating from you and protecting you in a safe space.

Now bring your awareness to each and every part of your body feeling the relaxing energy infuse every part of your being from the top of your head to the soles of your feet. You are completely bathed in this loving glow now and you are radiating it into the world in soft waves.

Now that you are in a safe and comfortable state of relaxation, take a deep breath and repeat quietly to yourself:

I am worthy of love. I am worthy of happiness. I am worthy of success.

Continue to feel the warm glow of light bathing you in its warmth and protection. Inhale slowly and deeply and exhale slowly through your mouth.

Repeat quietly to yourself:

I am worthy of love. I am worthy of happiness. I am worthy of success.

You are deeply relaxed and you feel any self-doubt and stress melting away. Your mind is completely relaxed and you have let go of any resistance. You are a source of light radiating a warm glow outwards.

Repeat quietly to yourself:

I am worthy of love. I am worthy of happiness. I am worthy of success.

Feel yourself connecting with your inner glow. Allow yourself to be drawn into the warmth of the light that is now illuminating every part of your being.

Let this light replace any darkness, fear, or doubts. You are enough. You have everything you need to be who you want to be. You are sufficient.

Repeat quietly to yourself. I am worthy of love. I am worthy of happiness. I am worthy of success.

Now take a deep breath and exhale slowly through your mouth.

Slowly bring your attention back to your physical body and your breathing. Gradually bring your awareness back to the present and let yourself soak in the feeling of self-love and acceptance you are feeling in this moment.

You may now open your eyes.

This guided meditation is now complete.

Gratitude is the Key – 10 minutes

One of the easiest ways to attract happiness and live positively is by being grateful. So often we get so caught up in what we want that we overlook what we already have. Yet if you could learn to appreciate what you already have in your life, it will be much easier to attract abundance and joy.

This meditation will help you train your mind to appreciate and be thankful for what you already have. By so doing you will reset your subconscious filter to project the happiness and positivity you need to manifest your deepest desires.

Let's get started.

Duration: 10 minutes

Start by sitting in a comfortable position. Now gently close your eyes and place both of your hands on your chest above your heart.

Relax your whole body and take a deep breath slowly inhaling through your nose, then exhaling through your mouth

Let everything else fade to the background as you bring your awareness and concentration to the fall and rise of your chest as you breathe in and out.

Feel your body sink deeper into relaxation as you continue to inhale deeply and exhale slowly.

Now think about the people in your life and think about who you appreciate. See their smile, feel their touch and remember how they make you feel. Embrace that feeling.

See them one by one in great detail. Maybe it is your spouse, your child, a parent, a friend, or all of the above.

Now take a deep breath and visualize yourself hugging them and bring them closer to you. As you continue to visualize them repeat this mantra:

I am thankful for you. I am happy you are in my life. I am a better person because of you.

Now inhale deeply and exhale slowly. As you exhale shift your focus to the things in your life that you are grateful for. A good job, a nice home, your health, anything in your life right now that you appreciate bring your focus to it.

See it in vivid detail. If it is your home, visualize every room, your favorite place in the home, the little treasures that make it home. If it is your career think of all the milestones you have achieved so far. Visualize all the things you love about your job, your home and your possessions.

See those moments that have brought you joy. See the days that you were strong enough to keep it together no matter what was going on. Find the things about yourself that you are grateful for.

Your inner strength. Your empathy. Your loyalty. Your kindness. What abilities do you have that you are grateful for? Name them one by one in your mind and express your gratitude for them.

Repeat this mantra: I am thankful for who I am, I am thankful for all the things I have. I am thankful for this moment.

Soak in this feeling of gratitude and the blissful feeling of knowing that everything you need, you already have.

Feel the love, compassion, and understanding that gratitude brings into your heart. What are the things you have now that you take for granted? How was you life before you had them?

Reflect on all the challenges you have been through? What have you learned? How have you grown? Are you a better person because of them? Did they help you find hidden strengths you did not know you had?

Take a deep breathe and exhale slowly.

Feel the gratitude take root in your mind and in your heart. Relish the blessings and abundance in your life. Right now, where you are, realize that you are already blessed in more ways than you can count.

Now take a deep breath and exhale slowly. As the air fills your lungs acknowledge what a miracle it is just to be alive. Bring your awareness to your body and how alive it feels right now in this relaxed state.

Now raise both hands in the air and open them up wide as if you want to embrace the air around you. As you do this imagine a beautiful white light shining above your head. Let this light fill your whole being with gratitude and love.

Let this light penetrate every cell in your body, every tissue and every organ. As you continue to open yourself to this light, picture yourself traveling into your ideal life, a life in which you have achieved all your dreams.

See the person that you are in that ideal life. You have everything you ever wanted. You are happy, you are confident, you are successful. You are exactly where you want to be. Look around you, where do you live? Who are you with? How do you feel? Yes, see it, feel it, live it and take a moment to absorb it all.

Take a moment to express gratitude for all you have seen in your vision. Then take a deep breath and exhale slowly through your mouth.

Now imagine yourself traveling back to the present. You are now confident that your ideal life is already waiting for you. You no longer need to worry or live your life in resistance. The universe already knows everything you need and it will bring it to pass. All you need to do is trust your journey.

Take another deep breath and exhale slowly. You can now let your arms fall back to your sides.

As your awareness comes back to the moment take another minute to relish the life that you are destined for.

Slowly open your eyes and take this feeling of gratitude and hope with you throughout the day.

This guided meditation is now complete.

Chapter 3: Attracting Wealth & Abundance

Look at your financial situation right now. Do you have the wealth and abundance you desire? If you have been chasing wealth and abundance with no success, it is important to understand that your beliefs about wealth and money are what are shaping your reality. Often people think that it is their reality that shapes their beliefs but actually it is the other way around; your core beliefs shape your outcomes.

To attract wealth and abundance it is important to disrupt any lack consciousness that you may be subconsciously holding on to. A lack consciousness is when you operate from a belief that there is not enough money, resources, opportunity, love and so on. You are always afraid of running out or falling short. This lack consciousness is what blocks your path to manifesting wealth and abundance. When you wish to create more, you must have the ability to focus on what you want and not what you do not want. A lack consciousness keeps you focused on what you do not have and this blocks the path to the manifestation of wealth and abundance.

To help you get past this barrier, the guided meditations in this section are intended to help you develop a wealth consciousness. This wealth consciousness will help to reset your beliefs about wealth and abundance and set you on the path to attracting all the wealth and abundance you have ever desired.

Manifesting Success with Consciousness - 15 minutes

This meditation will help you overcome any lack consciousness you may have and create a positive money mindset. This guided meditation will help you rewire and reset your relationship with money, wealth and abundance.

Let's get started.

Duration 15 minutes.

I invite you to make yourself comfortable in a quiet space free of distractions. Sit in a comfortable chair with your hands resting gently in your lap. Your feet should be squarely planted on the floor.

Now close your eyes and shut everything out by focusing on your breathing. Inhale deeply and feel the air fill your lungs and exhale slowly through your mouth.

Slowly breathe in and breathe out allowing each subsequent breath to become longer slower and deeper.

Your awareness in this moment should be fully focused on your breathing. Release any thoughts that come into your mind.

As you get deeper into a relaxed state now take a moment and think of all the abundance that is in the world. The abundance that surrounds you every day. The trees you see everywhere, the millions of leaves on all those trees.

The abundance of the air that you are breathing, the abundance of the water in the ocean. The abundance of the light radiating from the sun, the abundance of the stars in the sky at night. See all these things clearly in your mind in their vastness and infinite abundance.

You are a part of all this abundance and it is a part of you. You live in an abundant universe and the universe has everything you will ever need.

Now take a moment to create images in your mind of the kind of life you want. See the house that you want to live in. See it in vivid detail, with all the things that you want in that home. Walk through it from room to room and immerse yourself in its abundance.

As you look at this image of the abundance that is waiting for you, start to picture yourself having all the money you need to buy whatever you want. Feel the money in your hand and see yourself buying anything you want, investing in anything you want and never having to worry about money again.

It's all there in your hand already. Bind yourself to it and feel yourself connect with this wealth.

Now imagine living where you want to live, traveling anywhere you have always wanted to go and doing the things you have always wanted to do. Can you see yourself in those places, living your best life? Can you see yourself taking that trip you always wanted, living in that neighborhood you always dreamed of?

Now pick the specific amount of money you would like to make every month. See this number very clearly in your mind. Be very specific about it. As you think about that number see it on your bank statement, see it in form of a check with your name on it.

See yourself with that money already in your account. Relish the feeling of freedom, abundance and security that having that money gives you. Let that feeling permeate every part of you as you feel any worry about lack or financial insecurity slowly melt away.

Everything you want is expanding in your life. Everything in your life is increasing and you are aware that you can easily allow money to flow into your life. You are aware that abundance is within your reach if you only open and embrace it.

Now you also see yourself sharing your abundance. You do not just have abundance but you are sharing your abundance with the people in your life.

As you take your next breath, imagine money being drawn towards you and into your life. As you exhale see yourself exchanging that money for the things you have always desired. See it vividly and feel those things in your hand.

Luxuriate in the image of having them. Embrace that feeling of abundance. Let it permeate your entire being.

Now take a deep breath and exhale slowly through your mouth. Repeat this affirmation:

I love my abundant life. I choose to succeed and prosper in every area of my life. I have abundance and wealth. I have all the wealth I desire.

And now take a minute to simply be grateful for all the abundance flowing into your life this very moment. Feel the freedom, the security and the joy of abundance.

Repeat this affirmation: I love my abundant life. I choose to succeed and prosper in every area of my life. I have abundance and wealth. I have all the wealth I desire.

As you say those words, connect with this abundance and attach yourself to it. You are wealthy, you have abundance, you have all the money you want. Immerse yourself in this feeling of having everything you need.

Now slowly bring your awareness back to the present. Take a deep breath and focus on the sensation of the air filling your lungs, and then exhale slowly. Take another deep breath and slowly open your eyes.

This guided meditation is now complete.

Wealth Visualization Techniques - 10 minutes

When you want to manifest wealth, it is important to keep the following in mind. The key to manifesting the wealth and abundance you want is to always see yourself in the picture and visualize your life exactly as you want it to be. You must first see the things that you want in your mind before you can manifest them into reality.

This wealth visualization technique is a quick and simple meditation that you can do twice or thrice a day to manifest the wealth that you want.

Let's get started.

Duration: 10 minutes.

Sit in a comfortable position. You can sit in a chair or on the floor in a cross-legged posture. Just make sure your body is relaxed.

Start by closing your eyes. To bring your awareness inward, let us concentrate on breathing.

Take a deep breath in through your nose and exhale slowly through your mouth. Now take another deep breath and as you feel the air enter your body let your body sink deeper into relaxation.

In this relaxed state, with your eyes still closed imagine that you are looking towards the center of your forehead. This is the location of the third chakra. This chakra is a powerful manifestation point that will make your visualization even more powerful.

As you focus on this point on your forehead, continue taking deep slow breaths. As your mind gets calmer and more relaxed you will feel more centered.

Now in this relaxed state visualize yourself living in wealth and abundance. Be very detailed in what you see. If it's a new home that you are in, see it in vivid detail. The structure itself, the furniture in it and everything else that you want in that home. See yourself in this beautiful home, living in it with your loved ones.

Immerse yourself completely in the visualization. Touch the fixtures and furniture. Sit in a chair. Walk around the rooms in this home. Become one with it. Experience it.

Continue to visualize the thing you want the most. If it is money. Feel the notes in your hand, crisp and bundled up. See yourself walking to the bank and withdrawing all the money you need. Can you feel the money in your hands? Can you feel the freedom and security of having it?

Whatever it is that you want, see yourself having it. If it is a new car, visualize yourself driving it. Visualize the feel of the steering wheel in your hand, the quiet hum of the engine as you drive and the smell of the interior. See it, touch it, drive it. It is yours, experience it.

Now as you continue to soak up this feeling of abundance repeat this affirmation quietly in your mind.

I am grateful for my money. I am financially free. I make money easily. I always have enough money.

Now take a deep breath as you slowly bring your awareness back to the present. Repeat the afiirmation one more time.

I am grateful for my money. I am financially free. I make money easily. I always have enough money.

Stay with this feeling of abundance and wealth for a minute and allow yourself to keep that feeling with you throughout the day

You can repeat this visualization as often as you want throughout the door to keep you connected to the things you want to manifest.

This guided visualization is now complete.

Creating Opportunity - 15 minutes

If you constantly feel like there are obstacles in your path blocking your abundance and wealth, this meditation will guide you through the mental blocks. Whether you are yearning for your dream job, a business you have always wanted or any other opportunities, resetting your subconscious energy to align with your goals will help you manifest the opportunities you want.

Let us get started.

Duration 15 minutes.

Let us begin by settling down in a comfortable position. You can choose to sit or lie down with your eyes closed for this meditation. Find a quiet room that is free of distractions.

Now let's start by directing your awareness inward and shutting out everything else. Inhale deeply through your nose and exhale slowly through your mouth. Again, inhale deeply, letting the air fill your lungs completely then exhale slowly.

As your mind starts to relax, concentrate on the feeling of the air entering and leaving your body. If any errant thoughts come to mind, simply release them and let them float away.

Bring your awareness to your body starting from the top of your head. As you focus on each part feel it come alive.

Slowly work your way down from your head bringing your awareness to your neck and shoulders. If there is any tension there feel it ease as you continue with the deep breathing.

Now bring your awareness down to your spine and abdomen. Feel the warmth spread from your head downwards as you continue to scan your body. Your back is now comfortable and relaxed and this feeling is spreading down to your legs.

As you continue all the way down to your feet, your whole body is now fully relaxed and you feel light and calm.

Now in this relaxed state visualize yourself walking into your ideal job. See yourself walking through the doors and confidently walking to a bright and beautiful workspace. Feel yourself take a seat in this beautiful office. Look around you and take in your surroundings.

Take your time to explore this space. If it is the business you have always wanted to open. See the sign and branding on the window with your company's name on it. Walk through the doors and see the setup you have always wanted. Touch the furniture, look out the window, what do you see?

Whatever it is that you want to come into your life, see yourself having it now. The job, the business, the promotion, the leadership role. Picture yourself in that role and experience it vividly. You are there right now doing what you have always wanted.

You feel valued and abundant in this space. You are interacting with people in this abundant space.

You are confident in your accomplishments, your skills and your potential. This is who you are. This is the version of yourself that you want to be the most.

Feel the joy of being exactly where you want to be. Bathe in the confidence of knowing you can accomplish anything you want and that every opportunity you crave is opening itself up to you right now in this moment.

Notice how your body feels in this moment. Tune in to your emotions and fill the energy running through your body at this moment when you are in the role you have always wanted. Experience these sensations and radiant energy in your body and your mind.

Now imagine that this energy is vibrating and radiating outwards enveloping your body like a warm cozy blanket. This energy is now surrounding you and now filling your whole room radiating outside into the universe.

Let yourself release this powerful energy into the world and onto the deep space where opportunities are waiting for you to grab them.

See this radiant energy cover and infuse everything around you. Now stay connected to this moment for a little while.

Take a deep breath and begin to release all the concentration and expectations that you have. Simply allow yourself to bask in this positive energy trusting that what you want is going to manifest.

Slowly bring your awareness back to the present and open your eyes.

You can repeat this meditation twice a day to keep your mind open to opportunities.

This guided meditation is now complete.

Wealth Affirmations - 10 minutes

Everything that you want to manifest must first be birthed in your mind. These wealth affirmations are powerful tools to help you manifest abundance and wealth.

Repeat these affirmations every morning for 21 days to tune into the vibrations of wealth and abundance.

Let's get started.

Duration: 10 minutes

I am a money magnet.

I attract money and abundance easily.

I am a money magnet.

Money comes to me easily.

I live abundantly and money serves my highest good.

I am a money magnet.

I have all the money that I need.

I deserve abundance and wealth.

I invite wealth and abundance into my life.

I am getting wealthier each day.

I deserve to prosper.

I open myself up to embrace wealth and abundance.

Money flows into my life easily.

I am a money magnet.

I release my resistance to money.

I release my lack consciousness.

I deserve wealth.

I am wealthy.

I am a money magnet.

Money comes to me easily.

My income continues growing.

My finances are great.

I have all the money that I need.

I am a money magnet.

I am grateful for my wealth and abundance.

I am open to abundance and wealth.

I can feel my financial abundance daily.

I can feel my financial abundance increasing daily

Every day I become wealthier.

Every day my abundance increases.

I am destined to live abundantly.

I am grateful for my wealth.

I am thankful for my abundance.

The universe provides for me.

I will never lack.

I am getting wealthier each day.

Chapter 4: Manifesting Love

We spend a lot of time fighting off the creations of our own minds. In relationships, just like in wealth and abundance, we manifest our deepest beliefs and preconceived notions. This means that unless you can align your subconscious energy with the kind of person you want to attract you will keep struggling to find fulfilling relationships. Our beliefs follow us around like a shadow and they infuse us with whatever energy that we have created. This energy can then either manifest the love and relationships you want or take you further and further away from them.

Love is an integral part of abundant and fulfilling life. If you want to attract your soulmate or healthy relationships, the work starts on the inside before it can manifest on the outside.

For these sessions on attracting love, the guided meditations are intended to help you manifest the person of your dreams and have the relationships you yearn for.

Heart Chakra Activation - 15 minutes

This heart chakra activation meditation will help you open yourself up to love and attract your soulmate. It will help you overcome any self-limiting beliefs you have about love and relationships.

You can practice this meditation before you go to bed or when you wake up in the morning.

Let's get into it.

Duration 15 minutes

Start by sitting in a comfortable position. Your neck and spine should be aligned in a relaxed position.

Now place your hands on your thighs with the palms facing upward ready to receive what the universe has to offer.

In this relaxed stance close your eyes and take a deep breath in through your nose. As you exhale slowly, let your mind clear of all thoughts and distractions. Simply concentrate on your breathing and release any thoughts in your mind.

As you sink deeper into relaxation start to visualize a radiant light surrounding your heart and getting brighter with every breath you take.

You can feel the warm glow of this radiant light all over your chest and the warmth is slowly spreading throughout your body. You are opening yourself up to receive love and making room in your heart for your soulmate.

Feel this warm glow become a vibrant energy that is permeating every part of your body. As you continue to feel this positive energy repeat these affirmations quietly in your mind.

I am attracting my soulmate.

I feel my soulmate is strongly attracted to me.

I believe in my ability to attract my soulmate I feel it within every cell of my body.

My soul mates and I are being drawn closer and closer together each day.

I love being with my soulmate.

My heart is open to receive and give love to my soulmate.

I now attract the perfect partner in my life.

I have more love than I ever thought was possible.

I naturally and effortlessly attract healthy loving relationships into my life.

I am deeply connected to my soulmate.

I'm in the right place at the right time to meet my perfect partner.

I will let my soul and my spirit guide me into my soulmate.

I release everything that is standing in the way of love.

I am attracting my perfect partner.

I am attracting the love of my life.

I've now found the love of my life

I'm extremely grateful for all the love in my life.

I'm so thankful that I have attracted my soulmate.

I attract love and everything that I do.

I'm so grateful for my love life.

True love is my divine birthright and I claim it now.

I opened my heart to myself and I trust that true love will follow and flow through me.

I love myself and I attract loving relationships into my life.

This loving relationship enhances my being and brightens up my life.

I have entirely detached of any outcome and have for trust that my heart will lead me to where I need to go.

The more I love myself the more I love my soulmate.

I am in total acceptance and receive the love my soulmate has for me.

As I relax in this moment, in this very moment I feel this positive love and energy radiate through me and I become one with this love.

I become love. I am love and I attract true love to my life.

Now take a deep breath and slowly start to bring your awareness back to the present.

Take a deep breath in and out. And again, deep breath in and then exhale slowly.

Slowly open your eyes

This guided meditation is now complete.

Affirm Your Belief in Your Soulmate - 15 minutes

If you want to find the perfect partner, you have to be intentional about sending the right energy out into the universe. This meditation will help you affirm your belief in your soulmate and open yourself up to manifesting the partner that you want in your life.

Let us get started.

Duration 15 minutes

For this meditation find a quiet place and sit in a comfortable chair.

Keep your back straight and your shoulders back in a relaxed but upright sitting position. Your feet should be flat on the ground.

Place your hands on your lap with the palm facing upwards as a sign that you are open to receive what the universe has to offer.

Now gently close your eyes and allow yourself to focus on your breath. Inhale deeply making a point to focus on the rise and fall of your chest as you continue to inhale deeply and exhale slowly.

Let the calmness take hold and release any lingering thoughts in your mind. Simply focus on breathing and following the rhythm of your chest as it rises and falls.

With every inhale feel the clean air nourish your body while every exhale releases any resistance to love, any negative thoughts and any negative emotions. Let them all float away as you continue to inhale nourishing energy with every breath you take.

As you continue with the deep breathing, bring your awareness to the energy center of your heart which is at the center of your heart.

Focus all your awareness on this chakra point as you continue to open up your heart and your mind to accept your soulmate.

Now with your heart chakra fully receptive to the universe. Start to visualize yourself seated at the top of a peaceful lush hill. There is nothing but green healthy vegetation as far as the eye can see and you are surrounded by all this beauty and open space.

In this moment you are ready and open to connect with your soulmate. Now in this relaxed beautiful place repeat these affirmations.

I love and accept you. I welcome you in whenever you're ready.

Now take a deep breath, and fill the clean fresh air fill your lungs. Now exhale slowly and as you release the air release with it the need for your soulmate to be here right now. Instead, release this need for attachment trusting that your soulmate will come to you at the right time.

Your journey and your soulmates are intertwined and you are a magnet attracting them to you through the vast expanse surrounding you.

Allow yourself to be open to your soulmate without needing to control the timeline or where it happens. You are patient knowing that your soulmate is coming to you and you are ready to receive them.

Although they are not here with you now, allow yourself to relax into their love just feeling the energetic presence of their love. Notice how it feels to know that they are there. The comfort of knowing that you are going to meet your perfect partner.

Trust and know that even when they are not with you in the physical that you can connect with their energy feel their love and let them feel yours in return. You are connected now and your energies are aligned.

Notice the way you want to feel with them long before you ever are near them physically. You can just love them for wherever they are and whatever they're doing trusting that they will come into your life.

You simply enjoy the fact that you know they are out there. You know you are both going through whatever you need to go through so that you may meet at the perfect timing.

In the next few moments just send appreciation to them wherever they are, whatever they're doing.

Repeat this affirmation.

I love and accept you. I appreciate you. I know we will meet when the timing is right.

Now take this feeling of love, acceptance and appreciation with you and hold on to it until the time is right for your lives to come together.

Take a deep breath and feel the love in your heart as you hold on to the connection you feel to your soulmate.

Slowly bring your awareness back to the present by tuning into the rhythm of your breathing. You can now open your eyes slowly.

This guided meditation is now complete.

Manifest Your Partner, Lover, & Improve Your Relationship - 25 minutes

Sometimes the partner of your dreams is already in your life but your relationship has hit a snag. Or you want to mend a broken relationship. To attract your partner back into your life or heal your relationship, you need to manifest this desire by aligning your subconscious energy with the relationship you want to attract.

Let's get into this healing mediation.

Duration 25 minutes.

For this meditation, you can lie back in a comfortable position. Make sure you are in a quiet room free of any noise or distractions. You can also choose to sit on a comfortable chair or the floor.

If you are sitting up, make sure you are sitting up straight. Pull your chin down to aligning your neck with your spine in an upright but relaxed posture.

Place your palms face upwards by your side if you are lying down or on your lap if you are sitting down. This opens up to connect with the energy around you.

Bring your awareness to how you are feeling in this very moment. Become aware of how you feel, any thoughts running in your mind and how your body feels.

Now begin your cycle of deep breathing that will be our anchor throughout this meditation.

Inhale slowly and deeply through your nose and as you do so feel your mind start to clear. With every exhale you are releasing any errant thoughts and negative emotions.

Inhale deeply and exhale slowly. Inhale deeply and exhale slowly. Inhale deeply and exhale slowly.

As you continue with the deep breathing start to bring your awareness to your body. Start with your feet feeling a tingling sensation there as you focus on them. Now continue to scan upwards and feel this tingling sensation travel slowly up your body.

As you feel the energy spreading throughout your body, let your body relax and feel the energy infuse every part of your body.

Become aware of how your breath keeps you focused and connected with yourself and with the universe.

Your breath is a vehicle between your body and everything that you desire. Trust in the process of your breath.

Inhale deeply and exhale slowly. Inhale deeply and exhale slowly. Inhale deeply and exhale slowly.

Feel your body sink deeper and deeper into relaxation and the radiant energy coursing through your body.

Now set an intention for this meditation. Do you want to mend your relationship? Are you looking for your soulmate? Do you want a healthier relationship? Whatever your intention is be very clear about it.

If your desire is someone in particular, see them in vivid detail. Their face, their smile, their eyes. See them exactly as they are.

Get as clear as possible on what it is you desire.

Focus on your desire and intention. On your next deep inhale, repeat this affirmation:

I deserve this connection.

On your next inhale, repeat this affirmation - I am ready to call this connection into my life.

Now breathe in and repeat this affirmation - I can feel my desire.

As you breathe out repeat this affirmation - I am ready to experience my desire

Inhale deeply and repeat this affirmation - I can see clearly what I want

As you exhale, repeat this affirmation - I know that it is coming toward me

You are now consciously connecting to the powerful energy of the universe. And you are aware that what you seek is also seeking you.

Take a long moment and be grateful knowing that the love you are seeking is also searching for you.

Breathe in the gratitude of this surety. Embrace this feeling and let yourself feel it deeply.

With each grateful breath in, you are becoming a part of everything positive that is working in the universe.

You are calling in your perfect partner and the universe is releasing them to you. Feel them in this moment there with you, connected and sharing in your life. Hold their hand and embrace the feeling of being with the one you desire.

As you experience these feelings, you are bringing your desires closer and closer. You are feeling gratitude. You are feeling joy. You are feeling at peace. You are content.

You and the power of the universe are working together to bring your desire to pass.

Breathe in deeply and exhale slowly. Now visualize your lover or ideal partner moving towards you.

Imagine that you are standing in a giant, sunny field with your soulmate. Visualize them looking at you. See how they loom deep into your eyes and feel them take your hand in theirs. Feel the connection between you two.

Keep deep breathing and anchoring yourself to the present moment.

In this present moment is where your future manifestations are being born. In this present moment, all that you want is beginning to unfold.

Everything you want is already here, in front of you.

Deep breath in, slow exhale. Deep breath in, slow exhale and again a deep breath in followed by a slow exhale.

Now visualize your soulmate and you standing across from you in this sunny, peaceful, quiet field, imagine looking up at the beautiful sky.

As you begin to enjoy the view of the sky a golden light begins descending from the sky above you two.

The golden light begins to move slowly down to where the two of you stand. As you both look up at the light, you feel a sense of true calm and peace inside of your hearts.

This light continues to move toward you and enters your body through the crown of your head. You can both feel this warm glow spreading throughout your body and connecting you to each other. You are now bound by this radiant energy and you are one.

You see each other, full of light, full of connection and strong feelings for each other. The golden light wraps the two of you together, slowly and powerfully circling your bodies. It is bonding you together and healing any hurtful past or heartbreak.

This is a new, fresh start. You are safe and surrounded by the loving energy of the universe.

You see the sense of calm in your partner. You feel calm. You feel peaceful.

Continue with deep breathing and as you do so, bring to the surface all the feelings you long to feel.

You feel loved. You feel wanted. You feel appreciated. You feel like you belong. You feel safe. You are surrounded by your heart's deepest desires.

Stay connected to these feelings and let them permeate your being. You are living these feelings in this moment. Let them infuse you with positive energy and open you up to receive the love you deserve.

Keep visualizing that golden light surrounding the two of you. The light is pulling you together and keeping you connected.

You are one. You are not afraid. You do not doubt. You feel clarity. You do not bring fear into this relationship.

This light that surrounds you is pure, and nothing harmful can enter this energy you are experiencing.

You deserve these feelings, this light, and this person.

Now I want you to bring back your intention that you set at the beginning of the meditation.

Breathe into your intention.

As you visualize this person standing in front of you, imagine what your relationship looks like with them.

How you feel in the relationship, how you are treated, how you treat your partner, how attracted you are to each other.

Let your imagination run wild with future sensual, happy moments with your partner. Imagine what you are looking forward to the most.

Their presence is here with you now, and your longing is being fulfilled. Breathe into your partner's presence and begin to identify why they make you feel happy and fulfilled.

Now breathe in deeply and exhale slowly. Deep breath in, followed by a slow exhale. Breathe in breathe out

As you continue to breathe and dwell in this light, visualize your relationship freeing you from any limiting beliefs about love that you may hold in your mind.

Your relationship is limitless. This relationship will provide the full connection and freedom that you desire.

You and your soulmate are one. You feel strong. You feel secure.

Now with a deep inhale and exhale, start to bring awareness back to your body. Focus on the top of your head and slowly bring your awareness down your neck and shoulders. Now your back, slowly down to your thighs and eventually your feet.

Let your body awaken slowly and as it does so, bring your awareness back to the present by focusing on the rhythm of your breathing.

Now take in a slow deep breath then exhale slowly. Breathe in deeply and exhale slowly through your mouth. One more time, deep breath in, slow exhale.

Now you can open your eyes and take this feeling of love, security and freedom with you throughout the day.

This guided meditation is now complete.

Affirmations to Attract Your Soulmate and Attract Love -10 minutes

Affirmations help you to set your intentions and make them clear to the universe. This helps you send out the right energy to manifest the things you desire most.

You can repeat these powerful love affirmations before you go to sleep or first thing in the morning.

Let's get started:

Duration: 10 minutes

I radiate loving energy into the universe.

My heart is open to receiving and giving love.

I am a magnet to the love of my dreams.

There are countless opportunities to meet my love.

I trust the universe to send me my ideal.

I am worthy of a relationship filled with mutual respect and love.

I have attracted the most loving person into my life.

I am in the right place and at the right time to attract my soulmate.

I surrender to my soul and intuition to guide me to my soulmate.

I release anything that is blocking love out of my life.

Love is flowing to me and through me at all times

I are destined to be together.

Positive loving energy is growing between my partner and me.

The attraction energy between me and my soulmate grows each day.

I will meet my ideal partner.

I am attracting the partner I desire.

I will find my soulmate and the love that I deserve.

Love is flowing through my spirit and attracting my ideal partner to me.

I am a love magnet and my soulmate is coming towards me.

The soulmate I seek is also seeking me.

My mind and heart are open to receiving and giving love.

My relationship is healthy and happy.

My desires are coming true.

I am surrounded by a loving universe that is releasing love and abundance into my life.

I am aligned with the energy of my soulmate.

The universe is bringing me my perfect partner.

I am grateful for the love that is coming to my life.

I am thankful for my partner.

I release any past hurts and broken relationships.

I am ready to be in a loving and healthy relationship.

My heart and spirit are connected with my soulmate.

My heart is open and I radiate love.

I am sending the perfect energy out into the world and my arms are open to receive love from the universe.

I have the soulmate I desire. I have the love I deserve. I am surrounded by love.

Chapter 5; Manifesting Health & Wellness

If you struggle with chronic health conditions or constant stress and anxiety, meditation is not just a powerful coping technique but can also help to restore your vitality. Meditation helps you to create harmony between your mind and body and use this harmony to manifest good health. Your mind and body are in sync and the energy from your mind can affect your physical health. I am sure you have noticed that you are more prone to infections when you are stressed out or going through turmoil. This is simply because your mental energy affects your physical state.

This mental distress ends up manifesting physically in terms of illnesses, sleep disorders, eating disorders, and a host of other conditions that impact your health negatively. That is why healing often starts from the inside out because your mind and your subconscious energy need to be in the right place to attract good health and vitality. Fortunately, meditation is an effective way to nurture your body and mind back to wellness and enjoy a healthy life.

The guided meditations in this section are intended to help you attract and manifest good health and wellbeing. This includes your mental, spiritual and physical wellbeing. Whether you want to lose weight, overcome chronic stress or cope with an illness, meditation will guide you to a safe and healthy place.

Guided Morning Meditation for a Healthy Body -20 minutes

This guided meditation will help you tap into your body's self-healing mechanism to attract a healthier body.

Let's get started.

Duration: 20 minutes

Start by making yourself comfortable. You can choose to either lay down or sit in a comfortable position in a chair or on the floor.

Now close your eyes gently and begin to block all external input by bringing your awareness to your breathing.

Start by taking a deep breath feeling the air as it enters your body, then taking your time to exhale slowly.

Take another deep breath through your nose, hold it for a moment and then exhale slowly and as you do begin to fill your mind releasing any errant thoughts.

As you continue breathing deeply, you can feel your body start to relax. Tension is leaving your muscles, and you are releasing any negative energy from your body.

With each breathing cycle, allow your mind and body to sink deeper and deeper into relaxation. You feel calm and grounded to the present. Your mind is clear and open and your body feels light and relaxed.

Deep breath in, hold for a while then slowly exhale. As you exhale you are releasing negative thoughts, all feelings of anxiety, all worries and all fears.

As you inhale, you are feeling your body with a positive vibrant energy that is spreading a soothing warmness to every part of your body.

Deep breath in, hold for a while, then exhale slowly through your mouth. You feel peaceful and calm.

Each breath out is freeing you from anxiety, stress and negative thoughts.

Each breath in is cleansing your mind, your spirit and your body. You are filled with healing energy and your body is protected by this energy that is now flowing in you.

Notice how relaxed and calm you feel in this moment and now start to bring awareness to every part of your body.

Start at the top of your head and feel for any aches or pains. As your awareness move to each part, let the healing energy cleanse it and release it from any pain or tension.

Slowly move your attention down to your neck and shoulders. Feel for any tension in your muscles and slowly roll your shoulders back as the healing energy soothes and nourishes this part of your body.

Continue to bring your awareness down to your abdomen and back, slowly arch your spine as you feel the healing energy travel down and ease any aches and pains in this part of your body. Relax your spine back into a comfortable posture and continue to scan your body downwards.

From your upper thighs, feel the healing energy spread a healing warmth in your muscles, knees, calves and finally your feet. Your entire body is now at ease and you have released any tension, pain and discomfort in your body.

Lean into this feeling of wholesome wellness and appreciate how you feel in this moment. Notice how much lighter your body feels and how much clearer your mind is.

Now that your body is completely relaxed, open yourself up to receive healing of your mind and body.

Repeat this affirmation quietly in your mind – I am healthy. I invite healing into my body.

Deep breath in, hold for a while, now exhale slowly through your mouth and repeat this affirmation - I am physically and emotionally connected to an abundant source of healing.

As you repeat these affirmations you can still feel the healing energy within your body and radiating all around you. You are covered in it and it is protecting you from any illness, stress or pain.

Continue with the deep breathing as you scan your body from head to toe, again releasing any tension that you feel in any part of your body by bringing your awareness to it.

Repeat these affirmations:

Every time I think healing thoughts, my body gets healthier.

I treat my body with respect.

I choose food that nourishes every cell in my body.

I choose thoughts that feel like love to me.

I am choosing to get healthy.

I am choosing to be healthy.

I am grateful for my health.

My body is full of healing energy.

I deserve to be healthy.

As you continue to affirm your health you can feel every cell in your body aligning with this positive healing energy. You feel an overwhelming sense of wellness and wholeness.

Immerse yourself fully in this sense of well-being and take another deep healing breath and exhale slowly.

Repeat these affirmations one more time:

Every time I think healing thoughts, my body gets healthier.

I treat my body with respect.

I choose food that nourishes every cell in my body.

I choose thoughts that feel like love to me.

I am choosing to get healthy.

I am choosing to be healthy.

I am grateful for my health.

My body is full of healing energy.

I deserve to be healthy.

Now take a deep breath and as you exhale start to bring your awareness back to the present by focusing on your breathing.

Feel every breath as it enters your body and then exhale slowly noticing how your chest expands and contracts.

You can now gently open your eyes.

This guided meditation is now complete.

You can practice this meditation every night before you go to sleep to relieve your body of the physical and mental stress of the day.

Meditation for Weight Loss - 20 minutes

For those who struggle with weight loss, often the problem starts with an unhealthy relationship with their bodies and with food. If you have self-limiting beliefs about health and weight loss in your mind, these beliefs may be hindering you from manifesting the healthy body that you want. With meditation, you can reset any mental blocks that prevent you from having a healthy relationship with your body and manifest your weight loss goals.

Let us get into the weight loss meditation.

Practice this meditation daily for at least 21 days to start manifesting your weight loss goals.

Duration 20 minutes

For this meditation start by sitting on the floor in a comfortable position with your legs crossed. You can also choose to sit in a comfortable chair with your feet planted firmly on the ground.

Now place your hands on your lap with the palm facing upwards ready to receive from the universe whatever energy you need for your intentions.

Gently close your eyes and as you do so you are going to start taking deep slow breaths in through your nose and exhale slowly through your mouth.

Deep breath in, hold for a while, then exhale slowly.

As you continue with the deep breathing your awareness and focus are on the rhythmic rise and fall of your chest. You are releasing any errant thoughts in your head and focusing your attention simply on the sensation of breathing in and out.

As you breathe in, feel your chest rise as your lungs fill with air and as you exhale, feel your chest relax.

As your continue with the deep breathing, your mind is getting clearer and your body now feels more relaxed.

Now with your eyes still closed, focus on the center of your forehead or your third eye. You want to use this powerful chakra point to reset your mindset about your weight.

To focus on this chakra spot just imagine your eyes are fixed on the center point in the middle of your forehead.

Now with your awareness fully focused on your third eye, you are going to start releasing any unhealthy attachments as you breathe out.

Take a deep breath and as you continue with the deep breathing start to visualize yourself standing in front of a full-length mirror. You can see every inch of your body in this mirror exactly as you are in this moment.

As you look in the mirror next to you is a notepad with the number 10 written on it. This number symbolizes your current weight. Look at this number and then look at yourself in the mirror.

At the next inhale, see yourself flipping the page on the notepad. Now the number on the page is 9. When you look in the mirror you can see that you are starting to lose weight. You feel lighter and your body looks smaller.

Take a deep breath and exhale slowly.

Again, still looking at yourself in the full-length mirror flip to the next page on the notepad. The number on this page is 8. As you see this number look back at the mirror and look at your body. You are even slimmer now and you have lost a little bit more weight.

Notice how much slimmer you look right now. Your body also feels healthier and lighter. As you continue to look at your reflection in the mirror feel the relief and gratitude of knowing that you are losing weight already.

Look in the mirror and if you still want to lose more weight flip to the next page of the notepad. You are now at number 7 and you have lost even more weight. You have a much slimmer body and you feel healthier and stronger.

As you continue to look at your slimmer self, feel the joy of being in a slimmer body. Look at this slimmer version of yourself reflected in the mirror and imagine what you will feel like in this body. Revel in this feeling and connect to this new healthier you.

Notice every little detail of your smaller body. Notice how it looks and how it feels to be in the body you have always wanted.

As you continue to look at your slimmer body, flip to the next page of the notepad. You are now at number 6. With every page you turn, your body gets slimmer and the body you see reflected in the mirror looks better and healthier.

As you continue with this visualization, when the reflection that you see in the mirror is the body that you want to achieve, you can stop flipping the pages.

If the image you see at number 6 is exactly what you want your body to look like, you do not need to flip to the next page. Simply look at your new slimmer self and take in every detail of your slimmer body.

Notice the curve of your hips, your waistline, your abdomen and every other little detail of your body. See it, internalize it and commit to your mind that this is what your body looks like.

If you want to keep losing even more weight you can keep flipping the pages on the notebook until the image that you see in the mirror is exactly the body that you want to manifest.

When you find the perfect image of yourself, let yourself feel the emotional connection with your new slimmer body. See yourself, walking around in this body, dressing this slimmer body and connect with it as deeply as possible.

How does it feel seeing yourself fit and healthy? How liberating is it to let go of the excess weight and live in the body you desire? Notice what you are feeling right now in this moment looking at a slimmer and healthier you in the mirror.

Feel the joy and gratitude of no longer having to feel unhealthy or ashamed of your body. Feel the freedom of knowing you can wear anything you want and do anything you want.

You are healthier, you are slimmer and you look beautiful in this new slimmer body.

You are free of all the excess body weight and free of any unhealthy attachments to food.

As you continue to gaze upon your new slimmer self, bring your left palm up placing it above your heart. Now place your right palm above your left.

With both palms now above your heart, take a deep breath and repeat these affirmations quietly in your mind.

I am joyfully achieving my weight loss goals.

I am losing weight every single day.

I enjoy eating healthy foods.

I eat only when I feel hungry and control how much I eat.

I am becoming fitter and stronger every day.

I can easily reach and maintain my ideal weight.

I love and care for my body.

As you affirm your weight loss intentions stay connected to the image of a slimmer and healthier you. See it in great detail and feel the joy of having that body that is free of excess weight.

Now place your palms back in your lap and take a deep breath followed by a slow exhale through your mouth.

Slowly start to bring yourself back to the present by bringing your awareness to your breathing. Feel your chest rise and fall rhythmically as you breathe in and out.

When you are ready you can now open your eyes.

This guided meditation is now complete.

Healing Meditation for Pain Relief - 10 minutes

For people with painful conditions, this healing meditation is designed to help you activate your body's self-healing mechanism from the inside out. It will help you radiate the healing energy that you need to manifest a pain-free body and a healthier stronger you.

Let's get into it.

Duration 10 minutes

Find a comfortable spot to sit in a quiet and peaceful environment. You can sit on a chair or the floor. Just make sure you are sitting up in an upright but relaxed posture.

Now gently close your eyes and start to shut everything else out apart from the sensation of your breaths. Feel the air as it fills your lungs and then exhale slowly allowing yourself to release any pent-up stress.

As you continue to breathe deeply, start to feel the weight of your body. Your body on the chair or the floor.

Become aware of your body. Your body right here and now. Focus on the muscles and any tense areas as you start to relax them and release any tension with every exhale.

Feel your neck and your shoulders relax. Allow every muscle in your body to soften and let your body sink deeper into relaxation.

Now take a deep inhale, followed by a slow exhale through your mouth. Feel your mind open up as you continue inhaling deeply through your nose and exhaling slowly through your mouth.

Again inhale deeply and exhale completely

If your mind starts to wander just let any errant thoughts pass through and release them like water flowing down a stream.

Let your breath center you. Let your breath calm you. Let your breath soothe you.

As you breathe in, feel healing energy come into your body like a warm soothing breeze that infuses every cell in your body.

As you exhale you are releasing any aches, pains and dysfunction from your body. With every inhale you are breathing in health and with every exhale you are releasing pain and discomfort.

Feel your body get lighter and lighter as you continue to release anything that is weighing you down.

Physical pain, stress, discomfort, fear. Let it all float away from you as you welcome the healing energy with every breath you take.

Find relief in release and embrace the healing energy that you are inhaling every time you breathe.

As you continue to breathe, feel your body growing stronger and any areas of weakness getting filled with vibrant healing energy.

You are activating deep healing in your life and you can feel your internal energy shift as you receive wonderful healing energy from the universe.

Allow yourself to feel that healing happening now. Feel it in every bit of your mind and your body.

Continue to sit in this healing energy giving yourself completely to it. You are open and free of any attachments to pain or discomfort. With every breath, you are freeing yourself from pain and welcoming healing.

Now take your right hand and place it on any part of your body where you feel any pain or discomfort. Feel your palm transfer calmness and healing energy to ease any pain and discomfort.

Repeat this affirmation quietly in your mind – I am free from pain and discomfort. I am healthy. I am full of healing energy.

As you affirm your health, continue breathing in deeply and exhaling slowly. Let your hand fall back to your side and trust that the healing energy you feel in your body is manifesting to free you from pain and discomfort.

Take another deep breath and feel the gratitude of being whole again. Picture yourself in perfect health and sit with this feeling as long as you need to.

Connect with the healthy you that you have visualized. Feel yourself in that body and let yourself claim it for yourself.

Now take a deep breath, hold it for a while then slowly exhale. As you breathe deeply, start to tune in to your breathing and slowly bring your awareness back to your body.

You can now slowly open your eyes and keep this feeling of healing and restoration with you throughout the day.

This guided meditation is now complete.

Freedom from Addiction Meditation - 20 minutes

Addictions are coping mechanisms that we use to distance ourselves from our pain. You may be addicted to alcohol, cigarettes, smoking or even drugs. However, no matter what the addiction is, the key is to find the emotional and psychological traumas that trigger the addictive tendencies. With meditation, you can start healing your addiction from the source instead of just dealing with the symptom.

This meditation will help you learn to cope with the emotional trauma that drives you to addictive behavior. If you want to manifest good health and wellbeing, it is important to align your emotional and mental health with the physical health you want to manifest.

Let's get into it.

Duration 20 minutes

Find a comfortable place to sit. You can do this meditation sitting up in a comfortable chair or lying down in a quiet room free of distractions.

Start by taking in a deep breath filling your lungs all the way hold, and then release through your mouth. As you exhale release any tension or anxiety you may have.

Let us do this another three times to completely calm yourself and open up your mind. Deep breath in, slow exhale. Deep breath in, slow exhale. Deep breath in, slow exhale.

Release all that tension, any anxiety and any errant thoughts in your mind. Deep slow breath in, again slowly exhale freeing yourself from anxiety and tension.

Now, return to your normal breathing pattern. Continue to inhale peace and relaxation and exhale anxiety, fear and self-doubt.

You are strong. You are in control of your emotions. You are in control of your habits. You are in control of your health.

Now breathing slowly, slowly ask yourself - what am I afraid of? What am I hiding from behind the cover of this addiction? Whether it is alcoholism or overeating or smoking or any other addiction name it clearly at this point whatever it is.

Let the answer rise unbidden to the surface. Do not try to judge or analyze the answer simply let it float to the surface of your consciousness.

Whatever the answer is acknowledge it and accept it. Whether you are running away from emotional pain, whether you are afraid of facing the unknown, whether you are trying to soothe past hurts. Whatever the reason is acknowledge it without judgment and sit with it for a minute.

Now take a deep breath and slowly exhale. Calm your mind by breathing in deeply and exhaling slowly through your mouth.

Now that you know what you are running from, ask yourself - what do I have to gain by holding on to this fear? What am I losing by hiding from my pain?

Again, just let the answer rise to the surface unbidden. Let your subconscious tells you what it already knows that you may not be aware of. Open yourself up to the answer and receive it without judgment.

Without judging allow whatever answers you have hidden and buried under the surface to rise to the surface.

As you receive the realization, continue with the deep breathing allowing the deep slow inhales to bring in positive healing energy. As you exhale release the pain, the hurt and the fear that you are feeling.

Let it all out. Feel the pain and release it even as you continue to breathe in healing energy.

Now ask yourself - what will I gain by letting go of this addiction? Again name your specific addiction clearly.

When the answer comes to you sit with it for a moment. Acknowledge it and open your mind to it.

Now take a deep breath, hold for a minute and then exhale slowly.

At this point start to visualize yourself sitting in a vast green garden surrounded by lush greenery.

You are sitting under a magnificent tree and you can feel a calm breeze caressing your skin. All around you, it is quiet and peaceful.

As you look up into the horizon, you can see that the sun is about to set. As you watch this beautiful sun start to set, bring your palms above your heart and repeat this affirmation out loud.

I release my pain. I release my addiction. I release my fear.

As you say these words feel your body get lighter and lighter with every exhale.

Repeat this affirmation out loud.

I welcome healing. I welcome health. I am free.

As you affirm your intentions, raise your arms and open them up as if you want to embrace the air all around you.

Repeat this affirmation out loud – I welcome healing. I welcome health. I am free.

Now let your arms fall back to your sides. Continue to look at the beautiful sunset. Breathe in the crisp clean air and let the soothing breeze caress your face.

The universe is giving you its healing power. You are getting the strength you need to move forward with confidence without hiding from your emotions.

You are free. You are well. You are at peace with yourself.

Allow yourself to experience this feeling of newness and refreshment. Lean into the healing power that is enveloping you right in this moment. Feel it and connect to it. Carry it with you.

When you are ready, slowly start to bring your awareness back to the present. Tune in to the rhythm of your breathing. Focus on the sensation of air entering and living your body.

Slowly open your eyes.

This guided meditation is now complete.

Guided Meditation for Anxiety and Sleep - 20 minutes

Good rest is not just essential for your mental well-being but also your physical health. Sleep is important for a healthy body, weight management and even dealing with stress. If you often toss and turn because of an overactive mind, a calming meditation will help you get the rest you need to stay mentally and physically healthy.

This guided meditation is intended to help you overcome anxiety and sleep peacefully. Do not practice this meditation while driving or operating any kind of equipment.

Let us get started.

Duration 10 minutes

Start by lying comfortably in your bed. Lie in the last position you remember falling asleep in or your usual sleeping position.

Now close your eyes and focus your attention on your body. Scan from the top of your head to your feet. As you bring your awareness to each part, release any tension and soften your muscles until you start to feel completely relaxed and at ease.

Now you are going to create in your mind a home base where we can go whenever you feel overwhelmed, anxious or scared.

This home base will become the place where you anchor your attention when your mind is overrun with anxiety, worry and other negative thoughts.

To create this home base, you will need to anchor it by becoming aware of your breathing.

Whenever you want to bring your mind to a calm peaceful place, you will focus all your awareness on your breathing. You will take deep breaths through the nose, then exhale slowly through the mouth.

As you inhale you breathe in a calming soothing energy, and as you exhale, you are releasing worry, stress and fear.

The more you continue to breathe in and out, the more calm energy you bring into your body and the more negative energy you expel.

This deep breathing will be your anchor to your home base where you go to quiet your mind.

As you breathe your attention is on the pace of your breathing, the sensations in your chest, the rise and fall of your abdomen and the sensations in your body. Any time you feel your mind wondering simply refocus your attention on the rhythm and sensations of your breathing.

Deep breath in, slow exhale.

You are anchoring your attention using your breath. Your body feels more and more relaxed and your mind is calm and free of any anxiety.

Now just allow your breathing to fall into a natural rhythm.

Start to visualize yourself on a long quiet beach. You are in the shade deeply relaxed and comfortable on a reclining chair that cushions your limbs perfectly.

You can see the blue and green ocean. The water is calm under a beautiful summer sky.

You can see the water shimmer as it touches the sandy shore in gentle waves that advance and retreat slowly.

There is a gentle breeze that is caressing your skin and you can feel a warm glow as you lie in your beach chair feeling connected to the peace and tranquility around you.

Notice the perpetual movement of the water against the shore and feel it start to lull you slowly into a comfortable daze.

You are drifting off slowly and all you can hear are the gentle sounds of the ocean and the breeze around you.

The gentle breeze is warm against your skin and there is complete peace and tranquility.

You are drifting deeper into relaxation as you feel the flow of the ocean bring you healing and serenity in this quiet and peaceful place.

Let yourself drift off in this quiet place. You are enjoying the tranquility and your mind is completely calm and relaxed.

Abandon yourself to the quiet and now let the gentle waves soothe you as you sleep.

Chapter 6: The Healing Room; Manifestations for Your Spirit

The law of attraction depends on our subconscious energy to manifest the things that we want to see in our lives. However, for most people, the law of attraction does not work because they lack clarity not just on what they want but also about who they are deep down inside. Meditation helps to open up the deepest layers of your subconscious to allow you to find the answers you need to manifest your desires.

To attract love, wealth, abundance and good health, it is important to have clarity. Clarity about who you are and where you want to go and clarity about the kind of energy you are projecting into the universe. If your internal energy is different from the things you want to manifest, you will always struggle to manifest the things you want. Your desires and your intentions need to be aligned with the subconscious energy that you are anchored to.

For this section, the meditations will focus on bringing your clarity, self-acceptance and mending any broken spirit that may be tainting your subconscious energy.

Meditation for Self-Love and Self-Acceptance - 20 minutes

Clarity starts with self-acceptance. Knowing who you are, what is important to you and where you want to go will help you align your internal energy with the things you truly want to manifest.

Let us get into it.

Duration 20 minutes

Start by making yourself comfortable in a quiet room. Sit in a comfortable chair with your feet firmly planted on the ground. Your neck and spine should be aligned in an upright but relaxed posture.

Now close your eyes gently. Place your hand on your chest above your heart then take a deep breath in through your nose. Exhale slowly and as you do release any pent-up thoughts or emotions.

Keep breathing in deeply, as you relax and exhale any tension or stress releasing it from your body.

You are feeling calmer and more relaxed as you continue to breathe in deeply and exhale slowly.

Allow each inhale to be a bit deeper than the one before it. Feel your lungs expand out as you inhale, and feeling everything contract back in as you exhale.

Now allow your breathing to return to its normal rhythm but continue to follow the sensations of your breath weaving in and out of your body.

Let your body and mind relax completely letting go of any tension, anxiety or errant thoughts.

Now turn your attention to the bottom half of your body, everything from your hips all the way down to the tips of your toes.

Bring your awareness to this part of your body and as you do feel a warm sensation traveling from your feet all the way up to your hips.

As you become more in tune with this part of your body now imagine that the awareness and warm sensation in this lower part of your body are radiating love and appreciation.

You are releasing positive energy to this part of your body. Embracing every curve, every scar and everything else about this part of your body. Feel the love and appreciation flow from your mind to your lower body.

Gradually continue to move your awareness upward and now focus on the top half of your body. Feel the warm sensation travel from your hips up into your abdomen, to the arch of your spine, up to your shoulders and to the very top of your head.

Now you can feel every part of your body vividly. You are sending love and appreciation to every inch of your body and allowing your awareness to ease any tense muscles.

As you appreciate and send love to your body repeat this affirmation quietly in your mind.

I am beautiful. Every part of me is perfect just as it is. I accept who I am. I appreciate who I am.

Now take a deep breath in and slowly release it through the mouth feeling your body relax even more.

Repeat this affirmation one more time.

I am beautiful. Every part of me is perfect just as it is. I accept who I am. I appreciate who I am.

And now begin to call to mind other parts of yourself that you've held in judgment in the past.

All the little things you nitpick about yourself and constantly berate yourself for. A bad decision, a missed opportunity, something you lost, something you failed at. Recall all the things that you hold against yourself for whatever reason.

Think of all the things you say about yourself that highlight your flaws and overlook your strengths. Let all these things come to the surface as one by one you sift through all the negative and self-defeating beliefs.

As you allow these thoughts to rise to the surface, begin to release them one by one. Every time you exhale, release these negative judgments that you have about yourself.

Release the self-doubt, the regrets, the guilt, the shame, the need for acceptance from others. Disconnect yourself from these judgments by letting them float away with every exhale.

Feel your mind and body start to get lighter as you unload all these judgments and negative beliefs that you have been carrying around with you.

Feel yourself getting freer and freer as you keep breathing out the negativity and cleansing your mind with fresh positive energy.

As you continue to release the negative thoughts repeat this affirmation quietly in your mind.

I offer myself forgiveness. I free myself from these negative thoughts and emotions. I offer myself acceptance. I am okay with who I am.

Now take in a deep breath and as you exhale open up your arms and reach out on either side.

With your arms wide open, visualize a bright golden light bathing you from the top of your head all the way to your feet.

As this light touches you, any negativity or tension in your body is being washed away and you feel a renewing energy engulf you.

Allow yourself to luxuriate in this light as you feel it take away any self-judgment leaving only love and acceptance.

Now bring your arms around yourself, hugging yourself and as you do so feel the love and appreciation you have for yourself.

At this point I want you to focus on the parts of you that you cherish and love the most. Whether it is your smile, your kind spirit, your love of nature, your strength, your resilience, a feature that you love.

Everything you appreciate and love about yourself, focus on it right now. Whatever makes you proud, whatever milestones you have reached so far, whatever challenges you have overcome.

Call to mind all the positive things about yourself and go through them one by one. Note each of them with appreciation and love. Let yourself connect with these positive thoughts and emotions that you have about yourself.

Now you can bring your arms back down. But stay in the moment a while longer simply focusing on everything you love about yourself and appreciating who you are.

When you are ready, you can bring your awareness back to the present by focusing on your breathing. Slowly become aware of your surroundings and gently open your eyes.

You can practice this meditation every time you find yourself having negative self-talk or when you simply want to lift your spirits and self-esteem.

This guided meditation is now complete.

Guided Meditation for Healing Broken Hearts & Removing Negative Attachments - 25 minutes

When you have been in a failed relationship or any kind of toxic relationship, often the emotional trauma stays with you long after the relationship ends. This trauma often leads to dysfunction in your subsequent relationships and makes it impossible for you to attract and manifest healthy and loving relationships. It is important to work on being whole by releasing negative attachments before you can seek to invite and attract new relationships.

This guided meditation will help you train your mind to release negative attachments that keep you anchored to toxic situations and environments.

Let us get started.

Duration: 25 minutes

Start by sitting or lying down in a comfortable position and allow yourself to relax your muscles.

Now close your eyes and take a few long deep breaths to help calm you and ease any tension.

Take a deep breath feeling the air enter your body and into your lungs. Feel your stomach and chest rise and fall as you inhale and exhale.

Feeling any tension and stress leave your body every time you exhale.

Notice the relief that it brings to your body and mind to release some of that tension and stress.

Now repeat the deep breathing a couple more times and sink even deeper into relaxation and calmness.

Now I want you to focus on any comfort that you feel no matter how small it is. Maybe it is the cozy temperature in your room, the comfortable chair you are sitting on or anything else that is bringing you some comfort in this moment.

As you hold on to this feeling of comfort start to visualize yourself sitting in front of a warm cozy fireplace. The fire is burning nice and warm and you can see the bright flames rising gently into the air.

As you sit in the warm glow of this fire, call to mind an experience, a memory or any past hurt that you would like to take and burn and be free of.

Let the image or memory come to you unbidden. Do not try to force it or rush it. Know that whatever image comes to mind first is the correct one.

Now take that image on the mental screen of your inner mind and let it be as big as a portrait. You can see it clearly in vivid detail as you hold it in your hand.

Now just toss it gently into the fire and watch it start to burn. See the flames starts to eat it up as it shrivels and starts to turn into ash. Watch it disappear completely into the flames until nothing is left but the warm glow of the fire.

Now I want you to take the next memory that brings you pain, hurt or regret. As you see this memory on the mental screen of your mind, see it as a portrait with that memory clearly painted on it.

Hold that portrait in your hand and then toss it into the flames and watch as it burns. Watch the smoke rise slowly into the air as the portrait catches fire. Watch it start to shrivel until it is completely engulfed in flames and there is nothing left.

Now repeat the same process for as many toxic memories, situations and people that you want to detach yourself from because they are keeping you from growing.

Clear all the residual hurts and attachments by burning them one by one in the fire until there is nothing left of them in you.

As you continue to release these attachments, feel your heart and mind get lighter and more open with each attachment that you release.

The bad relationships, the hurtful memories, any past hurts, you are releasing them all and unburdening yourself. You are freeing up space for the things that you want to manifest in your life.

You are releasing negative attachments to create room for new healthy relationships, new love, new happy memories and a life of abundance and joy.

Notice your level of peace or satisfaction as you untether yourself from all these unwanted attachments that have kept you from abundance and jot. Lean into this feeling of freedom, and peace.

Continue to gaze into the fire as it burns brightly bathing you in its cozy warmth. It is feeling you with a positive energy and you feel open and clear about who you are and where you want your life to go.

You have unshackled yourself and now there is room in your heart and your mind for new experiences, new memories and healthier relationships.

Allow yourself to sit with this realization for a moment. Revel in your release and detachment from all the things that were not serving you.

Now take a deep healing breath in and fill the crisp clean air fill your lungs before exhaling slowly.

Repeat the deep breathing two more times, then allow your breathing to go back to its normal rhythm.

Slowly start to bring your awareness to the present by focusing on your breathing. When you are ready you can gently open your eyes.

This guided meditation is now complete.

Guided Meditation for Forgiveness and Letting Go - 20 minutes

Nothing burdens your spirit and weighs down your mind like holding on to grudges, past hurts and judgments against yourself and others. If you want to radiate the positive energy that you need to manifest love, abundance and wealth, it is important to clear your conscience and unburden yourself.

The freedom that forgiveness brings allows you to direct your energy into the things you want rather than getting caught up in what you do not like. If all your energy is going towards grudges, hate for others, self-hate and other destructive emotions there is no way you can manifest a happy abundant life.

This meditation will allow you to forgive and let go freeing yourself to receive all the blessings the universe has in store for you.

Let us get into it.

Duration 20 minutes

Make yourself very comfortable in a seated position on the floor on a meditation cushion or in a chair. You can also choose to lie down with a pillow beneath your knees and another pillow supporting your neck and head.

Make sure you are as comfortable as possible. If any of your clothing is tight release it so that your body is not constrained in any way.

Your spine should be straight and your arms and legs uncrossed to ensure the natural flow of energy throughout your body

Now take several slow deep breaths feeling them all the way up through the top of your head and all the way down through to your legs.

Your breath is a life force so as you breathe in allow this life force to move deeply into your body bringing fresh life and energy into your body.

As you exhale allow this life force to wash away any physical and emotional toxins that you need to release.

Repeat this inhale and exhale cleansing a few times and with every inhale allow the life force to go deeper and with every exhale just let go of negativity and toxins.

Now allow yourself to be supported in this moment by calling on the universe to surround you with love and light. Allow the universe to surround you with its healing and protective energy and bring you healing.

Notice all the points of contact between your body and wherever you are resting and allow your body to melt more and more into relaxation with every breath.

You are safe. You are comfortable. You are in a good place.

Now start to picture pure white light beginning to fill up your room. This light is filling the entire room covering every inch of open space in your room.

Feel the white light wash over you in a gentle wave that brings nourishment and protective energy.

Now still enveloped in this light, picture a shimmering door before you. You know instinctively that this door is inviting you to a beautiful place beyond.

Notice the door in every detail. The color, the size, the shape, the texture. As you take in every little detail, now bring your attention to the doorknob.

Reach out and touch the doorknob feeling its coolness in your palm. Now take a deep breath, turn the knob and open the door.

On the other side of the door, you are standing on a serene white sandy beach overlooking an expansive crystal-clear blue ocean.

The sand beneath your feet feels warm and soft to your bare feet.

The warm rays of the sun feel warm and inviting. The air smells fresh and clean and every breath in feels like a cleansing energy working its way into your body.

Feel the gentle breeze caress your skin gently. It all feels so peaceful.

Now take a deep breath and inhale the fresh salty scent of the ocean as you listen to the soothing sounds of the waves.

Slowly walk to the water's edge and stand there feeling the gentle waves touch your feet as they advance and retreat from the shore.

You can feel the pure energy of a healing wave coming towards you. As you stand here at the edge, you open up your palms and as you do so, breathe in deeply and exhale slowly.

With every exhale you release from your mind and heart any grudges, any hate any past hurts that you are holding on to.

Continue to breathe in the cool healing life force of the pecan air and as you exhale, let all the things that you are holding against yourself and others go.

As you release these negative emotions repeat this affirmation quietly in your mind.

I forgive myself. I free myself from grudges and hate. I am opening myself up to love. I am radiating love. I am letting go.

As you affirm your intentions continue to breathe in the healing life force of the ocean and with every exhale continue to unburden yourself.

You are releasing from your heart anything you feel needs forgiving within yourself. Past actions, unhealthy habits, toxic behaviors, negative thoughts and all those negative beliefs that block your essence.

You are releasing any animosity you feel towards others and choosing to let go of grudges and unresolved issues because they are only clouding your clarity and preventing you from manifesting your desires.

You are releasing it all into the ocean and as you stand there you can feel all these negative thoughts and emotions get swept up in the waves.

With every release, you feel freer and more in control of your heart, your mind and your destiny.

You are no longer going to be driven by negative emotions. Instead, you will lean into your positive emotions and direct your energy to the things you want to attract in your life. Health, wealth, abundance and love.

At this point repeat this affirmation quietly in your mind.

I forgive myself. I free myself from grudges and hate. I am opening myself up to love. I am radiating love. I am letting go.

Now take a deep breath, hold it for a moment and exhale slowly. Another deep breath and as you inhale feel the healing life force touch every cell in your body.

Exhale slowly and let your breathing go back to normal.

Let this feeling of utter and complete unburdening and freedom wash over you. Feel the warm rays of the sun on your face and as you do, roll your shoulders back to open up your heart and your mind to the positive energy of the universe.

Gradually, bring your awareness back to the present. As you breathe, tune in to the sensations of the rhythmic rise and fall of your chest. Focus on these sensations until your awareness is back to the present.

You can now open your eyes.

This guided meditation is now complete.

Affirmations for Body, Mind and Soul - 10 minutes

Affirmations rewire your brain to create new core beliefs that create the reality that you want to manifest in your life. When you use affirmations to state and clarify your intentions you reset your beliefs to align with the things that you want to attract to your life and manifest.

You can repeat these affirmations every day in the morning or just before you go to bed.

Let's get started.

Duration: 10 minutes

Sit in a comfortable position. You can sit on a chair or on the floor wherever you feel most comfortable.

Straighten your spine and tuck your chin slightly inward to align your neck with your spine.

Now close your eyes and start to connect with your mind and body.

Tune in to your breathing and feel the air enter and leave your body. If any errant thoughts come to mind, simply release them and turn your focus back to your breathing.

As you feel your body and mind relax completely you can now repeat these affirmations. You can do it out loud or quietly in your mind.

I am a magnet for positivity and happiness.

I see the beauty of everything around me.

I am surrounded by love and I freely give my love to others.

I wake up every day excited to embrace the day.

I accept myself unconditionally.

I love and accept myself for who I am.

I am grateful for all the good things in my life.

I choose love over hate.

I choose forgiveness and freedom.

I am at peace with myself.

I am in tune with the universe and allow it to guide me.

I embrace joy and positivity every day.

Every day I get closer to my dreams.

My life is filled with possibilities and potential.

I focus on the positive and celebrate who I am.

I choose to be confident.

I choose to be at peace.

I choose to be free.

I am proud of who I am and the person I am becoming.

I am strong mentally physically and spiritually.

I live my life with grace and courage.

I am always surrounded by positive energy.

I am full of boundless positive energy

I trust the universe to guide me to my heart's desires.

I attract joy and positivity everywhere.

I focus on what I can control and let go of what I can't.

I have everything that I need to be happy and fulfilled

I give myself permission to be happy.

I embrace everything the universe is releasing to me right now.

Chapter 7: Overcoming Limiting Beliefs

When you think of the law of attraction, it is easy to assume that as long as you know what you want you can manifest it. However, since your subconscious is the reservoir of the energy you put out into the universe, you can only manifest the things you want if your beliefs are in alignment with what you want to manifest. You cannot manifest wealth if you are constantly thinking about lack. You cannot manifest love if you are convinced that you are unworthy of it. Your beliefs and your intentions must be aligned for the law of attraction to work.

Self-limiting beliefs will always be the biggest barrier to manifesting your desires. You must first believe in yourself and in what you want to achieve before you can call it into reality. Ultimately the universe will only give you what you have enough courage and belief to ask for.

To make it easier to reset your subconscious and rewire your mind, the meditations in this section are all about overcoming self-limiting beliefs that block your path to abundance.

Guided Meditation for Overcoming Self-Sabotage -25 minutes

If you find yourself constantly holding yourself back from going after the things you want either due to fear, lack of confidence or any other limiting beliefs, this meditation is for you. Self-sabotage is something that we do both consciously and subconsciously and it can make it difficult to live up to your full potential.

Let's get started.

Duration: 25 minutes

Start by sitting comfortably in a relaxed but upright posture. Relax your shoulders and make sure that your feet are firmly planted on the ground.

Now you are going to direct your awareness inward by shutting out all external input.

Take a nice big deep breath and as the air fills your lungs, feel yourself relaxing and releasing any tension. Exhale slowly through your mouth and feel the tension leave your body.

Now close your eyes and take a couple more deep breaths followed by slow exhales that lead you deeper into relaxation.

You can now allow your breathing to go back to normal.

I want you to now bring all your awareness to the bottoms of your feet. Imagine that there are cords connecting your feet to the ground, anchoring you and supporting you.

Now visualize a relaxing energy flowing up from the ground into your feet. You can feel your feet get warmer as this energy rises up into them filling them with a soothing warmness that starts to travel throughout your body.

You are feeling completely relaxed and every tension in your body has dissipated. Your muscles are loose and soft and all you feel is the comforting warmth of the energy coming from the ground and into your body.

Continue to focus on this pleasant and soothing feeling that is spreading throughout your body. You feel like a great weight has just been lifted from your shoulders.

It is so calm and peaceful and you feel yourself open up to receive the energy that is soothing and relaxing your entire body.

Now take a deep breath and as you do so think of a pattern of behavior or habit that you repeat even when you know it is not good for you.

I want you to see this pattern clearly and identify it in the way you live your life. Maybe it is procrastinating over important decisions. Maybe you always shy away from anything that challenges your perceived comfort zone. Maybe you always worry about failure.

Whatever it is that you repeatedly do, focus on this particular pattern and acknowledge it without judgment.

Now I want you to go back to the time to when the pattern began. Move as far back as you can in time until you uncover the source of the limiting belief.

Was it something you experienced as a child, something someone said that maybe made you question your self-worth? Is it a failure that you have trouble getting over?

Delve deep and allow yourself to find the trigger that created the pattern that you find yourself constantly repeating in your life.

You are right there now in the past. Take note of the details. Are you indoors or outdoors? Are you alone or is someone with you? What are you feeling in this moment?

As you immerse yourself in the memory notice the conditions that existed at this starting point of your pattern of self-sabotage. What is your mental state? How are you feeling emotionally? What is going on around you?

Now take time to think about how in similar circumstances you revert to this pattern because your subconscious is holding on to the negative experience or memory.

Take a moment to absorb any information in the scene from the past that will help you detach yourself from this negative pattern.

Are there any emotional ties that are causing you to keep repeating this pattern of behavior? Does it help you escape your fear or mask your emotions? Are you using this pattern to avoid challenging and pushing yourself?

Be open to receiving the answer without judgment or shame. Open yourself up to the realization that your self-sabotage is really just a reflection of your emotional resistance to things that you are not comfortable with.

As you start to become aware of the answers, see yourself moving back to the future from that time in the past that set off your destructive pattern.

As you withdraw from the memory, feel it fade further and further away from you until it is nothing but a tiny speck on the horizon.

You are releasing that memory right now and freeing yourself from its attachment in your life. You will not live your present based on your past and you are opening your mind up to new perspectives and new belief systems.

Keep withdrawing from that past memory and the further away you go, feel it sink deeper and deeper into oblivion. Picture yourself shutting a door and leaving that experience behind the closed door as you walk towards a different door.

You are standing before this new door and you can see it vividly in your mind. You can see the doorknob and you reach out and touch it. The cool metal feels soothing in your hand and you take a deep breath and open the door.

On the other side of the door, you are standing in a lush green field surrounded by a vast expanse of greenery and trees.

The air is clean and fresh and all around you are the nurturing sounds of nature.

A cool gentle breeze rustles the trees and you feel the crisp clean air fill your lungs as you breathe in.

You feel confident and relaxed in this peaceful place and your mind is fully receptive to the loving positive energy of the universe.

You immerse yourself in this feeling of confidence and positivity that is coursing through your body right now.

Your mind is free of mental blocks, you are sure of yourself and your intentions, you are at ease with where you are. You are trusting the universe to manifest your deepest desires for success, love and joy.

Now as you continue to stand in this lush field surrounded by positive uplifting energy start to see all the things that you want to manifest in your life.

See the career that you have always wanted but been too afraid to chase after. Think of the relationship you have always wanted but never dared to pursue.

Think of all the things and desires you have kept buried out of fear or self-doubt. See them clearly in your mind and as you continue to visualize them open up your hands with your palms facing upwards ready to receive.

Feel the universe start to release all these things to you one by one. It is giving you all the things you have ever desired and all you have to do is reach out and take them.

Now bask in the confidence of knowing what you want is still out there waiting for you. Relax in the knowledge that what you are seeking is also seeking you if only you will allow yourself to find it.

Feel yourself yield to the infinite power and positive energy of the universe.

Remain in this space for a moment, attaching yourself to the positive energy and letting it fill you completely from the soles of your feet to the top of your head.

You are in sync with your desires, you know what you want and you are no longer afraid to reach out and take it.

Now slowly start to bring your awareness back to the present. Take a deep healing breath, hold for a moment then exhale slowly. Another slow deep breath followed by a long exhale.

Start to bring awareness back to your body. feel your arms, your feet and your chest as it rises rhythmically every time you breathe in and out.

When you are ready, open your eyes.

This guided meditation is now complete.

Reprograming Limiting Beliefs & Finding Your Power -15 minutes

Limiting beliefs can keep you feeling small and prevent you from living up to your potential. This meditation is intended to help you reprogram the negative thoughts and beliefs you have about yourself that are blocking you from manifesting abundance, success and wealth.

Let's get into it.

Duration: 15 minutes

You can choose to lie down or sit down in a comfortable position. Sit in a quiet room free of distractions and noise.

Now gently close your eyes and as you do so start to center and calm your mind by breathing deeply and bring all your awareness to the rhythm of your inhales and exhales.

Feel the sensations in your chest and abdomen as you inhale deeply letting the air fill your lungs. As you exhale slowly feel your chest relax.

As your body and mind start to relax, sink deeper into your chair or bed, allowing your muscles to soften and relax completely. Allow your body to sink deeper and deeper into relaxation with every breath you take.

Now that your awareness is fully focused inward, allow your breathing to return to its normal rhythm. Feel yourself fall deeper into yourself and sinking to a safe space within where there is no judgment or fear.

Now picture yourself walking barefoot on a soft thick bed of grass that is softly caressing your feet as you walk. Feel the coolness of the grass under your feet and fully allow it to support and anchor you.

You feel safe and at peace.

Your mind feels wide open and you are ready to open yourself up to new truths and release any beliefs that no longer serve you.

Take a deep breath and prepare yourself to absorb new truths into your subconscious.

Now repeat these affirmations.

I am worthy

I am lovable.

I exist. I matter. I am meant to be here.

I have a purpose.

I am confident and sure of myself.

I am surrounded by love and I attract it effortlessly to myself.

I am surrounded by wealth and I attract it effortlessly to myself.

I am beautiful inside and out.

I trust myself and my decisions.

I trust in my abilities and my potential.

I attract abundance like a magnet.

I embrace and accept who I am.

I trust the universe to manifest all my desires.

I exist. I matter. I am meant to be here.

Take a deep breath in and as you exhale, allow all of these new truths to sink in deeper into your unconscious mind.

Now repeat these affirmations.

I now cut all cords from negative beliefs in my life.

I detach myself from self-doubt, fear of failure and negativity.

I release all the dysfunctional circumstances and people in my life.

I am releasing negativity and making room for positivity and love.

I cleanse myself of all misconceptions and judgments about myself.

I free myself from the judgments of others.

As you affirm your new beliefs, feel the energy surging from the green grass beneath your feet into your body. It is a healing energy. It is a restoring energy. It is infusing you with love and self-acceptance.

Allow yourself to feel this positive energy permeate every cell of your being. As you breathe in, let the positivity flood your mind and your emotions and cleanse you of any dark limiting thoughts.

Now take a deep breath and repeat these affirmations.

I exist. I matter. I am meant to be here.

I have a purpose.

I am confident and sure of myself.

As you complete these affirmations, go into deep breathing to slowly start bringing your awareness to the present.

Deep breath in, hold for a moment, now exhale slowly through your mouth. Again slowly deep breath in through your nose, followed by a long exhale. Now allow your breathing to go back to normal.

Slowly open your eyes when you are ready.

This guided meditation is now complete.

Meditation for Eliminating Your Abundance and Success Blocks - 15 minutes

It is natural to see opposition and resistance when it is coming from external sources. However, we often overlook the ways in which our belief systems and subconscious energy block our own paths to success.

If you want to eliminate the self-imposed blockages that are keeping you from manifesting abundance in your life. Practice this guided meditation. It is intended to help you get out of your own way and reframe your mind to reflect all the things that you want to be manifested in your life.

Let us get started.

Duration 15 minutes

Find a comfortable quiet spot and sit in a comfortable posture. Relax your neck and shoulders and plant your feet firmly on the ground.

Now, I want you to look up as if you're looking into your eyebrows. Try and focus on the midpoint on your forehead which is a powerful chakra point that helps to open up your subconscious.

Now close your eyes with your awareness still focused on this chakra point.

Breathe in deeply and breathe out. Again, breathe in deeply and exhale slowly. You are starting to feel relaxed and calm.

Take another deep breath followed by a slow exhale and as you exhale release any tension that you are holding in your body. Let your muscles soften and allow your body to sink deeper and deeper into relaxation.

Now allow your breathing to go back to normal.

Slowly stretch your arms out in front of you as if you're holding onto the handlebars of a bike

Now with your arms still extended, visualize that you have a bucket in your left hand. This bucket is a vivid red and it is full of sand. The bucket is heavy and you can feel it weighing your extended arm down.

Your left arm is becoming heavier and heavier as you continue to hold the heavy bucket of sane. You can feel the tension start to grow in your left arm muscles.

On the other arm, your right hand is still extended. However, in this arm, all you have is a balloon. This beautiful balloon is not heavy at all so there is no strain on your right arm.

The beautiful balloon is pulling your arm up and you can feel your right up floating weightless before you.

As the weight of the sand bucket in your left hand continues to weigh you down, the helium balloon is trying to pull you up into the sky with it.

You are now being pulled in two different directions and you have a choice to let go of one of the things you are holding on to.

In your left hand is the red bucket full of sand. This bucket is a reflection of all your negative beliefs that keep you anchored in lack, unhappiness and emotional turmoil.

This red bucket contains your beliefs that there is not enough money, your belief that no one will love you as you are, your belief that you can only be rich if you came from wealth. This bucket is holding all your limiting beliefs and the longer you continue to hold it the more the strain on your left hand is.

You can feel the muscles in your left arm start to tire. This fatigue is slowly creeping into other parts of your body.

Now, look at the beautiful balloon on your right arm. This balloon is doing its best to help you float but the bucket in your other hand is too heavy to lift.

In this moment I want you to feel the weight of the red bucket on your left arm and feel the lightness in your right hand.

At this point, you have a choice. You can let go of the balloon and continue to struggle with the heavy bucket or you can let go of the bucket and allow the balloon to pull you up.

In this moment, you are realizing that you cannot hold on to both. The beautiful balloon is the abundance and success you want to achieve. It is all the things you want to manifest in your life.

However, to hold on to this balloon and let it pull you as high as you can go you must first release the bucket in your left hand.

Now take a deep breath and exhale slowly. Now tell yourself- I'm ready to let go of my fear. I'm ready to rise to my full potential. I'm ready to release these beliefs that have held me down for so long.

Now slowly open the palm of your left hand and let the bucket of sand fall to the ground. Your arm is no longer weighed down by the weight and you can feel the tension in your muscle start to ease.

Your whole body starts to feel lighter and lighter and slowly the beautiful balloon starts to pull you up into the sky. You are floating off the surface now, and the higher you rise the easier it becomes.

You are elated by this feeling of freedom and discovery that is engulfing you right now. You are ready to reach new heights and you have completely detached yourself from all the beliefs that were holding you sown.

Feel yourself rise steadily into the air as positive energy starts to fill your body with confidence and trust that you are on your way to meet your heart's desires.

Your wealth is weighting for you, your abundance is just a breath away and fulfilling relationships are in your sights.

See yourself steadily floating away from negative beliefs and rising higher and higher. It feels great to be free. You are allowing yourself to trust the universe to guide you to your dreams.

You have given up all resistance, all negative anchors and are opening yourself up to receive from the universe.

Let this feeling permeate every part of your being and sit with it for a moment. See the doors that are opening up for you right now after unburdening yourself. See the boundless possibilities that await you.

Now take a deep breath in, hold it in and then exhale slowly. Again, breathe deeply, and exhale. Now slowly let your consciousness return to the present. Become aware of your body, your surroundings and your breathing.

When you are ready, you can open your eyes.

This guided meditation is now complete.

Feeding Your Passions Using Meditation - 15 minutes

Do you often find yourself losing your motivation to pursue the things you want? Have you ever started to do something and then given up halfway through? If you keep birthing dreams that never come to pass because you cannot summon the energy to keep them going, mindful meditation can help you to keep feeding your passions.

In this meditation, you will learn how to reconnect to the things that are meaningful to you in order to manifest your desires.

Let's get into it.

Duration 15 minutes

Start in a comfortable position. You may sit cross-legged or with your knees together back on your heels. If you are sitting on the floor, get some cushy pillows to make yourself as comfortable as possible.

Now sit up nice with your spine is elongated and in alignment with your neck for an upright but relaxed posture.

Roll your shoulders back without straining to open up your chest and leave yourself open to receiving energy from the universe.

Now take a deep breath in and as you inhale roll your shoulders up towards your ears.

Exhale slowly through your mouth and roll your shoulders down. Start to ground yourself by bringing awareness to the surface beneath you. Become aware of all the parts of your body that are in contact with the surface you are sited on.

Take a moment to get grounded here and really root yourself down by visualizing cords connecting to the ground beneath and keeping you grounded and supported.

Now that you are truly centered I want you to ask yourself – what do you really want? What are you passionate about? If you could have everything you wanted right now what would you pick?

Listen to the answer that comes unbidden to the surface. Do not try to analyze or judge the answers just acknowledge what your subconscious is telling you.

Whatever the answer is feel it take hold in your mind and see it in vivid detail.

Maybe you want to start a business, maybe you want to pursue a different career, maybe you want to start a family, maybe you want to buy your first home. Whatever the answer is, recognize it and internalize it.

Feel yourself connect to whatever goals and passions you have uncovered for yourself. Imagine yourself having those things right now in this moment and how it would make you feel. Allow yourself to experience this feeling deeply and stay connected to it.

Now take a deep breath in, and then exhale slowly. Two more deep breaths in, followed by a slow exhale.

Now focus all your attention on your heart space by imagining a radiant bright light burning in your chest area. Feel the energy start to spread out from your heart into your arms, your eyes, your legs, your feet and every single cell in your body.

Feel yourself start to vibrate with this powerful energy that is filling you on the inside and radiating outside.

With this energy still coursing through your body, I want you to picture the passion or goal that you uncovered earlier. As you visualize this goal open up your mind and let this energy breathe life into this goal.

Now it is not just a house that you want, but you can see yourself living in it in your mind right now. It is not just a new job you want but you can picture yourself walking into your new office and sitting behind the desk.

Whatever your goal is breathe life into it by attaching yourself to it as the powerful radiant energy continues to radiate from you.

Don't just see yourself achieving it but also put yourself in that moment and feel what it will feel like to see your goal come to life.

Take a deep breath in and slowly exhale. Another deep breath in and a slow exhale. Now repeat this affirmation out loud.

I am committed to my goal. I have what it takes to achieve my purpose. I am attracting all the things I desire to my life.

As you voice your affirmation, bring your hand up to your chest and repeat these affirmations.

I can do anything I put my mind to.

I will pursue my goals to the very end.

I have what it takes to manifest my goals.

I am capable. I am strong. I am confident.

Sit with the power of your intentions and let these affirmations sink deep into your subconscious. Allow yourself to connect with them deeply and carry them with you.

Now slowly start to bring your awareness back to the present. Listen to the sound of your breath, feel the rhythm of your chest moving up and down and reconnect with the present.

When you are ready open your eyes.

This guided meditation is now complete.

Affirmations to Achieve Your Goals - 10 minutes

When you speak affirmations you are not just voicing the things that you want to manifest but you are also setting a clear intention that will guide you in the right direction. The following affirmations are powerful statements that will help you reset your mind when you start to lose motivation and commitment to your goals.

Repeat these affirmations in the morning for at least 21 days to reawaken your commitment to your goals.

Duration 10 minutes

Take a sit in a comfortable position and close your eyes.

To clear your mind and tap into your subconscious take a couple of deep breaths making sure to release any tension in your body as you exhale.

Again, breathe deeply and focus all your awareness on the air as it enters your body and fills your lungs. Exhale slowly through your mouth releasing any tension, errant thoughts and pent-up emotion.

One more time, deep inhale, hold for a minute then exhale slowly. As you feel your mind start to relax and calm down, allow your breathing to return to normal and repeat these affirmations.

Every day I take action to achieve my goals.

My mind is focused on getting things done.

Achieving success comes easily to me.

Nothing that can stop me from achieving success.

Being focused and motivated comes easily to me.

I act with courage and confidence.

I will take action to get things done.

My mind is energized, clear and focused on my goals.

All of my goals are well within my reach.

I am focused and consistent.

Everything I am seeking is also seeking me.

I have intense passion and belief in my goals.

I am aligned with the abundance of the universe.

I have everything I need to reach my goals.

The universe brings me success every day.

Chapter 8: Manifesting Personal Growth Through Healing

Progress is proof of life and every day we strive to be better than who we were yesterday. If you have been struggling to attract the things that you want, you can use meditation to boost your personal growth by rewiring your mindset. When you move from strength to strength and milestone to milestone, it is only a matter of time before you can manifest the wealth, abundance and love that you desire.

Just like everything else in life, manifesting your desires is an inside job that starts with having your mind and subconscious energy in the right place.

Guided Meditation for Self-Assertion-Discovering your Ideal Self - 25 minutes

It is so easy to lose yourself in the hustle and bustle of life. This guided meditation is designed to help you reconnect with your ideal self. You will start manifesting growth by rediscovering your worth and your higher purpose.

Let us get started.

Duration: 25 minutes

Start by finding a quiet space that is free of distractions and noise.

Now sit in a comfortable chair or on a meditation pillow on the floor. Relax your body and allow yourself to ease any tension in your muscles.

Now close your eyes and begin to bring your awareness to your breath without changing your normal breathing rhythm. Simply tune in to the gentle rise and fall of your chest as you breathe in and out.

Notice how your breath flows in through your nose and fills up your body with life. Notice how each exhale flows out taking with it emotional and physical stress.

Feel the stress and tension gradually melt away as you continue to focus your awareness on your breathing.

If you still have thoughts going through your mind simply let them flow through your mind without attaching to them.

Any time an errant thought pops into your mind simply draw your focus away from it by focusing on your breathing.

Gradually start to take deeper and longer breaths as you ease your mind and body deeper and deeper into relaxation.

Notice the stillness that comes between each inhale and exhale.

As your breath deepens focus your attention on the stillness between the breaths.

Take another deep slow breath in and fill your lungs completely and then release the breath through your mouth slowly and gently like a sigh.

Empty your lungs completely and feel all the tension in your body ease then allow your breathing to return to its natural rhythm.

Each breath is carrying you deeper and deeper into a calm, centered and relaxed state.

Your mind is open to possibilities and you feel a sense of clarity that is connecting you deeply with your subconscious.

Now allow yourself to let go of expectations, of the need to control and any resistance. Simply open your heart and your mind to what the universe has to offer. You are receptive and open.

Now bring your attention to the top of your head and imagine there is a warm light surrounding you and protecting you.

Visualize this light as a bright yellow light that is glowing softly and calming you as it passes over your body and bathes you in its radiance.

Every part of your body that this light touches feels lighter and softer.

Notice the glowing nature of the radiant light and lean into the relaxing and comforting energy that it is infusing you with.

You can feel your forehead soften. The muscles around your eyes are relaxed and your neck and shoulders are perfectly at ease. As the light travels down your body, you feel the relaxing warmth spread downwards and cover every inch of your body.

Each part of your body is connected to this radiant energy and you can feel the energy grounding you and supporting you.

With each breath begin to feel that you are fully supported by the surface beneath you and protected by the energy surrounding you.

Notice how calm and at peace you feel right now in this moment.

Now I want you to visualize yourself outside on a wooded trail. As you walk on this trail take in your surroundings in vivid detail. The feel of the breeze on your skin, the rays of sunshine peering down the tree branches, the slope of the ground beneath your feet and the path outlined ahead of you as you walk.

You can feel the gentle warmth of the sun on your skin and the clean crisp air feels divine every time you inhale.

As you walk along the trail, you can see a small lake up ahead. It is full of striking blue water that is calm and gently rippling with the breeze.

You are walking towards the lake and when you get to the bank you are now looking out at the sparkling blue with its reflections of the sky and the trees.

As you stand by this beautiful lake start to explore your innermost desires and values.

What do you want to manifest in your life? Who is the person you wanted to grow up to be when you are young?

What is the last thing you think about when you go to bed? What is the first thing you think about when you wake up in the morning?

As you begin this self-inquiry the answers will start to surface from your subconscious into your conscious thoughts.

Take time to explore what your subconscious is telling you. Now as you start receiving your answers reflect on whether the way you live is in alignment with the values you are uncovering.

When was the last time you did something that truly made you happy? How often do you take time to simply take care of yourself and appreciate yourself? Are you pursuing any of the dreams that are close to your heart?

As you continue with self-inquiry your gaze is still on the beautiful lake scenery before you. You are accepting the answers to your question without shame or judgment.

Now start to reflect on how you live your life and ask yourself how much of your life is dedicated to pleasing others as opposed to doing what is meaningful to you. How often do you compromise your values just to fit in or go along with everyone else?

Let every answer reveal to you where you are going and whether you are making progress towards your goals, standing still or walking backward.

Accept these revelations without fear and judgment knowing that with this awareness you can make different choices and steer your life in a direction that reflects your innermost values and desires.

As you continue to gaze at the lake, connect with your innermost desires that your self-inquiry has revealed to you.

Attach to those things that have been lying dormant under the surface waiting for you to pick them up, dust them off and give them the attention you deserve. These are your dreams, your values and the things that matter to you most.

Pick them up one by one, holding them tightly in your hand and committing to staying true to them.

Now take a deep breath and repeat these affirmations.

I choose to live with passion.

I choose to be true to my innermost desires.

I choose to live with my whole heart.

I choose to live life on my own terms.

I choose abundance in all aspects of my life.

I choose an authentic life.

I choose growth and progress.

I choose me.

Now that you have affirmed your commitment to living in alignment with your personal values, slowly allow yourself to feel deeply connected to your innermost desires and passions. Open your mind to being true to these desires and making them come true.

Now gradually start to bring your awareness back to the present moment. Start to feel your breath flowing in and out of your body. bring your focus to your legs, your arms, your neck and your spine.

You are feeling relaxed yet energized. You have clarity in your intentions and you feel centered and at peace.

When you are ready, gently open your eyes.

This guided meditation is now complete.

Finding Growth Through Struggle Guided Meditation - 20 minutes

Even with our best-laid plans, sometimes life simply does not go our way. While failure is a natural process of any growth curve, often constant disappointment and struggle can sour your spirit and diminish your hope for abundance, success, and joy.

This next meditation is designed to help you find the sun even in your darkest times and stay anchored in your dreams and goals trusting the universe to manifest them.

Let's get into it.

Duration 20 minutes

Find a comfortable place to practice this meditation. You can choose to sit on a comfortable chair or lie down.

Now close your eyes and start to calm your body and mind by taking a slow deep breath followed by a slow exhale through the mouth.

As you exhale, release any tension in your muscles and any pent-up emotions.

Simply concentrate on your breathing and releasing any stress that you are feeling right now.

Continue to breathe deeply sending the air all the way to the bottom of your diaphragm. Hold the breath for a moment then exhale slowly through your mouth.

With every deep breath, your body is relaxing, your muscles are softening and your mind feels centered and calm.

Every exhale is bringing your release from negative thoughts, anxiety and stress.

You feel more relaxed and peaceful now.

Your entire body is at ease and there is a calming soothing energy settling all around you.

Now allow your breathing to go back to its normal rhythm. In this relaxed state, I want you to call to mind the challenge or challenges that have drained you and left you feeling empty or broken.

Maybe it is a broken marriage, a relationship that did not go the way you wanted, losing the job of your dreams, illness, loss or anything else that has drained you of hope and faith.

Sit quietly with these thoughts and allow this memory to rise to the surface. It may be painful and you can probably still feel the hurt right now. But the only way to detach yourself from it is to acknowledge it, feel it and release it.

Sit with this experience and notice how it makes you feel thinking about it. Now take a deep breath and with this experience still in your mind, bring your hand up to your chest and inhale deeply, as you exhale. Now feel yourself releasing this experience with the breath that you are letting out.

See it float away from you and disappear into thin air. Take another deep breath, hold it for a few seconds.

Again as you exhale, release the memory of the struggle that you went through or are going through. Feel it leave your body and see it float away from you and disappear into thin air.

Now the next time you inhale, I want you to feel the fresh life force in the air come into your body and start to replace all the negative emotions that the experience triggered in you.

Feel the disappointment and the hurt get replaced by hope. Feel the need to control the outcome get replaced by surrender to the universe. Feel yourself replace stress with hope and joy.

The dark energy is leaving your body and renewing energy is replacing it. As you continue to inhale and exhale you are trading positivity for negativity, joy for sadness, despair for hope and control for surrender.

In this moment you are aware that even when you cannot control every external circumstance, you can always control how you let them affect you. You are reclaiming power over your emotions, your mindset and your reactions.

With every deep breath, you feel new life being breathed into every organ of your body. With every exhale you are unburdening yourself of disappointments, frustrations and fear.

You realize that you do not need to always control everything because the universe knows what you need.

Your desires are manifesting now as you change negative energy into powerful positive energy.

With your hands still over your heart repeat these affirmations.

I am attracting new opportunities and positivity.

I am freeing myself from the struggles of my past.

I deserve to succeed.

I am manifesting my deepest desires.

I trust the universe to give me exactly what I need.

I deserve happiness.

I deserve joy.

I am hopeful and confident about my future.

I can handle any challenge that comes my way.

I yield to the positive energy and open myself to it completely.

I will trust my journey and enjoy the process.

I am taking the first step towards a positive new life now.

Every day I will wake with hope and confidence.

Every day I will align my intentions with the energy of the universe.

I am attracting joy.

I am attracting abundance and wealth.

I am attracting good healthy and emotional healing.

I am whole.

As you affirm your intentions feel these words connect deeply with your subconscious. Do not just say them, feel them and understand what they mean. For every affirmation feel it happen as you say it. Allow it to manifest in your mind so that it can manifest in reality.

Now take a moment to repeat the affirmations that particularly resonate with you. Make your own declaration right now and attach yourself mentally, emotionally and spiritually to it.

Take a deep breath in and allow yourself time for these uplifting affirmations to sink in. Let yourself attach to them deeply and commit them to your heart and mind.

When you are ready, start to bring your awareness back to your body and your surroundings. Take a deep breath in and then exhale slowly. Again, inhale deeply and then exhale slowly through your mouth.

Embrace the feeling of optimism and positivity that you are feeling right now in this moment. You can now gently open your eyes.

This guided mediation is now complete.

Emotional Healing and Liberating Yourself From Toxic Relationships - 25 minutes

If you have been wounded by a partner or a loved one in a way that left you emotionally damaged you can still manifest healthy and fulfilling relationships. This mediation is best practiced in bed just before you sleep to help you nurture your emotional health and manifest the kind of love you deserve.

Let's get started.

Duration 25 minutes

Start by lying in bed. Lie in your normal sleep position ensuring that you are comfortable and that there are no distractions in your room.

Now gently close your eyes and listen to the sound of my voice as I take you deeper into relaxation.

If you hear any sounds, let them calm your mind and soothe you.

If you have any tension in your body, bring your awareness to that part of your body and as you breathe out release that tension and feel your muscles soften and relax.

Concentrate on your breathing, each breath relaxing you more and more until you feel your body sinking and melting into the bed.

Now, visualize yourself in a garden. The air is clean and fresh and all around you is the beauty of nature and its tranquility.

It's as if the world has not touched this magical garden. The colors are vibrant and rich. Just ahead of you there are beautiful flowers of different shades and as you get closer to them you can smell a sweet inviting fragrance that is drawing you in.

Take a deep breath in and inhale the warm and perfumed air and as you breathe out, relax deeper and deeper.

As you continue walking in this magnificent garden, you can feel the cool grass under your feet.

As you breathe in the fresh air of the garden you can feel your body getting more refreshed with each breath you take.

You feel safe and relaxed.

As you continue walking you come to a pathway lined with stones that lead to a beautiful beach.

There are 10 stones on this pathway and each has unique healing properties.

As you step on that first stone, you feel yourself becoming more relaxed and at ease with yourself.

You come to the 9th stone and as you step on that stone, you're surrounded by a protective bubble that makes you feel safe and protected.

Take the next step to stone number 8 and feel a deep sense of peace settle within you.

Seven, you feel a sense of confidence. This is the stone that invokes the brain and awakens your subconscious.

Six, you are feeling calm and relaxed.

Five, your subconscious is fully listening to everything I say

Four, you feel yourself letting go of any tension and stress in your body.

Three, the mind, body and spirit are all aligned and in tune with the healing energy of the universe.

Two, breathe deeply and sink into the warm embrace and positive energy the universe is giving you.

One, sleep, deeper down as you reach the beautiful beach.

You are now at the beach and as you gaze into the distance, you see the vastness of the sea.

You are watching the waves roll gently towards the beach then retreat once they reach the shore.

As you walk to the water's edge, you can see your reflection in the water. Your face looks calm, happy and content.

Your feet sinking into the warm sand and you know without a doubt that you are exactly where you're supposed to be

As you drift deeper into this world you strip away the negative things that surround you.

You release the toxic attachments in your life that are stealing your joy.

You release yourself from relationships that only cause you pain.

You accept yourself as you are with all your strengths and flaws.

You can see all the positives that surround you in your life.

You now realize that the hurt and the pain of the past are only a minor part of who you are.

You start to have gratitude for who you are and who you'd become.

You forgive yourself. For your past. For your choices. For settling for less than you deserve. For forgetting that you are an amazing person.

Now you are stripping away any guilt that keeps you tethered to a toxic situation. You are freeing yourself from shame, from responsibility for other people's choices and constant pain.

You deserve better. You can do better. You will do better.

Let go of the past because the past doesn't serve you anymore.

Now, I want you to just take a moment and let your mind drift. Enjoy how relaxed your body feels.

I just want you to think of the word 'love'. Let it permeate your mind, body and spirit. Connect with it for a moment.

What does this word mean to you? How do you want to be loved? How do you want to love? What would your ideal relationship look like?

The answers to these questions are what you are going to manifest from this point onward in your life. Here them clearly and internalize them in your mind.

Today is the day you create the love you want and start to live a life you love. Today, you choose, and there is so much power in that choice.

Today is the day you love and respect yourself. You feel self-worth welling up inside of you, flowing through your body inspiring and healing you

Feel that energy flow through your heart and heal your spirit. It's time for your heart to heal.

It's time to leave the past in the past. It's okay to let go

Now, you can allow yourself to drift off safe and secure in the positive energy surrounding you.

This guided sleep meditation is now complete

Affirmations for Manifesting Growth - 5 minutes

Thoughts have the power to shape your reality and that is why affirmations are one of the core ways that you can use the law of attraction to manifest your goals and desires.

These powerful affirmations will help you align your mindset and your intentions to manifest the things you need in your life.

Duration: 5 minutes

Start by clearing your mind and making yourself comfortable.

Take a deep breath in and hold it for a while before exhaling. As you exhale feel any tension and stress in your body start to dissipate.

Take another deep breath in through the nose, hold for a moment and exhale slowly. Ome more deep breath in, hold and then exhale slowly through your mouth.

You feel calm and your mind is receptive. In this relaxed state, repeat the following affirmations.

I accept that my well-being and happiness are my responsibility.

I am embracing this day with gratitude.

I am opening up my mind and heart in gratitude for the good things that are on their way to me now.

I am aligning with my values, my intentions and my goals.

I will pursue my dreams with courage and passion.

I allow my light to shine brightly from today.

I am awakening to the greatness within me.

I am grateful for the healing energy of the universe.

I am grateful for the freedom I have to be myself.

I am grateful for everything in my life right now.

I gratefully and graciously accept all the things that I manifest in my life.

I am grateful for the lessons life has taught me.

I choose to learn from my challenges and move courageously forward.

I choose to move into abundance.

I choose to appreciate myself just as I am.

I choose to love myself fully.

I choose to show up in my life and live with hope and love.

Now you can open your eyes and breath in deeply allowing these affirmations to connect deeply with your subconscious.

You can repeat these affirmations every day in the morning to stay grounded and committed to your personal growth.

Chapter 9: Meditations for Your Mind

One of the reasons why meditation is such a powerful manifestation tool is because it is one of the most effective ways to reset your mind. When you want to get past destructive habits, negative emotions, limiting beliefs and any other success blockers, mediation provides the tool that you can use to tap into your subconscious.

Every outcome that you are living right now is a direct result of your mindset and your subconscious energy. This means to manifest success, abundance, wealth and even good health you must first create all these things in your mind then release them into the universe to become reality.

The meditations in this section are going to help you tap into the infinite power of the mind to manifest and attract success, abundance and wealth.

Meditation for Productivity and Focus - 10 minutes

If you struggle with productivity and getting things done, this guided meditation is a great way to start your day.

Let us get started.

Duration: 10 minutes

Start by making yourself comfortable. Sit in a comfortable chair with your feet planted on the ground.

Now relax your shoulders and sit upright with your neck and spine aligned. Now gently close your eyes.

Bring your awareness and focus to your breathing and let everything else fade into the background. Release any thoughts and simply tune into the rhythmic rise and fall of your chest as you breathe in and out.

As you inhale, feel the breath enter and nourish your body. As you exhale feel any stress and tension leave your body.

Continue to focus on your breathing and allow yourself to get into a relaxed state with every breath you take.

Now I want you to sit quietly and call to mind all the things you want to achieve today. See them clearly one by one and connect these things with your short-term and long-term goals.

As you continue to see these tasks, I want you to visualize yourself doing them. If it is an office or school project, visualize yourself working on it and finishing it. If it is a decision you need to make, visualize yourself having made it.

Whatever it is that you know that you need to do today, see yourself doing it and doing it well. Once you visualize this, allow yourself to feel the sense of accomplishment you will feel once you have completed it.

You are proud of yourself for having taken a step towards your goals and you know that each task you complete brings you closer to manifesting the things you want.

Now allow yourself to focus on your upper chest, really feel it puffing out as you breathe in and contract as you breathe out

Let the energy circulate up into your chest and wake up your mind and body. You are feeling invigorated, focused and energized.

Allow yourself to feel the rejuvenation of fresh breath, a fresh new perspective and a new day.

Your mind and body are eager to experience this new day and you embrace the things that you will do today.

Your mind is alert, your body is energized and you are radiating positive energy and manifesting productivity and success for your day.

Today you are in alignment with your intentions, your goals and your deepest desires.

You cannot wait to start taking steps to the things you want by doing everything you need to do and do it well.

You are grateful for the opportunity to manifest success, abundance and wealth.

This is your day and you will walk into it with confidence and purpose.

Now I want you to visualize yourself at the end of the day. You are feeling content and happy because you accomplished everything you wanted to do today.

Tune into this feeling of accomplishment. Connect with it and know that this is exactly how you want to feel at the end of the day.

Now take a deep slow breath in through your mouth. As you do this bring your awareness to the present. As you exhale slowly feel any trepidation about your day dissipate.

You are breathing in confidence and exhaling self-doubt. With every breath in you are surer of your purpose and your goals. With every breath out you feel any self-doubt and resistance disappear.

Now allow your breathing to go back to normal. When you are ready you can open your eyes.

This guided meditation is now complete.

Guided Meditation for Overcoming Procrastination - 20 minutes

One of the biggest blocks people face to manifesting wealth and abundance is procrastination and putting off action. To attract the things that you desire, you must be willing to act and set in motion the opportunities that will create the outcomes you want.

This guided meditation is meant to help you become more decisive and proactive.

Let's get into it.

Duration: 20 minutes

Make sure that you are in a comfortable position. You can choose to sit on a chair or a meditation pillow on the floor.

Place your arms gently on your lap and close your eyes to begin focusing your awareness inward.

Now, start to focus all your attention on your breathing. Release any thoughts in your mind by simply turning all your attention to your natural breathing rhythm.

Breathe in, breath out.

Feel the sensations in your chest as you breathe in and out and let your awareness only focus on these sensations.

As you continue to breathe in and out, you are releasing any tensions in your body. You are also releasing any pent-up emotions as you sink deeper and deeper into relaxation.

Simply enjoy your breathing and the feeling of calmness that is increasing with every inhale. You are relaxed. All the muscles in your body are soft and loose.

Now I want you to visualize yourself standing on top of the hill looking down onto a city or suburb.

It is autumn and as you stand on top of the hill you are in a cozy and warm jacket that is keeping you warm.

You are breathing in the cool crisp outdoor air and your mind feels refreshed and alert.

The is a gentle breeze caressing your face and you can smell the scent of ripe apples in this breeze.

You feel relaxed and at ease surrounded by the tranquility and vibrant energy of the beautiful nature all around you.

As you look down at the city down below let your imagination bring you the sights sounds and smells of this beautiful place.

As you breathe a little deeper start to walk down the hill towards the city down below. With every step you take closer to this city, the sounds and the colors get more pronounced.

You can see the colored rooftops, hear the bustle of the cars and the people in the city and you know that you want to get there as soon as possible.

As you walk down the path, there are a lot of beautiful scenes all around you, calling out to you and enticing you. However, even though you look around, you keep moving forward towards your destination without stopping.

You know where you want to go and you understand that the sooner you get there, the sooner you can settle in and start enjoying yourself.

With every step you take your destination gets closer and you can see it clearly. You are confident in your step because you can clearly see where you are going and you know what is waiting for you there.

A few more steps and you can hear the sound of laughter, cars and activity. You are drawn to the life within the city and although the nature surrounding you is beautiful; you know that your shelter lies in the city below.

As you draw nearer and nearer your step is getting lighter and you start to feel excited at the thought of reaching your destination.

Now at this moment, I want you to connect with that feeling of excitement and joy that you are feeling as you keep drawing closer and closer to your destination.

Doesn't it make you even more motivated to finish the journey? Does it not get easier the closer and closer you get to the city?

As you ask yourself these questions, let the answers come to you from deep down within. Let yourself come to the realization that the first step is the hardest part. After that, the action will be its own motivation and the rest of the steps will get easier.

Realize that everything you use to distract yourself and procrastinate is just like the beautiful scenery you are walking past as you walk down to the city. The scenery may be beautiful but come nightfall it will not offer you the shelter and security you need.

In this moment realize that your destination is only far if you are not moving towards it. Come to the realization that every step you take is one step closer to manifesting your dreams.

At this point, you are at the foot of the hill and you have made it to your destination. I want you to take a deep breath and tune into how you are feeling in this moment when you have reached the shelter of the city.

This feeling of safety and accomplishment is what you deny yourself every time you procrastinate. Let yourself experience it and feel what it feels like to get to your destination in time.

As you lean into this feeling I want you to internalize it and connect to it deeply. Tell yourself that you want to feel this sense of accomplishment and safety from now on.

You want to have the courage to keep moving towards your goals no matter what distractions are along this path.

Take a moment to connect with these realizations and commit them to your mind. Every time you want to put off doing something or distract yourself, I want you to remember walking down the hill to the city below and how it feels to arrive at your destination.

Now take a deep breath in, and then exhale.

Feel yourself breathing in focus and motivation and letting go of any resistance to your purpose.

Take another deep breath in and as you exhale start to bring your awareness back to the present.

When you are ready, open your eyes.

This guided meditation is now complete.

Guided Meditations for Manifesting Good Grades 20 minutes

Duration 20 minutes.

Find a nice comfortable spot. You can close your eyes or leave them open.

Make sure you are sitting comfortably in an upright but relaxed posture. You can place your hands on your lap with the palm facing upward in a sign of openness to receiving and letting the universe guide you.

Let's start by getting centered and grounded in the present moment.

Breathe in deeply through the nose feeling the air fill your lungs completely then exhale slowly through the mouth.

Now repeat this deep breathing technique five more times. Deep inhale, slow exhale. Deep inhale, slow exhale. Deep inhale, slow exhale. Deep inhale, slow exhale. Now one last time, inhale deeply, then exhale slowly.

Now place your hand over your chest and allow yourself to feel the rhythm of your breathing as you allow your breathing to go back to normal.

Shut everything else out apart from the gentle rise and fall of your chest as you breathe in and out.

With every breath, you are going deeper and deeper into relaxation. Your mind is open and you feel a sense of clarity and calmness in your mind and body.

At this point I want you to think about your favorite thing in nature. Maybe it is majestic waterfalls, the beauty of a snowcapped mountain, the untamed beauty of wildlife or anything else that takes your breath away about nature.

When you find that thing that is most striking to you, I want you to now think of yourself as having the same magnificent energy of nature as the striking thing that came to your mind.

The same energy that fuels the water gushing down the waterfall is in you, lying dormant waiting for you to activate it. The same natural energy that fuels the volcanoes is available to you if only you will allow yourself to tap into it.

Whatever natural feature takes your breath away, I want you to come to the realization that the same energy that fuels it is also available to you from the universe.

You have limitless potential because the universe is ready to give you anything you need provided that you reach out and ask for it.

Nothing is out of reach for you because the powerful natural energy that fuels nature is also fueling your brain.

You are so powerful and capable of accomplishing anything you put your mind to because you have unlimited reserves of positive energy available to you from the universe.

Now I want you to take a deep breath and as you inhale, feel yourself inviting in radiant and powerful energy with every inhale.

As you continue to breathe in deeply, you are taking in more powerful energy and this energy is permeating every part of your being.

You feel your confidence grow with every exhale because you know that with this powerful energy from the universe, you can manifest the grades you want in any subject.

Nothing is too difficult for you. You have everything you need to take on any challenge and succeed.

Feel this power and confidence swell within you. Clear your mind of all self-imposed doubts and limiting beliefs.

Breathe in intelligence and confidence and as you exhale release any self-doubt.

Now I want you to visualize the grade you want to manifest. See it written clearly on your exam paper. As you look at that grade see your name written beside it. This is your grade.

How does it feel to see it on paper? Imagine yourself sitting at your desk with the paper marked A in your hand. How do you feel?

Now I want you to take this feeling and immerse yourself in it. The sense of accomplishment, the pride in passing, and the relief you feel at this moment. Take a moment to experience these feelings clearly and vividly.

With this mental picture in your mind, I want you to repeat these affirmations.

I am gifted.

I am intelligent.

Good grades come easily to me.

I learn fast and everything I learn I remember clearly.

I am attracting good grades right now.

I can accomplish anything I set my mind to.

The universe is fueling me with powerful energy to take on any challenge.

I am grateful for my intelligence.

I am grateful for my good grades.

As you affirm your intentions, I want you to connect with them deeply and let them resonate in your mind. Sit with them for a moment and let them penetrate your subconscious.

Now, gradually start to bring your awareness back to the present. Bring your awareness back to your body by tuning into the sensations of your breathing. Feel the air enter your body as you inhale and notice how your chest relaxes when you exhale.

When you are ready, you can open your eyes.

This guided meditation is now complete.

Manifest Your Life's Purpose - 10 minutes

If you want to manifest your life's purpose by resetting your mind, this meditation will help you attract your dharma and find your purpose.

Let's get started.

Duration:10 minutes

Start by getting comfortable. Sit in a quiet spot with your feet planted firmly on the ground.

Roll your shoulders slightly back to open up your chest> your back should be straight in an upright but relaxed posture.

Now close your eyes and let's start by getting you centered. To relax your mind and your body take a couple of deep breaths through your nose and then exhale slowly through your mouth.

One more time, breath in nice and deep, hold for a few seconds and then exhale.

Now let your breathing go back to its normal rhythm and allow yourself to sink deeper and deeper into relaxation.

Your whole body is relaxed and your mind is calm and receptive.

Now I want you to imagine that there is a glowing golden light at the top of your head.

This light is full of positive and peaceful energy that is now flowing into your body starting from the top of your head and flowing downwards all the way to your feet.

Allow this energy to calm your mind and relax your entire body as it continues to flow into every part of your body in warm gentle waves.

The more you are bathed in this energy the more relaxed and centered you feel.

Feel your body responding to this soothing energy. All your muscles are loose and soft. Your facial muscles are relaxed and your whole body feels energized and alive.

Now feel this cleansing energy start to dissipate all your stress and negative emotions. The more it courses through your body the more it frees you from negative thoughts and emotions.

You are covered in positivity and gentle soothing energy that has guided you to a peaceful and grounded state.

Now in this relaxed state, I want you to visualize yourself one year from now. Where do you see yourself? What are you doing? Who are you with?

As you visualize yourself at that point in the future, look around you. What do you have that you do not have now? How has your life changed? Are you content and happy where you are?

As you answer these questions, I want you to go back a little further into the future> Now you are five years into the future. Again, look around you and take in your surroundings. Where are you? What are you doing? Who are you with? Are you happy with what you see?

As you internalize the answers to these questions now let's go even deeper into the future. Now it's ten years from now, where do you see yourself? What has changed in your life? Who are you with? Are you fulfilled and content?

Now take all these three versions of yourself and in your mind hold them up side by side. You as you are now. You as you want to be in five years and you as you want to be in ten years.

As you compare these different stages of your life, ask yourself – what do I need to do now to get where I want to be in five years or ten?

Let this self-inquiry reveal to you your life purpose and the direction you need to steer your life in to manifest the outcome you want.

If you see yourself in a new home or at a better job in the future, what can you do now to manifest this reality? What steps can you take to attract the wealth, abundance and fulfillment you see in your future?

To manifest your purpose you need to create a link that aligns your intentions and actions today with the future that you want to create.

Sit with this realization for the moment and allow yourself to connect to the future versions of yourself that you want to manifest.

See yourself exactly as you want to be then. See the home that you want to be living in. See the car that you want to be driving. See the relationships that you want to have.

All these revelations will connect you with your purpose and connect you with your goals.

Now with this awareness, you can take a deep breath and bring your consciousness back to the present.

Take a series of deep breaths and exhales and feel yourself gradually return to the present.

When you are ready, you may open your eyes.

This guided mediation is now complete.

Chapter 10: A New Beginning

The power of affirmations in attracting the things you want is that they set a clear intention and purpose that seeps into your subconscious. If you want to change any sphere of your life, using affirmations to create the reality you want is one of the most effective ways to do it.

In this section, we shall focus on powerful affirmations that will help you create the future that you want.

Affirmations for Healthy Eating Habits - 10 minutes

You can repeat these affirmations daily to reset your mindset about food and manifest the body you want.

Duration 10 minutes:

In a quiet comfortable space, sit comfortably and bring your awareness inward by shutting out all external input.

To enhance clarity and open up your subconscious take a series of deep breaths until you feel calm and relaxed.

No in this relaxed state, close your eyes gently and repeat these affirmations.

I am attracted to healthy food.

I love to nurture and nourish my body.

I pay attention to how food makes me feel.

I respect my body and only feed it healthy and wholesome food.

I make healthy eating choices.

Healthy food makes me feel good.

Eating healthy is part of my lifestyle

I prefer healthy food over junk food

I eat to fuel my body

My body is a reflection of what I put in it.

I am grateful that my diet nourishes and keeps me healthy.

I choose healthy foods because they keep me strong and energized.

I choose healthy foods because my body is important to me.

I take care of my health by eating healthy.

I have a healthy relationship with food.

I feel great when I take care of myself.

I feel great when I eat right.

I manifest good health by eating healthy food.

Eating healthy comes easily to me.

Good food nourishes my body and my soul.

I make healthy eating choices.

I avoid any food that does not nourish my body.

I choose to be healthy.

I choose to eat right.

I choose to nourish my body.

After you affirm your intentions, take a deep breath and allow yourself to connect with these affirmations deeply. When you are ready you may open your eyes.

Affirmations for Manifesting Self Control and Discipline - 10 minutes

If your emotions often get the better of you, these affirmations will help you in staying calm and manifesting better self-regulation.

Duration: 10 minutes

Start by sitting comfortably with your feet planted firmly on the ground. Now take a few deep breaths to center yourself and direct all your awareness inward.

Now repeat these affirmations stating each clearly in your mind or speaking it softly out loud.

My self-control is growing stronger by the day.

Self-discipline comes naturally to me.

I have control over my impulses.

I am completely focused on succeeding.

I am committed to my goals.

I start each day with purpose and confidence.

I am in control of my habits.

I am in control of my emotions.

I do not make emotional decisions.

My mind is strong, capable, and disciplined.

I can tap into my willpower.

My choices are in agreement with my desires and my habits.

Every day my willpower becomes stronger.

I am in charge of my behavior and actions.

I exercise self-restraint.

I finish all tasks that I start.

I have the power to choose my thoughts and actions.

I am capable and I am disciplined.

I set and achieve goals effortlessly.

I align my actions with the outcomes I want to manifest.

Affirmations for Trusting the Universe to Manifest Your Desires - 10 minutes

Sometimes giving up the need for control can be the reset you need to attract the things you want to manifest. This short affirmation session will help you trust your journey and have faith that your desires will manifest.

Duration: 10 minutes

Recite these affirmations first thing in the morning before you start your day.

I am on the right path.

I am in alignment with my desires.

Everything always works out for me.

Everything is working out for me.

I will trust the universe to manifest my desires at the right time.

I do not need to always control the outcome.

I trust my journey.

I am manifesting the things I want right now.

I am exactly where I should be.

Everything I want is already available for me.

I am grateful for everything I already have.

My future is bright no matter what today looks like.

Nothing can block my abundance.

Nothing can block my wealth.

I trust the universe to provide me with all the things you need.

I can keep my focus on the present confident that my future is manifesting my desires.

I am free of anxiety and worry.

Every day I get closer to my dreams.

Morning Gratitude Affirmations - 10 minutes

Setting your day with gratitude is the best way to send out the right energy into the universe to manifest abundance and joy.

You can recite these affirmations daily first thing in the morning to reset your energy to gratitude and appreciation.

Duration: 10 minutes

You can repeat these affirmations while seated in a comfortable chair. To really connect with your subconscious, close your eyes and focus all your attention inward.

When you feel calm and centered, repeat these affirmations slowly and with clarity.

I am grateful to be alive.

I am grateful to this day.

I am grateful for the abundance I create.

I am grateful for the prosperity I attract.

I am grateful for the people in my life.

I am grateful for the riches that flow into my life.

I am grateful for the presence of love in my life.

I am grateful for where I am right now.

I am grateful for all I have experienced in my life.

I am grateful for the amazing potential the future holds.

I am grateful for this moment right here, right now.

I am grateful for everyone who loves me.

I am grateful for everyone who challenges me.

I am grateful for the wonders of mother nature.

I am grateful for plants and animals.

I am grateful for the wind and the weather.

I am grateful for all my skills and talents.

I am grateful for endless opportunities.

I am grateful for the full range of emotions I feel.

I am grateful for the things that excite me.

I am grateful for the many things that bring me joy.

I am grateful for this day, teeming with potential.

I am grateful for another opportunity to serve and live life to the fullest.

I am grateful for being a beneficial presence on the planet.

I am grateful for all that I have.

When you finish the recitations take a moment to sit with your intentions and commit them to your mind. You may now open your eyes.

Total Hours - 11

Conclusion

The power of the universe is infinite. Every day we are surrounded by miracles and the giving nature of the universe. All you have to do to tap into this infinite reservoir of abundance, wealth, and joy is to align your inner energy with that of the universe. This means being aware of your subconscious beliefs, values, and intentions. Unfortunately, the subconscious exists just below the surface of your consciousness. Even when you are not aware of it, it is directing your thoughts, habits, and actions.

To tap into this subconscious layer of your mind that determines the energy you project into the universe, it is important to become more mindful and in touch with your inner self. This is why meditation is one of the most effective tools you can use to attract and manifest wealth, abundance, love and everything else you yearn for. Meditation does not just show you how to tap into your subconscious but it also allows you to reset your subconscious to project energy that is in alignment with the goals you want to manifest.

Throughout this book, we have equipped you with the tools you need to manifest the outcomes you want in different spheres of your life. With these meditation tools, you can harness the law of attraction to create the reality that you want to live in. If your subconscious energy is not aligned with the things you want to manifest, the law of attraction cannot work for you.

Now that we have shown you exactly how you can reset your subconscious energy to start manifesting everything you have always wanted, all you need to do is find a comfortable space and start meditating. Meditation is one of the most powerful mind control tools that will help you project the right energy into the universe. once you are in control of your subconscious energy then everything you need to manifest is right within your control.

We hope this book helps you to manifest your deepest desires using the principle of the law of attraction. You now have all the tools you need to create the life you have always wanted so all you need to do is get started.

Table of Contents

Introduction

I don't know about you, but I have often wondered why the world works the way that it does. What I mean is that there have been things that I really wanted for my life. As hard as I worked for them, I frequently fell short of achieving them. I also wondered why others, who seemed to apply less effort than I did, got what they wanted. Some were of questionable character that also seemed to come out ahead of me. These thoughts used to come up frequently when I was younger. However, all that has changed since I got older and wiser.

No longer do I have the attitude that there is no rhyme or reason to how life unfolds for me and others. I have gained some little-known knowledge that has left me no longer guessing or judging why my life is the way it is or why the lives of others turned out the way they did. This knowledge did not come by easily for me. I had to earn it.

Years ago, I was sitting in my backyard on a warm sunny day when I saw a cocoon tethered to the branch of one of our shrubs. The cocoon was moving when I saw a butterfly emerge. This butterfly crawled out of the cocoon and then perched itself on a branch. It remained perfectly still, except for the pulsing of his abdomen as it drew in the fresh morning air into its body. Gradually, it began opening and closing its wings as it pumped them full of blood.

This creature was far removed from the caterpillar that it used to be. In fact, it bore absolutely no resemblance to it. I remember thinking to myself, what was it within the caterpillar that allowed it to make such an extraordinary transformation? Something was going on within the caterpillar that caused its cells to reconfigure their functions for this new creature to emerge.

As I thought about it, I realized that this amazing transformation was not restricted to the caterpillar. Extraordinary transformations occur throughout the natural world. For those who are sensitive and curious enough, there lies an opportunity to transform themselves. For those that are drawn toward this path, there lies a whole new way to experience life. From this vantage point, all sense of separation ceases to exist. It becomes evident that everything in existence is interconnected.

All that we experience blends together. A spider's web is such that the mere touching of one strand will be experienced by the entire web. In the same way, the one who leaves the safety of their cocoon will touch the far reaches of the universe by just the movement of their wings. The wings that I speak of are the wings of a liberated mind.

A butterfly has a completely different perspective than a caterpillar's. A caterpillar can only experience life at the ground level, though they can detect odors from above them. Because they are not restricted to the ground, a butterfly can view the world from high up in the air. They can perceive things the caterpillar could never know. In a way, the Law of Attraction is like this.

Most people think of the Law of Attraction as a way to bring that which they desire into their lives. Those who have a deep understanding of the Law of Attraction know that it is more than just about attracting what you want. For them, the Law of Attraction goes so much deeper than that. For them, it is a vehicle to a deeper understanding of the true nature of the self. A deeper understanding of the self gives one the perspective of a butterfly as opposed to a caterpillar.

There are plenty of books available on the Law of Attraction; however, most of them are of limited scope. They offer a surface understanding of how to attract what you want. This book is different. It will explain the mechanics of the Law of Attraction and point you to a place where you can discover your essential nature. If you can go to this place, the ability to attract your desires will seem superficial. Instead, you will experience a state of life where you can make a real impact on the life of others. It is for this reason that this book was written.

How far you go in your understanding of the higher realms of consciousness is up to you. At the very least, this book promises you a deeper understanding of how to make the Law of Attraction work for you. At most, this book will point you in a direction beyond what the mind can phantom.

Chapter 1: What is the Law of Attraction

When Rhonda Byrne's book, *The Secret*, came out in 2006, it became an international sensation. With its release, the Law of Attraction became part of popular culture. The Law of Attraction is a philosophy for manifesting one's desires through thought. It is based on the premise that everything in this universe is made of energy, including our thoughts.

Suppose that someone wants to attract financial wealth into their lives. In that case, they can make this happen by focusing on thoughts of financial success. The vibrational energy of these thoughts will align with the vibrational energy of abundance. Because of this, financial success will appear in this person's life. There are other components to applying the Law of Attraction, which we will get into later, but this is the essence of this philosophy.

However, Byrne's book was not the first to discuss the Law of Attraction. The Law of Attraction was part of a growing New Thought movement in America that emerged in the early 19th century. The New Thought movement was centered on the theory of mind over matter. There was a growing interest as to how the mind could affect matter.

The New Thought movement can be traced back to New England transcendentalism, Hermeticism, Hinduism, and even parts of the Bible. In transcendentalism, it is believed that the mind is more powerful than matter. At the same time, Hermeticism led to the study of alchemy. From the bible, some verses speak of the mind's ability to manifest. Mark 11:24 reads: "Therefore I tell you, whatever you ask in prayer, believe that you have received it, and it will be yours." Toward the end of the 19th century, America was introduced to teachers such as Swami Vivekananda. He gave lectures on the mind's ability to affect matter from a Hindu perspective.

In America, one of the founders of the New Thought movement was Phineas Quimby. A clockmaker, Quimby was also a self-described mentalist. Quimby contracted tuberculosis. At the time, there were no established cures for the disease. Quimby took up horseback riding as a way to distract himself from his predicament. Horseback riding gave him a sense of exhilaration, and he noticed that it temporarily relieved him of his symptoms. Quimby's experience led him to study the relationship that the mind had over the body. His study was the genesis of the mind-body medicine movement in America. The term "Law of Attraction" had yet to be created, but Quimby made reference to it when he wrote:

"The trouble is in the mind, for the body is only the house for the mind to dwell in, and we put a value on it according to its worth. Therefore if your mind has been deceived by some invisible enemy into a belief, you have put it into the form of a disease, with or without your knowledge. By my theory or truth, I come in contact with your enemy and restore you to your health and happiness. This I do partly mentally and partly by talking till I correct the wrong impressions and establish the Truth, and the Truth is the cure."

The actual term "The Law of Attraction" did not appear in print until 1877. Russian author Helena Blavatsky used the term when writing about the occult and the powers of attraction between matter and spirit.

The first time the Law of Attraction was discussed in detail was in an essay titled, *The Law of Success. The Law of Success* was part of a larger work titled *Your Forces and How to Use Them.* Published in 1887, the essay's author, Prentice Mulford, became a central figure in the New Thought movement. *Your Forces and How to Use Them* laid the groundwork for understanding the Law of Attraction, though it never referred to it by name.

Other authors of the New Though movement began to emerge in the late 1800s. These included Henry Wood, who wrote *God's Image in Man,* and Ralph Waldo Trine, who wrote *What All the Word's A-Seeking.* These authors expanded Qumba's approach to the New Thought movement. They believed that thought could affect all areas of our lives, not just our health.

It would not be till 1906 that Blavatsky's term "Law of Attraction" would reappear. *Thought Vibration or the Law of Attraction in the Thought Word* was written by William Walker Atkinson. In his book, Atkinson discussed the importance of strengthening one's focus and willpower to manifest one's desires. Atkinson's teachings were based on Hindu philosophy.

By the time the 20th century appeared, interest in the New Thought movement had exploded in America. Two notable books were published: Napoleon Hill's *Think and Grow Rich* and Norman Vincent Peale's *The Power of Positive Thinking.*

A journalist, Hill drew his inspiration not from spiritual teachers but from poets like Ralph Waldo Emerson. Hill's contribution to the New Thought movement was the effect of negative thoughts on our lives.

One of the most influential spiritual leaders of the 20th century, Peale wrote the best seller *The Power of Positive Thinking.* The book discusses how to make faith practical by applying it to our lives. Numerous other books that were based on the Law of Attraction soon followed.

Chapter 2: Our Energetic Universe

To have a deeper understanding of the Law of Attraction, we first need to understand the nature of the universe. Most of the universe is nonphysical. Only a small fraction of the universe is made of matter, meaning that it has a physical form.

The traditional scientific approach to studying the universe involved focusing on matter. After all, scientists want to study that which can be measured or quantified. They are not interested in studying phenomena that cannot be measured. Physics seeks to understand how the universe works by studying energy, forces, and matter. Those of us who are 50 years or older had our understanding of the natural world molded by physics, namely Newtonian physics. Born in 1643, the mathematician Issac Newton's ideas of the universe created the groundwork for modern physics.

Newton believed that we live in a mechanical universe where solid objects were in constant motion. These solid objects would later become known as atoms. Atoms were considered the smallest unit of matter. By studying the movement of matter, physicists attempted to explain the laws of the universe. Our view of the natural world is based on the idea that we live in a physical world where solid objects and forces interact. By studying these interactions, physicists sought ways to apply them for the development of new technology.

Newtonian physics was the unquestioned approach to understanding the universe until the 1920s. That was the time when quantum physics emerged as a scientific field of study. Quantum physics turned traditional theories of physics on their heads. It questioned even the most basic theories of Newtonian physics. With quantum physics, there came a dismantling of the sacred principles used to explain the laws of the universe.

The atom, which was long considered the smallest unit of matter, was no longer considered solid. The subatomic particles that form the atom are now considered to be fields of energy.
These "particles" constantly move in and out of existence, and they influence other "particles."

Imagine if you had a ping-pong ball at the goal line of a football field. On the other end of the field, you had a second ping-pong ball. You rotate the first ping-pong ball and the second ping-pong ball rotates on its own, even though it is a great distance away. This is what happens at the quantum level of existence.

Further, these "particles" can take on the form of a particle or a wave. This means that you can have a solid particle in one instance, and in the next instance, it behaves like the ripples of a pond or lightwaves. What is amazing is that what determines if the particle is a solid or wave is whether it is being observed or not.

This brings us to the next point. In traditional science, there is the object and the subject. The scientist is the object. He or she is the one who observers the subject, that which is being studied. For ages, the object and subject were considered independent of each other. In quantum physics, the object and subject are interdependent. Through the act of observing, the object can influence the behavior of the subject.

When monitoring devices were used to observe atomic particles, they behaved as solid objects. When there were no monitoring devices used, the atomic particle behaved like a wave. In other words, the atomic particle behaved like a bullet that hit the center of its target. At other times, it acted like a flood light that illuminated the target and the surrounding area.

What quantum physics demonstrates is that we affect the world around us just by our observing it. Further, at the most fundamental level, we and everything we experience is grounded in the same energy field. We experience ourselves and the world around us as being of a physical nature. In fact, this entire universe, including ourselves, comprises energy that expresses itself as physical form.

The illusion of physicality comes from our limited sensory ability to discern the substratum of an energetic universe. It is like when we look in a mirror. The reflection that we see in the mirror appears to be a solid physical body made of flesh and bone. However, the body is made of trillions of microscopic cells. In turn, each cell is made of numerous cell components. These components are made of smaller components. In turn, these smaller components are made up of even smaller components, and so on. Diving down deeper, we would eventually reach the atomic level. Go down even further, you guessed it....all that we would find is energy.

The energy that I speak of is not to be confused with the energy we use in our daily lives to power our homes or run our vehicles. Instead, the energy that I speak of has intelligence, and it contains information. It is this intelligence and information that creates the unlimited expressions of life that we experience. It is for this reason that we can refer to this energy as conscious energy or Prana. Whether it is a cell from the human body, an embryo, or a rock, this energy provides the blueprint for the physical world to take form.

In whatever form this energy manifests, its manifestation is not separate from this energy. Not only are you a manifestation of this energy, but you are also inseparable from it. It is like a drop from the ocean. The drop shows no resemblance to the mighty ocean; however, the drop and the ocean are identical in their chemical composition. In the same way, you are inseparable from the universe. Whether it is a constellation in the evening sky, the mighty Himalayan Mountains, or bacteria, the essence of who we are is one with all of these things. This means that, at the fundamental level, you and that which you desire are also one and the same.

Since everything is one, just a single thought by you reverberates across the universe. Everything that we can experience is found within conscious energy, and everything that we experience is conscious energy. What follows is an exploration of the ways this conscious energy is expressed. We will begin with the mind and body.

The Mind and Body as Energy Fields

From our perspective, the world that surrounds us is separate from us. At the quantum level, there is no distinction as we and our environment are the expressions of the same energy. Further, this energy can be influenced by us, just by giving it our attention. How we affect this energy has to do with our energetic frequency or vibration. What affects our vibration is our thoughts and emotions. Our thoughts and emotions can affect the vibrational frequency of our entire body and beyond. In the next few sections, we will explore how the mind and body are part of the universal energy field.

The Role of the Mind on the Energy Field

Thoughts and the Energy Field

Before discussing thoughts, it is important to understand how we experience ourselves and the world around us. First, there is no such thing as a thought that exists independently of our minds. In fact, nothing that we have any knowledge of exists beyond the realm of our minds. To better understand this, let us begin with two presumptions. The first is that thoughts exist and the second being that our thoughts reflect the nature of reality.

Starting with the first presumption, the only thing that we know about thoughts is our conceptual understanding of them. What do I mean by this? No one has ever seen a thought. No one has ever studied them or identified what they are made of. Has there ever been an investigation as to where thoughts come from or where they go when they leave our awareness? Is there anything that we can say about thoughts other than that we have them?

As with everything else that we experience, thoughts are mental constructs that are created by our minds. The following example will illustrate this. Let us say you are looking at a flower. Your eyes take in the visual information that is obtained from it. This information is converted into electrical impulses and transported to the brain via the optic nerve. Your brain receives this information and then reassembles it, creating an image of the rose.

Information collected from your other senses (hearing, smell, taste, and touch) is processed similarly. They are added to the image that is created by the brain. When we see a rose, we do not perceive something that exists outside of us. Instead, we perceive a mental image.

We have learned that this mental image is a "rose." Because we believe that we are separate and distinct entities in a physical world. We believe that the rose exists outside of ourselves. Besides being taught that this mental construct is known as a "rose," we learn to associate meaning with it. We may believe that the rose is beautiful. Attaching meaning to a mental image creates what is known as a concept. Everything that we experience is a concept.

Concepts are a form of thought; they are a representation of our experience of reality.

Earlier in this section, two presumptions were made:

- Thoughts exist.
- Our thoughts reflect the nature of reality.

How we experience reality is determined by our thoughts. Further, we know nothing about thoughts other than that we experience them. What we are left with is the inescapable conclusion that there is no world that exists outside ourselves, of which we can prove. Further, the only thing that we can know about this world is that we experience it.

However, we can go deeper with this. How we experience ourselves is a concept as well. Could it be that you and I are just a thought? I make these philosophical statements for a reason. The traditional view of the Law of Attraction is that we can attract what we desire into our lives by thinking about it.

This view assumes that there is a world outside of ourselves and that which we desire exists outside ourselves as well. It also assumes that we are in control of our thoughts. Lastly, it assumes that whom we experience ourselves to be actually exist! Regardless of which viewpoint is correct, they are grounded in thought. Everything that ever existed began with a thought.

I have presented this philosophical analysis for one important reason. Whether it is the Law of Attraction or anything else that you want to learn about, realize that all knowledge is based upon our limited understanding of the universe. Whatever knowledge that is derived from the minds of humans is superficial at best. The reason for this is because we believe that our mental representations are reality itself. Now that we have this perspective as a backdrop, we will discuss thoughts and their role in the energy field.

As previously mentioned, we are unable to discern the qualities of thoughts. Thoughts do not have a shape, color, or size. We do not know where they originate from or where they go. Further, we do not know what they are made of.

The only thing that we know about thoughts is that they exist. We lack an understanding of thoughts due to the same misconceptions that we have of ourselves. Just as we see ourselves as a distinct and separate entity, we perceive our thoughts in the same way. We view thoughts as a distinct entity that exists within our minds. When viewed from higher levels of consciousness, it is understood that thoughts are neither separate entities nor are they found within our minds.

When we see a wave travels across the ocean's surface, it has a distinct quality to it. However, the wave is not a separate entity. Rather, the wave is a temporary configuration of the ocean. In the same way, thoughts are a temporary configuration of the universal energy field, known as consciousness. Further, it is not us who are having thoughts. Instead, we are attracting thought from the universal energy field. We attract thoughts that are of the same frequency as our life's condition. To understand this, we first need to understand who we are.

We are the physical manifestations of consciousness. We are to a wave as is consciousness is to the ocean. Though our manifested self is consciousness, it is a more limited version of the greater consciousness. We lack the unbounded awareness of the greater consciousness. If this was not the case, we would not be able to function. We would be so overloaded with information that we would not be able to experience the world, which will be discussed in more detail later on in this book.

We, as manifestations of consciousness, are experiencing the information of the larger consciousness system. A simple metaphor for understanding the nature of thought and its relation to us involves boiling water. If water is boiled, bubbles will appear on the surface. The greater consciousness is to the water as thoughts are to the bubbles.

What we refer to as thought is the tapping into the greater consciousness. However, the content of our thoughts does not belong to the greater consciousness. Rather, it is us, the manifested self, which creates the content of our thoughts. The content we derive from these "bubbles of consciousness" comes from the mind.

The content of our thoughts is derived from our conditioning. I may notice that every time I go running in the morning that I feel better emotionally. Eventually, my running and emotional well-being become linked. I associate emotional well-being with running. This association becomes part of the information of the larger consciousness. When I tap into that association, it is experienced as a thought. Thoughts only exist within our manifested form.

Thought is the product of having an experience, which is why we manifested as physical expressions of consciousness. Thought does not exist in pure consciousness because there is nothing to experience. The relationship between the sleep state and waking state is similar to that of our manifested self and pure consciousness.

When we are in the waking state, we experience thoughts resulting from the associations that we make with our environments. When we enter deep sleep, the flow of thoughts ceases to exist. Our deep sleep state is like pure consciousness, while our waking state is like consciousness manifested.

One of the most important things you can do to become a conscious manifestor is to learn how to not personalize your thoughts. It is when we personalize our thoughts that we allow them to define who we are. You cannot manifest what you want if you identify with your thoughts, especially if your thoughts have self-doubt as their content! The following is a simple exercise for demonstrating to yourself that who you are is not your thoughts.

1. Take a moment to relax and close your eyes.
2. In your mind, imagine a full moon.
3. Next, imagine a red sports car.
4. Lastly, imagine a red rose.
5. Now open your eyes.

Did you learn anything from this exercise? If you are unable to answer this question, do not let it bother you. Most people would have difficulty answering it. So, just in case, let me help you by guiding you to the answer.

First of all, you imagined a full moon, a red sports car, and a red rose. Your visualizations are a form of thought. Most likely, you did not confuse any of these images with who you are. You did not think that you were the full moon, the red sports car, or the red rose. Why didn't you? There are two reasons for this. The first reason was that you were the observer of these images. Second, these images lacked significant meaning for you. You are not your thoughts! You are the observer of thoughts.

The Collective Consciousness

Most of us believe consciousness is found somewhere in our heads. From this perspective, we are physical beings that contain consciousness within us. As described before, consciousness is the source of all manifestations. So, based on this definition, we are found within consciousness. That which we perceive to be "mind" and 'body" are, in fact, expressions of consciousness that are found within consciousness. It is like a wave is made of the ocean and is found within the ocean.

There is no individual mind that exists within us. Rather we are accessing thoughts from the collective consciousness. The collective consciousness is not a component of consciousness. Rather, it is the flow of information within the consciousness stream.

A metaphor for this would be the ocean. The ocean has salts and other minerals within it. These minerals are not found in a specific part of the ocean. Instead, they are distributed throughout the ocean. Thoughts (which are a conceptual construct of the mind) are the informational aspect of the conscious energy that permeates all of existence. When we have a thought, we, the illusionary or manifested self, are tapping into conscious energy.

The collective consciousness contains all information that has ever existed or will ever exist. From the far distant past to the far distant future, information about it is found there. This is possible because consciousness is not bound by the same limitations that we experience as manifested entities. Where we experience time and space, consciousness is timeless and boundless. Time and space are mental constructs that exist exclusively within our minds.

Emotions and the Energy Field

It is a popular misconception that we attract into our lives that which we think of, that our thoughts are what create our manifestations. While our thoughts are definitely a component of the manifestation process, our emotions are even more powerful. If you are looking to find inner peace, a sense of well-being, or become a conscious manifestor, the less you depend on your thoughts, the better off you will be. Depending on our thoughts to manifest is unreliable because our thoughts are unreliable. Our minds are all about self-preservation, the preservation of our ego. I offered an example of this from my own experience when I started off learning about the Law of Attraction.

I meditated to develop a quiet mind and then made the intention that I wanted to know what book or magazine cover I would encounter when I went to the library later that day. I received an image of the cover that I would see, which I quickly forgot about it as I went on with my day. When I got to the library, I walked around the book aisles just to browse. As I browsed, I came across a magazine with the same cover I had experienced in my meditation.

I was so excited that I had successfully manifested it intentionally! I then decided to test out my abilities again. The next day, I went into my mediation and made an intention that I wanted to see a certain object when I was out and about. At first, I did not think about the object, but then my mind got actively involved. I was actively looking for the object, which later led me to start doubting myself. Needless to say, I never encountered the object.

There is a term in spirituality known as detachment. Detachment is the ability to not cling on to anything, including our thoughts. Detachment was a characteristic of my first manifesting experience; it definitely was not in my second experience.

Learning to become dethatched from your thoughts takes practice and patience as it is very easy to engage with the mind. Another challenge is that you have thoughts that you are not aware of. More accurately known as subconscious beliefs, subconscious thoughts can easily act as a counter force against any conscious thoughts that you may have.

Let us say that I am trying to manifest money in my life. I place my attention on thoughts that align with my desire. I may have a subconscious thought telling me that I do not deserve to have more money. In this case, my subconscious thought will override my conscious thought if I do not deal with them.

Your emotions are more dependable as a point of focus than are your thoughts. Your emotions are a reflection of your thoughts, including your subconscious thoughts. Additionally, by making your emotions the center of your focus, you avoid the influence of the ego. This is exemplified by my story of my second attempt to manifest. Unlike my first attempt, my second attempt was infiltrated by my ego.

As with thoughts, emotions are also energy forms. As energy forms, they have a vibrational frequency. What we commonly refer to as positive emotions are emotions that have a high vibrational frequency. Negative emotions have a low vibrational frequency.

The following is a list of emotions that are ranked according to their vibrational level.

1. Apathy
2. Shame
3. Guilt
4. Grief
5. Fear
6. Anger
7. Acceptance
8. Joy
9. Gratitude
10. Appreciation
11. Love/Compassion
12. Enlightenment

Apathy: Apathy is ranked the lowest of the emotions on the list. This is because apathy is actually the condition where emotions are suppressed. Since emotions are energy, apathy is the suppression of energy.

Shame: The emotion of shame is the second-lowest emotion. Shame occurs when we negatively focus on ourselves. Since we are focusing on low-frequency thoughts, we attract other thoughts of the same frequency.

Earlier in this chapter, you were asked to imagine a full moon, a red sports car, and a red rose. You placed your focus on these images; yet, you did not identify with these images. At no time did you believe that you were these images.

These images were a form of thought. Unlike these thoughts, there are other thoughts that you do identify with. If you ever found yourself caught up in anger, jealousy, or frustration, you had identified with a thought. The emotion of shame takes self-identification to an all-time low.

Guilt: Guilt is the next lowest emotion. The emotion of guilt is intended to be a message to you that you need to change your beliefs about your relationship with other people. If you change your beliefs for more empowering ones, then guilt has performed its function. If you dwell on how inadequate you are as a human being, you have thrown yourself to the mercy of your mind. Where shame is based on self-worth, guilt is based on behavior.

Grief: Grief is the emotion of loss, and the sense of loss is based on a sense of separation. From the point of higher levels of consciousness, it is impossible to experience grief because the sense of separation does not exist.

Fear: While grief is the emotion of loss, fear is the anticipation of loss. One of the biggest challenges in life is to overcome our fear. Fear has an important role in our survival. The emotion of fear causes mental and physical changes that put us on high alert and prepare us to fight or flee. The problem is that we have allowed this evolutionary mechanism to be activated over mundane matters such as public speaking or approaching someone to ask them out for a date.

Anger: Anger is a reaction to fear, and it has a higher frequency than fear. We experience anger when we feel that something that we have identified with is being threatened. If you did not identify with that which is being threatened, you would not get angry. Most likely, you would not feel angry if someone rear-ended another driver. On the other hand, you are likely to experience anger if the rear-ended car was yours.

Satisfaction: The emotion of satisfaction is a higher vibration than anger because it involves less identification. Both anger and fear are experienced as the result of identifying with something outside ourselves. The emotion of satisfaction is an indicator that the emotion of fear is temporarily absent. Because the emotion of fear is absent, we loosen our grip on our attachments. While it is a higher frequency than anger, the emotion of satisfaction will be fleeting as long as we identify with our thoughts or the people and objects around us.

Happiness: The emotion of happiness has a higher frequency than satisfaction. However, the happiness that most of us experience is dependent on the conditions of our life being to our liking, which is a challenge given that everything in life undergoes changes. To seek relationships or possessions to become happy is like building sand castles on the ocean edge; they will remain standing only until the next wave.

Joy: Joy is a higher vibration than happiness; however, it is an unstable emotion if the source of joy is found outside of ourselves.

Gratitude: Gratitude is a higher vibratory level than joy because gratitude is an energy that is directed toward others for what they have given us. I may have gratitude for a co-worker because of how they helped me complete a project. Because I am directing my attention toward another, my ego-based mind does not get involved. Because gratitude has an outward focus, it is a more stable energy frequency. The problem with gratitude is that it is often expressed in response to the receiving of a gift. For this reason, it is an energy frequency that is still vulnerable to change as external conditions change.

Appreciation: Appreciation is a higher frequency than gratitude because the emotion of appreciation can be unconditional. We do not have to receive something to feel appreciation. For example, we can appreciate how some people go out of their way to help others.

Love: Many consider love to be the most powerful force in the universe, which is true if that love is unconditional. Since the love that we experience is normally conditional, it is subject to the changes of our external conditions. An example of this is when our partner does not meet our expectations.

Enlightenment: Enlightenment has the highest vibratory level of any energy. Unconditional love can be equated with enlightenment; however, enlightenment can be achieved without first developing unconditional love, which is extremely rare. A more practical approach to enlightenment can be achieved by practicing meditation and self-inquiry.

Both of these practices can lead to the expansion of awareness as we begin to realize that who we are is beyond our mind and body. However, this awareness must be achieved through the direct experience of it. It cannot be achieved intellectually or by just reading about it.

In describing the energy levels of the various emotions, you may have noticed a pattern. The lower the emotion, the lower its vibrational level will be. The lower frequency is due to the greater amount of identification with the mind and body. The lower vibrational frequency leads us to experience ourselves as being separate and limited entities. It is from experiencing ourselves this way that causes us to be reactive when the conditions around us change.

The higher the vibrational level of the emotion, the less identification there is to the mind and body; hence, we become less reactive toward changes in our circumstances. A person who identifies with their mind will become angry if they feel insulted by another. They become angry because they have identified with the emotion of anger. One who is enlightened may experience anger, but they will not personalize this emotion.

What determines the vibrational frequency of your life state is the level of identification that you have with your thoughts and emotions. High-frequency emotions (which reflect high-frequency thoughts) have an outward orientation (meaning that they are centered on others). Lower frequency emotions (which reflect low-frequency thoughts) have an inward orientation (meaning that they cause you to focus on yourself).

Because of this, higher frequency emotions transcend the ego-based mind. By transcending the ego-based mind, one's life state will rise. When one's life state rises, one will be able to employ the Law of Attraction more effectively.

The Body as an Energy Field

Before launching into this section of the book, I want you to try a simple experiment:

1. Sit down and make yourself comfortable.
2. Now turn your hands so that your palms are facing each other. Keep your hands relaxed.
3. Next, slowly bring your hands together without touching them and then slowly pull them away. As you pull them away, make sure that your palms remain facing each other.
4. As you do this, do you feel anything? What you are feeling is your body's energy.
5. If you do not feel anything, keep practicing until you do.

The ability to feel your body's energy is not limited to your palms. Your entire body is an energy field; however, detecting that energy is easier in some areas of the body than in others. Your palms are one of those areas where energy detection can be experienced by most people.

Though the body may appear to us as being of a physical nature, this is just an illusion of the mind, created by our limited perception. Our limited perception prevents us from perceiving that our body is composed of billions of cells. These cells are made of numerous cellular organelles. The cellular organelles are, in turn, made of molecules, and molecules are made of atoms. Atoms are made of subatomic particles. In turn, these subatomic particles are made of energy.

Any sense of solidity in this physical world is just an illusion. Everything in this universe is made of atoms, except for sound and light. It is our limited perception that gives us the impression that we have a physical body. From the perspective of higher consciousness, that which we experience as a body is actually an energy field. This energy field has some key energy centers that help distribute energy, known as chakras. This is the subject of the next section.

The Wheels of Energy

The study of charkas can be traced back to Buddhist and Hindu traditions. The word "Chakra" comes from Sanskrit; its English translation is "wheel." Found throughout the body, these "wheels" of energy are located near the major nerve centers of the body. Chakras are the energy centers of the body, and they regulate the flow of energy.

There are seven main chakras in the body. They include the root chakra, sacral chakra, solar plexus, heart chakra, throat chakra, third eye chakra, and the crown chakra. The seven chakras create a network; hence, they are interconnected. Besides being correlated with various parts of the body, each of the seven chakras is associated with a specific element and color. Elements include the various earth elements as well as psychological states. The color provides a reference to any given chakra when meditating.

What happens in one chakra can affect all the other chakras. Because of this, the seven chakras are continuously changing in their ability to regulate the flow of energy. An analogy of this is a car's engine. When fuel is added to a car, each of the engine's various components interacts with the fuel in a certain way that eventually allows the engine to run.

If any of the engine's components is not functioning properly, there will be problems with the car's performance. If not corrected, other engine components can become affected as well.

Our sense of wellbeing, both physically and emotionally, depends on whether our chakras are balanced with each other.

With even a basic understanding of chakras, you can learn how to maintain them so that your energy flows properly. In turn, properly flowing energy leads to physical and emotional well-being and the ability to attract what you desire.

The Seven Chakras

The following is an overview of the seven chakras:

Root Chakra (also known as Muladhara)

Regarding the root chakra:

- It is associated with one's sense of emotional stability and security and one's basic needs. When this chakra is open, we feel calm and confident. When blocked, we experience fear, anxiety, or doubt.
- It is located near the lower spine.
- It is associated with the color red.
- It is associated with the Earth element.

The Sacral Chakra (also known as Svadhishthana)

Regarding the sacral chakra:

- It is associated with one's sense of creativity, sexuality, and ability to adapt to new situations. When we doubt our creative potential or experience anxiety over any aspect of our sexuality, we create an imbalance in this chakra.
- It is located approximately two inches below the navel.
- It is associated with the color orange.
- It is associated with the element of Water.

The Solar Plexus Chakra (also known as Manipura)

Regarding the Solar Plexus Chakra:

- It is associated with our sense of autonomy, self-esteem, and determination. When balanced, the solar plexus chakra leads to having clarity as to how to move forward with one's goal. For this reason, this chakra is important if we are to achieve success in our pursuits. Conversely, this chakra can become unbalanced if we focus on our perceived failures in life. Blockage of this chakra can cause low self-esteem.
- It is located in the upper abdomen, just below the center of the ribs
- It is associated with the color yellow.
- It is associated with the element of Fire.

The Heart Chakra (also known as Anahata)

Associated with our ability to experience love and compassion, the heart chakra is the most powerful energy center. Emotions are energy forms, and they have a hierarchy as it relates to their vibrational frequency. Fear has the lowest frequency, while love and compassion are at the top. The reason for that is the emotion of love and compassion reflect the qualities of our essential nature, which is Oneness and wholeness. The energy of love and compassion dissolves the mind's illusion of separation and our egocentric tendencies. The heart chakra unites the mind, body, and soul, resulting in a sense of inner peace. The heart chakra becomes balanced when the happiness of others becomes our focal point and when we experience compassion and empathy for what they may be going through. There are various popular sayings about love, such as:

- Love conquers all
- All that you need is love
- Love makes the world go around
- Love is the answer

These sayings are more than "feel good" adages. They depict a timeless, though possibly subconscious, understanding of love's power. Love is more than just a sentiment, for its energy is the energy of creation. Love is the substratum of all of existence. It is made experiential to us in the form of a feeling.

The illusions of the mind create a sense of separation within ourselves, which creates the ego-centered mind. From such a mind, fear, a sense of scarcity, and a lack of compassion and empathy are given birth. The energy of love dissolves the ego-centered mind. It reminds us of our higher nature, which is the energy of love. If you did nothing else but opened your heart chakra, you would regain balance in the remaining energy centers.

What causes the heart chakra to close are any negative perceptions that we hold regarding love, be it a failed relationship, the loss of a loved one, or the experience of heartbreak. From the level of everyday consciousness, such events create a sense of pain and loss within us. From the perspective of higher consciousness, pain and loss do not exist, for love is eternal. Regarding the Heart Chakra:

- It is located in the area of the heart.
- It is associated with the color green.
- It is associated with the element of air.

The Throat Chakra (also known as Vishuddha)

The throat chakra provides a passageway for energy from the lower body to the head. It is associated with our ability for self-expression through the use of sound. The voice is our original instrument for communication, predating the written word. More than just sound, the energy from the throat chakra reveals the heart's desires which speak more loudly than words alone. This energy center is the reason why the words of others sometimes deeply resonate with us and touch us at the deepest level. In fact, the Sanskrit word "Vishubba" means "pure" or "purification." When we speak with directness and honesty, it is filled with the energy of the throat chakra.

When the throat chakra is balanced, one speaks from the heart and is understood by others. The communication of such a one is forthright yet respectful of others. Imbalances of the throat chakra can result from the ego-based mind taking charge of communication when trying to prove others wrong or trying to prove themselves worthy.

Anytime the motive of our words is to justify who we are, we have removed ourselves from the throat chakra's energy. When the throat chakra is blocked, we have difficulty communicating what we want to say. We also may believe that others are not interested in what we have to say.

Regarding the throat chakra is:

- It is located in the throat area.
- It is associated with the color blue.
- It is associated with the element of air.

The Third-Eye Chakra (also known as Ajana)

As our level of consciousness rises, we experience things that we did not experience at the lower levels. Phenomena such as intuition, spiritual contemplation, self-reflection, extrasensory perception, and visions of past lives are just a few examples of this. The potential to experience these things was always there; it is just that we did not have the awareness to experience them.

The energy center that makes metaphysical experiences possible is the third-eye chakra. The Sanskrit word "Ajna" can be translated as "to perceive or to command." Those with a balanced third-eye chakra trust their intuition or gut feeling and plan accordingly, even when there is nothing in their current reality to validate that feeling. Those whose' third-eye is open are more effective in employing the Law of Attraction. When one learns to use the third-eye chakra, one transcends the ego-based mind and can view all of reality with non-judgment and acceptance. In other words, one becomes a silent witness to all that is. This witnessing is not just of the outer world but the inner world as well. Such a person can observe their thoughts without becoming entangled in them or personalizing them. For this reason, there is clarity of thought. What causes the third eye to become unbalanced is not trusting our intuition and relying too much on the rational mind.

Regarding the third-eye chakras:

- It is located in the center of the brow.
- It is associated with the color indigo.
- It is associated with the element of light.

The Crown Chakra (also known as Sahasrara)

Along with the heart chakra, the crown chakra is one of the most important energy centers. The crown chakra determines the level of our spiritual alignment. The crown chakra makes it possible to experience inner peace and attract into your life that which you desire. Other spiritual benefits include a deep appreciation for beauty and the feeling of joy. When the crown chakra is balanced, it serves as a conduit to our highest self.

We are multidimensional beings. We simultaneously inhabit the non-phenomenal realm of higher consciousness and the physical dimension of this Earthly plane. When the crown chakra is balanced, we are aligned with the higher aspect of ourselves. When it is unbalanced, it leads to self-doubt and a sense of lack of purpose.

Regarding the crown chakra:

- It is located on the top of the head.
- It is associated with the color violet.
- It is associated with the element of thought.

Later in this book, we will explore what causes these energy centers to be balanced or not. The state of our chakras plays into how effectively we are able to utilize the Law of Attraction. In the next chapter, we will explore how we inhabit different levels of consciousness.

Chapter 2: The Multidimensional Being That You Are

As you are about to discover, you are both the source of what you want while at the same time the one who wants to attract it. To understand this, we will look at you as your separate self and as your essential self.

Our sense of self is that we are a person with a mind and body. This sense of self is created by us personalizing our experience of the mind and body. When viewed from a higher perspective, the mind and body are expressions of consciousness, while our true identity is consciousness. It is for this reason that we are multidimensional beings. As consciousness, we have identified with mind and body. This is like a light that is shining on a rock, believing that it is the rock. The difference is that the light did not create the rock. You, as consciousness, created the mind and body. When consciousness identifies with the mind and body, it experiences itself as being a separate self.

The Separate Self

There is a joke that I once heard about two fish swimming in the ocean. One fish turned to the other and said, "I have been looking for water. Have you seen any?" The other fish replied, "No, I have not. I will let you know if I do." Most of us are like the two fish, while consciousness is like the water. As a species, we have deeply identified with what could be referred to as the "I" thought. This thought leads us to believe that we are separate and unique entities unto ourselves. This identification leads to consciousness energy believing that it is a separate entity as well.

The belief that we are a separate entity leads to further identification. For example, the belief that we are a separate entity leads us to believe that consciousness is found in the mind and contained within us. Most do not even question these assumptions.

It is the sense of separation that ultimately diminishes our connection with the pure consciousness energy field. This sense of separation then leads us to pursue the objects of our desires. We live out our lives pursuing status, relationships, acceptance, money, power, or material objects.

It is this type of existence that ultimately lowers our vibrational frequency. Our lower vibrational thoughts attract other low vibrational thoughts, reinforcing the belief systems that we are separate entities. Part of raising your vibration involves critical reflection. For example, I pose this question to you: Have you ever had an experience that you were unaware of? Obviously, the answer is "no."

Nothing can be experienced without the awareness of it. Are you aware of yourself? Of course, you are! So, if you are aware of your experiences and aware of yourself, who is aware of you? Consciousness energy is the ocean, and all that we experience is found in that ocean, including our sense of self.

We are projections of consciousness that appear in manifested form. Because we appear in manifested form, we become an object within consciousness. To understand what this means, all you need to do is examine your own experience. Take a look at your surroundings and select an object to observe. How do you know that this object exists? Is it not because you are aware of it? You are aware of this object. Can you distinguish the awareness of this object from the object itself? Can you separate the knowing of this object's existence from the object itself? The answer is no! Yet, the awareness of the object and the object itself are not the same thing. If you remove the object, are you not still aware? Of course, you are!

Awareness is closer than close to the object that is known, but it is not the object. Awareness is like a light. A light that shines on a rock illuminates it. When the light shines on the rock, you cannot separate it from the rock. Yet, the light and the rock are not the same.

When awareness (consciousness) shines its light on its manifested self, it and the manifested self become inseparable. The consciousness identifies with the manifested self and experiences itself as a separate entity. You and I are examples of consciousness experiencing itself as separate entities. As separate entities, we experience ourselves as being separate from the world around us. From the perspective of higher consciousness, you and I are but a thought within consciousness.

While sleeping, you may have a dream where you appear in a foreign land. As the dream character, you are actively engaged with this world, and it becomes your reality. As real as this world may be to you, it is just a dream. It is a dream that was created by you, the dreamer. While dreaming, you, as the dream character, are unaware of your illusionary nature, nor are you aware of the real you, the dreamer.

The real you, the dreamer, are unaware of your true nature as you believe that you are the dream character. This illusion persists until you wake up the next morning. It is then there is a realization that what you experienced during the night was just an illusion.

As a separate self, you are like the dream character, and your essential self is like the dreamer. You are unaware of your essential self because you are caught up in the dream. Your essential self, who is like the dreamer, identifies itself as being the separate self, which is like the dream character. To break through this illusion of separation, we need to raise our frequency. How to do this will be explained later in this book.

What is the Ego

It is this sense of being a separate self that is the ego. The ego-based mind experiences itself as being separate from the rest of the world. Because of this, it is driven by the need to acquire or possess things. The ego-based mind has lost all memory of its true nature, which is pure consciousness.

In pure consciousness, there is only oneness. As everything is one, there is no sense of separation. If the purpose of the Law of Attraction is to manifest our desires, what purpose would it serve in a realm where everything is one? The Law of Attraction exists only in our realm, the realm of the separate self. It is the ego's way of seeking fulfillment as a result of having amnesia. It has no memory of its infinite self.

Your Essential Self

Who you are is the pure consciousness experiencing itself in the manifested form. You are the awareness (also known as pure consciousness) of all that you experience, including your sense of self (also a thought). It is impossible to know pure consciousness at the experiential level as anything that can be experienced is being observed by it. The closest thing that pure consciousness can be compared to is deep sleep.

Deep sleep is that period of sleep when you are not dreaming. Try to reflect on what was your experience of deep sleep was from the previous night. If you are having a difficult time doing this, that is okay. The reason why is because it is not possible. It was earlier stated that pure consciousness is free of thought and having an experience requires thought. Without thought, there can be no conceptualization of experience.

Though you have no memory of deep sleep, you know whether or not you experienced it the night before. How can you know this when you have no memory of it? As your ultimate self, the answer is that you are always aware, even in deep sleep. Your essential self is aware of deep sleep and dream sleep; it is aware of confusion and clarity, and it is aware of thought and the absence of thought. It is aware of all that is! In the next section, we will explore your relationship with the universe.

Chapter 3: Your Relationship with the Universe

What is the universe? However we define it, we believe that we are located in it along with everything else that we experience. Whether it is galaxies, oceans, or a blade of grass, all of these things appear to be separate from ourselves. However, just as the body's appearance of physicality is an illusion, so are our impressions of the universe. To begin with, no universe exists outside of us. As quantum physics has demonstrated, everything that exists is at the most fundamental level, energy. What we perceive as being the universe is an extension of the same energy field that we are comprised of. If the universe was a pool of water, each of us would be a drop merging with that water. The illusions that we experience, such as a universe that exists outside ourselves are created by the mind.

Since the advent of Newtonian physics, scientists have considered matter to be the building blocks of the physical world. With all their references to matter, scientists have yet to prove the existence of matter beyond their mental concept of it. In the same way, no one has ever proven the existence of a thought other than our concept of it.

All of us have experienced thoughts, but has anyone ever found a thought? Has anyone located where thoughts arise from or discovered what they are made of? Most of humanity has fallen for the superstition of materialism. Just as there is no supporting evidence that black cats are bad luck, so it is true that no one has offered any evidence for the existence of matter or thoughts.

All that can be said is that we have mental concepts of these things.

The only thing that we can be sure of is that we have an awareness of the existence of physical objects and thoughts; however, we lack any knowledge of what these things are. In fact, we lack any knowledge of anything that we experience. After all, knowledge is experienced as a thought, but what is a thought?

Any attributions to the nature of the universe, including ourselves, are all conceptual. Meaning, anything that we experience is a construct of the mind. Unknowingly, we project our concepts onto that which we are experiencing. This process of projecting concepts onto our experience is exactly what happens when we dream at night.

When dreaming, your dream self inhabits a dream world. The dream self, which is your sense of self, actively engages with this dream world, fully accepting its world as being reality. Unless you are lucid dreaming, the dream self cannot perceive the fact that it, and its dream world, are the projections of you, the one who is having the dream.

Dreams are mental concepts that are projected by the mind. What is the substance that dreams are made of? Has anyone collected this substance for analysis? Of course not! Our dreams are a perfect metaphor for an alternative explanation to what we experience in our physical existence. Could not our daily experience of reality be the projection of the mind as well? Could not the same be true of ourselves?

Whether it is a dream that we are experiencing while sleeping or the "reality" that we experience in the waking state, there is one thing that we can be certain of. We are aware of both the dream and the waking state. Awareness is the force that brings to life all that we experience. Without awareness, there can be no experience.

It is for this reason that you and the universe are not separate entities. Both you and the universe are brought to existence by awareness. But whose awareness makes this possible? This awareness that I am pointing to does not belong to anyone or anything. Rather, awareness is an entity unto itself. We and all that we experience are its manifestations, and all of existence is found within it.

The Oneness of Existence

It was once believed that the atom was a solid structure that contained subatomic particles. It is now known that neither the atom nor its subatomic particles are solid; instead, they are made of energy. Everything that we experience, at the most fundamental level, is made of energy.

You are not only a manifestation of this energy; you are inseparable from it. It is like a drop that is removed from the ocean. The drop shows no resemblance to the mighty ocean; however, the drop and the ocean are identical in their chemical composition. It is only our minds that make distinctions between these two. In the same way, you are inseparable from the universe.

Instead of focusing on the physicality of life and your sense of separateness from it, I encourage you to challenge your preconceived notions of reality. Consider the possibility that you are part of an energetic system from which you create your experiences, which is the subject of the next section.

The Greater Consciousness System

Your life and all that you experience are part of a conscious energy system. This system encompasses all that is. There is a continuous flow of energy in this system, and this flow of energy creates the manifestations of existence. It is the manifestation process that leads to the expansion of consciousness.

In this system, there is the unmanifested and the manifested. The unmanifested is the realm of pure consciousness. Pure consciousness is the most fundamental aspect of the manifested realm; its qualities include wholeness, oneness, timelessness, unboundedness, and infinite potentiality for expression.

By manifesting into form, consciousness learns about itself, resulting in it creating new expressions of itself. Our connection with pure consciousness is restricted in our manifested form due to the world of form monopolizing our attention. This obsession with the world of form is not a mistake; rather, it allows us to have experiences.

We can think of the conscious energy system as a video game. When you play a video game, you, the gamer, are represented by an avatar that interacts with its cyber environment. By interacting with its environment, the avatar can accumulate points and moves to the next level, or it can be killed off and have to start over.

Your avatar is restricted in what it can do by a rule set programmed into the game. If it was not for this ruleset, playing the game would be impossible because there would be too much information to consider. How would you navigate your avatar if there were no guidelines or limits?

To illustrate this, here is another computer analogy. You can chat online and converse with another user with relative ease. You type your message, and it is formatted on the screen so that the other user can read it. In turn, the other user would respond to you by following the same procedure.

While you are chatting with the other user, hundreds of conversations are being carried out by other users simultaneously. What if the rule set that isolates your conversation from all the other users did not exist? It would be impossible to make sense of your conversation with all the other conversations flooding your screen.

Your essential self, which is pure consciousness, is like the gamer, while your manifested self is like the avatar. Your experience of this physical realm is like the avatar's experience of its cyber world. And just as the avatar cannot know the gamer, you cannot know your essential self experientially. However, you can know it intuitively.

Just as the avatar and the gamer are intimately connected, so are you and your essential self. Further, any limitations that you may perceive are rule sets that allow you to make sense of your experience. You are here to have a human experience so that you can score points and move to the next level. How do you score points? You raise the vibrational frequency of your life's energy. What happens when you move to the next level? You raise your level of consciousness.

It is raising the level of consciousness that is the purpose of our existence. However, the purpose of raising your level of consciousness is not for your benefit alone. It is for the benefit of all living things. By raising your vibrational level, you affect the vibration of all other beings. You ultimately win the game by contributing to the rise of the collective consciousness. Before you can raise your vibrational level, you first need to understand this energy field and the manifestation process, which is the topic of the next section.

Your Frequency and the Manifestation Process

We have covered a tremendous amount of information so far in this book. In this section, we will summarize the main points but present them in a way that explains the manifestation process. Your true self is conscious energy, also known as awareness. You are the awareness. The world of form, which includes thoughts and emotions, is conscious energy manifested.

There is an aspect of consciousness that is deeply identified with the "I" thought, which leads you to believe that you are a separate entity. By identifying with the "I" thought, you experience yourself as being separate from other energy forms. Further, the "I" thought acts like a magnet. It attracts other thoughts that have the same vibrational frequency.

Because you experience yourself as being separate from other energy forms, you also develop an ego-based mind. The ego-based mind forms judgments regarding other energy forms. It is the meaning that you project onto your experiences that creates your reality. Further, the meaning that you give to your experience of reality determines the vibrational frequency of your life's energy.

If you are an optimist, your vibrational frequency will attract thoughts that have a high frequency. If you are a pessimist, you will attract thoughts of like kind, and your vibrational quality will be low. In both cases, the thoughts you attract will reinforce your beliefs about life. You will continue to attract the people and situations into your life that match your frequency.

However, neither the optimistic view nor the pessimistic view is the correct perspective. Rather, they are different perspectives that are projected by your illusionary self onto the field of energy that you know as life or reality.

From the perspective of higher consciousness, there is no absolute truth. Truth is relative to the level of awareness that one inhabits. The manifestation you experience, the meaning you create, and the reality you perceive are one and the same. They are all found within consciousness. It is like you being the movie producer, the director, the actors, and the movie itself all wrapped up in one!

Keeping with the movie theme, here is another metaphor. In the old days, we used film projectors in movie theaters. The movie was in the form of a film strip that ran through the movie projector. Using a beam of light, the movie projector would project the film strip images onto the screen. You, as the awareness, are like the beam of light. The thoughts you attract are like the film strip, and the projected image on the screen is your experience of reality.

The projector's light beam is to the film strip as the pure consciousness is to its manifested forms.

However, you, as pure consciousness, are also like the movie screen. When a movie is projected onto the screen, they appear to be one. There is no distinction between the movie and the screen while the movie is playing. However, when the movie ends, the screen remains and is untouched by the movie.

As pure consciousness or awareness, you remain untouched by anything that is experienced. If you touch a hot stove, you will feel pain. You will also be aware of the pain; however, the pain will not be experienced by the awareness.

What is popularly known as the subconscious is the field of awareness that does not receive the light of attention. Referring back to the movie metaphor, the movie screen is the "object of attention" for the projector's beam of light. However, the remainder of the theater will remain dark. If the house lights in the theater are turned on, the entire theater will be illuminated.

The higher the vibrational frequency, the more your "subconscious" will be exposed to the light.

How Strong is your Signal?

Before the advent of electronic devices like CD or Mpg players, my generation listened to music on the radio. When I dialed to the station that I wanted, I was able to listen to music with clear reception. If I was not properly tuned in to the station, the quality of my listening experience would be significantly compromised. I would hear static, the music fading in and out, or have other stations appear. The strength of the radio signal determined the quality of the sound.

Have you ever gone to a party and noticed how some people seem to fade into the background? Either the other guests do not approach them, or they do but find it awkward to build rapport with them. On the other hand, you have probably seen how some people attract the attention of everyone in the room as soon as they make their entrance. They effortlessly make everyone around them feel good, which is why others want to engage with them.

These two examples of the radio and the party illustrate how energy can affect our experience of the world. When the radio signal was strong, the music was clear. When the signal was weak, there was distortion. Similarly, how the guests at the party were received by others was determined by their signal strength. To understand what causes our signal to be weak or strong, we first need to understand the two realms of consciousness and how energy is affected by each of them. This is the topic of the next section.

Two Realms and One Consciousness

The universe is divided between the non-phenomenal realm and the phenomenal realm. The non-phenomenal realm cannot be perceived through our five senses, nor can it be comprehended by the intellectual mind. The non-phenomenal realm is the realm of pure consciousness, and it has the highest vibratory frequency.

The phenomenal realm is the world that you and I experience. It is characterized by shapes and forms and has a sense of physicality to it. Everything that we experience, be it a thought, another person, or a building, is an energy form. All energy forms are an expression of pure consciousness; they are energy manifested. The higher your vibrational frequency, the closer you become aligned with pure consciousness. The lower your vibrational frequency, the less access you will have to this higher realm.

In comparison to the non-phenomenal realm, the phenomenal realm has a lower vibrational level. Further, each physical manifestation has its own vibrational frequency. The higher the vibrational frequency that the object has, the purer it is. Plants, animals, and the newborn of humans have the highest vibrational frequency because they lack an ego-based mind.

In contrast, most of us are deeply identified with the mind and body. More specifically, we have confused the ego-based mind as ourselves. The ego-based mind refers to the aspect of the mind that leads us to believe that we are a separate and limited self.

As we perceive ourselves to be a separate and limited self, we see ourselves as being a separate entity from all that is around us. This sense of separation causes us to be reactive. This reactivity results from us believing that to get our needs met, we need to depend on something that exists outside ourselves. To understand this, think about your own life. Suppose you are looking for companionship, acknowledgment, or a sense of connection. Do you not look toward others for these things? If you want to feel significant, do you not need others to demonstrate this to? If you want to feel accepted, do you not need others to make you feel this way?

Whenever we turn to others to get what we want, we do so because we believe that we lack it within ourselves. I believe that to feel loved, I need someone to love me. If I need reassurance, I need someone to reassure me. If I feel lonely, I need to be with someone. These are just a few examples of the many ways that we look toward others to get what we need. Because we feel that we need to rely on others to get what we need, we become reactive. If we get our needs met, we become happy or satisfied. If we do not get our needs met, we become hurt or disappointed.

How we respond emotionally shapes our sense of identity. If I am able to get my emotional needs met, I will most likely feel good about myself. However, if I cannot get my emotional needs met, I may feel inferior to others. Because we have allowed the reactions of others to shape our sense of identity, how we feel about ourselves is in constant flux. Our sense of self is unstable. For this reason, our vibrational frequency will be low.

Our vibrational frequency is low because we have built our sense of identity on the emotions that we most commonly experience. How others react to us is not constant. The people we look to in order to get our needs met will not always respond the way we want them to. Our self-image has been constructed on shaky ground. It is vulnerable to the whims of a world that is in constant flux. To better understand how experience and self-identification affect our lives, the following scenario is provided.

Jon is like 99% of the rest of humanity in that his sense of self is largely determined by external circumstances. Being toned, athletic, and fit, Jon's physical appearance is a great sense of pride for him as he knows that he looks good. Jon also has a high-paying job that allows him to live a rich lifestyle, which only adds to his feeling good about himself.

The challenge for Jon is that his sense of self is not permanent; rather, it is in constant flux. His looks and finances do not offer him true confidence. There are times when John experiences the fear of not being good enough when his feelings of insecurity appear. These feelings occur when he remembers how he felt as a child when he did not receive the validation he craved from his parents. John also questions his desirability when he sees others getting more attention. Jon's sense of self is object-oriented, meaning that how he feels about himself depends on his body, career, memories, and how others respond to him.

Most of us are like Jon. We have lost touch with our higher truth; we suffer amnesia and have forgotten who we are at the most fundamental level. Everything that we experience is impermanent; nothing is in the phenomenal world is lasting. Our physical shape, financial success, and how others respond to us will change. The word "phenomena" refers to something that we can detect using our five senses or experience from within. For this reason, thoughts and feelings are also constantly changing. Whenever we base our sense of self on that which is impermanent, we experience suffering.

Your Vibrational Frequency and the Subconscious

Many people who have tried to use the Law of Attraction experienced disappointment because they were met with results that were, at best, inconsistent. They were taught that all they had to do was think about what they wanted, and they would attract it. Many of them visualized what they wanted, got in touch with their desire, and yet ended up not getting what they wanted. We will now explore why this is so.

There is only one life force (pure consciousness), and that life force permeates all of its manifestations. As a species, we humans have developed a mind that is highly developed. Unlike other species, our mind is ego-based. What this means is that we see ourselves as being a separate entity unto ourselves. This kind of mindset leads to a sense of separation, and a sense of separation leads to a sense of fear. What kind of fear? It is the fear of loss, be it the loss of an important resource, the loss of approval, the loss of a relationship, the loss of health, and so on. It is this fear of loss that lowers our vibrational level.

Often, these fears are found within our subconscious. Even though we may not be aware of them, their vibrational frequency remains active. In fact, their vibrational frequency is often stronger than our desires. The result is that these subconscious vibrations cancel out the vibrational energy of our desires. I can give an example from my past that illustrates this.

I was raised in a critical environment. My father was often critical of me, and he was dogmatic in his ways. Because of my self-doubt, I had attracted low energy thoughts, which accumulated. These thoughts formed my beliefs about myself. When I got older, the view that I had of myself was a major challenge for me when it came to meeting members of the opposite sex and establishing long-term relationships.

Whenever I faced rejection, I blamed myself. At the conscious level, I craved a loving relationship. At the subconscious level, I was attracting experiences that matched the energy of my self-doubt. However potent these sabotaging thoughts were, they were no more damaging than the thoughts of a full moon, a red sports car, or a rose. The only difference was that I had laid claim to my thoughts of inadequacy while being indifferent to my thoughts of those three objects. It was not until I turned to the spiritual path that I developed the insights that allowed me to transcend my conditioning. One of my challenges in learning how to utilize the Law of Attraction was the fact that there was nothing to learn! Rather, I needed to unlearn what I was taught in the past. This is the topic of the next section.

Unlearning What You Know about the Law of Attraction

What is misunderstood about the Law of Attraction is that we have always attracted things into our lives, whether it is people, situations, or events. What we refer to as the Law of Attraction is an inescapable fact of our reality. However, most of us are not aware of this.

For this reason, you do not need to learn how to attract things into your life. Instead, you need to learn how to be intentional in what you attract. However, before you can learn how to be intentional in what you attract, we first need to explore how and why you manifest anything in your life.

The reason why pure consciousness expresses itself through manifestation is so that it can experience itself. Since there is only oneness in pure consciousness, any sense of differentiation is non-existent. By expressing itself in manifested form, consciousness becomes aware of what it is like to be a separate entity.

A manifested entity experiences itself separate from its environment, and this sense of separation creates contrast. I experience myself as a separate entity, so I see myself as being separate from my environment. I can experience the contrast between being in my living room when it's pitch dark compared to when the lights are on. Contrast leads me to formulate my preferences: I prefer the illuminated room over the darkroom.

My preferences inform the pure consciousness, which then creates a new manifestation based on my preferences. You may be thinking to yourself at this moment: "If pure consciousness responds to my preferences, why do I experience things that I do not want?" The answer to this question brings us back to the subconscious. Our subconscious thoughts compete with our preferences when it comes to informing the pure consciousness. Because we are unaware of our subconscious thoughts, they win out.

The vibrational frequency of our subconscious thoughts causes counter the frequency of our preferences. Pure consciousness responds to our intentions, and the intentions that are received come from the energy with the strongest vibration. Because of this, subconscious thoughts normally win out if they are not acknowledged. It was like when I shared my experience of growing up wanting a loving relationship.

Consciously, my intentions were, "I want someone to love." However, my subconscious thought was, "You are going to mess up with anyone that you meet." My subconscious thoughts created a sense of doubt whenever I thought of my intentions. What manifested in my life was having no confidence in myself, making it difficult to meet someone. The pure consciousness did its job; it manifested in my life what it took to be my preferences.

Our subconscious beliefs are formed in childhood. A major source for them is our parents, caregivers, and societal indoctrination (which were the source of our parents' and caregivers' subconscious beliefs). The following is another example of how subconscious beliefs affect the way we perceive ourselves:

Jane was born to parents who were critical of both her and her siblings. Like any child, Jane wanted her parent's approval, but nothing that she ever did was good enough for them. As a child, Jane was naturally curious, fun-loving, and liked to explore new things. Her parents perceived her as being undisciplined and restless.

With time, these natural qualities of hers gradually diminished as Jane strived to win her parents' approval and live up to their expectations. As she became older, she became self-critical and developed perfectionist tendencies. She felt that she always had to prove herself.

Jane cultivated this critical aspect of herself until it became her dominant personality. Because she was self-critical, she also became critical of others. Her natural qualities of being friendly and loving to explore were suppressed in her subconscious; she lacked any awareness of them.

Based on the Law of Attraction, you would think that Jane would attract people into her life who were also self-critical. However, this is not necessarily the case. Jane's qualities of being friendly and loving to explore while being repressed still gave off their energetic vibration.

Because she was unaware of these qualities, they played a stronger role in what she attracted into her life! It is why we sometimes see a couple who seem so different from each other that we find it puzzling that they ever got together. It is also why sometimes we have an instant dislike or attraction toward someone we do not know.

As an adult, Jane may see someone who exhibits her natural qualities and become judgmental of them. At some level of her being, she remembers the pain that she experienced for exhibiting these same qualities.

The following exercise will help you identify your subconscious beliefs. To show you how this exercise works, I will provide you with an example.

1. The first step is to think of an ongoing challenge that you are experiencing in your life. This challenge can be in any aspect of our life. My example will be: I want to be in a relationship but have difficulty approaching other people.
2. My next step is to start a line of inquiry using the phrase "What would be so bad if..." So my first question to myself would be, "What would be so bad if I approached someone whom I was interested in?"
3. After reflecting on this, I come up with the response, "I am afraid that I would be rejected."
4. Now that I have an answer, my next step is to drill down further by asking: "What would be so bad about being rejected?"
5. My answer to that question would be, "If I were rejected, I would feel that I was not good enough."
6. I would then use my response and rephrase the question: "What would be so bad if I felt that I was not good enough?"
7. My response to that question would be: "It would make me feel that I was undesirable."
8. I would continue to repeat this question by asking: "What would be so bad if I felt that I was undesirable?"
9. My answer to that would be: "It would mean that I am unlovable."
10. Keep going through this line of questioning until you are unable to any further. In this example, the belief "I am unlovable" is as far as I can take the exercise. For this reason, it is my core belief that I hold within my subconscious.

It is important to remember that who you are is not your thoughts or your beliefs. You are just a witness to them. In the example that I just shared with you, my vibratory frequency was low when I was very young due to how I interpreted my experience at that time. My low frequency attracted the belief, "I am unlovable." Additionally, being of low frequency also means that I personalized my thoughts and emotions. So, I allowed my sense of identity to be defined by the belief, "I am unlovable."

If I could look from the perspective of higher consciousness, such thoughts would have no impact on me. Such a thought would be as significant to me as the thought of a full moon, a red sports car, or a rose. There would be no identification with this thought. In the next chapter, we will explore ways to raise your vibration.

Chapter 4: Reclaiming Your Power as a Manifestor

From the perspective of higher consciousness, the ultimate goal of any spiritual practice is to raise one's vibrational level. In its purest sense, spirituality is less about our beliefs and more about learning to let go of our attachments to them. To release one's attachments to the phenomenal world is to be no longer held prisoner by the illusions of the ego-centered mind. This chapter will provide instructions on a variety of ways to increase your vibrational frequency.

When doing these exercises, it is important to keep a number of points in mind. First, you are not working toward becoming something different than you already are. Secondly, you are not learning something new. Instead, you are unraveling the layers of societal conditioning to reveal that part of you that you have forgotten about.

What is commonly known as enlightenment is returning to who we were before our societal conditioning had set in. By becoming reacquainted with that part of us that transcends our mental activity, we will experience an expanded sense of calm and liberation. The experience of this is not something new. Instead, it has always existed within us, but it eluded us due to our entrenchment with our manifested form. In this chapter, we will begin our exploration of ways to reclaim your power as a manifestor. We will start with the importance of unlearning our past.

Learning to Unlearn Your Past

In the previous chapters, we discussed the foundational components that make the Law of Attraction possible. These components include consciousness and the physical manifestations of it. These manifestations include our perceptions, thoughts, emotions, and how we experience our sense of self. These elements are aspects of consciousness, are made of consciousness, and are found within consciousness. It is for these reasons that we live in a conscious universe. With this understanding, we can now discuss the Law of Attraction from a deeper perspective.

The Law of Attraction is inherent to the nature of consciousness, which is our true nature. The Law of Attraction is not something we need to learn or develop; rather, we need to unlearn all the tendencies that prevent the Law of Attraction from occurring. The following are some of these tendencies that we need to unlearn:

Not Understanding Your True Nature

When you go to bed at night, do you have to think about having a dream? Do you have to make an effort to have one? Of course, not; dream just happens. When you have a dream, you experience a whole new reality. In deep sleep, you lose all sense of yourself. No trace of your personal identity exists.

Further, there is no sense of existence in deep sleep. Do you have to take any kind of action or make any effort to experience deep sleep? No, you do not. Dreaming and deep sleep does not require any effort on your part because these are different dimensions of consciousness, as is your experience of being a separate self.

In truth, you experience the Law of Attraction all the time, though you may not be aware of it. An example of this is your thoughts. Your thoughts are a perfect example of the Law of Attraction. Your thoughts attract other thoughts. The thought, "I should go grocery shopping today," is not a single thought. The first thought is "I." The "I" thought is the most fundamental thought; it is the thought that is created by your sense of being a separate self.

The "I" thought is the thought that attracts all other thoughts. The "I" thought is like a magnet, while all other thoughts are like metal filings attracted to it. Which thoughts are attracted is determined by where we (our illusionary selves) place our attention. Suppose your attention is being placed on a near-empty refrigerator. In that case, you could attract the second thought, "should go grocery shopping." If you are hungry, you may attract the third thought, "today." If your attention was placed on something else, you would attract different thoughts. If you are waiting to get paid, you may attract the thought "tomorrow" instead of "today."

Everything that we experience is thought-based. Anything that you see requires the addition of thought to give it any meaning. The same is true with anything that you hear, taste, touch, or smell. Even your sense of existence is created by the thought, "I." For this reason, it can be said that you are practicing the Law of Attraction in every moment of your life, except deep sleep.

Deep sleep, which is the deepest level of sleep, is void of thought. It is your essential state. For this reason, any experience of thought is an experience of the illusionary self. It is for this reason that everything that you experience is the result of the Law of Attraction. As most people are deeply identified with their illusionary self, a concession is made to treat the Law of Attraction as a spiritual teaching. It is from this perspective that the remainder of this book's content will be presented.

Attachments

Our sense of separation results in us forming attachments, particularly those things that we want to attract. By forming attachments, we reinforce the belief that we are incomplete unless we can attract the object of desire into our lives. If someone wants to attract more money into their life, that desire may reinforce a belief that they cannot be happy unless they have more money.

Naturally, there are situations where we may be going through difficult times where having more money would help relieve our suffering. It would be completely understandable to want more money for this reason. However, two subtle points get overlooked. Suppose there is a sense of desperation in our desire to attract more money. In that case, that desperation will lower our vibrational level. This occurs because we are operating out of fearful thinking. Because our thoughts attract other thoughts of like kind, we will attract other fearful thoughts.

The second thing to consider is that the Law of Attraction can be used as a crutch. Someone may believe that they will feel better about themselves if they can manifest their desire. In that case, they may continue looking for fulfillment outside themselves instead of developing themselves from within.

It is for these reasons that it is important to learn detachment. The probability of attracting what you desire will greatly increase if you no longer feel that you need to have it in your life. By giving up the need, you increase your vibrational frequency. This happens because you move from the emotions of fear and neediness to that of acceptance.

This shift comes from transferring your attention from fear-based thoughts to the acceptance of the present moment. The emotion of acceptance has a much higher frequency. In turn, a genuine acceptance comes about when we realign ourselves with our essential nature. Anything less than acceptance would indicate that we are identifying with our illusionary sense of self.

For this reason, attempts to attract anything into our lives are more effective when the happiness of others is our motive. Focusing on how we can create value for others will more likely manifest what we desire. This is because we are moving our attention from the ego-based mind and placing it on others.

At the level of higher levels of consciousness, there is only oneness. Even though we focus on manifesting to create value for others, we will receive what we desire. As the adage goes, we reap what we sow.

Expectations and Doubt

When asking the universe to turn your desires into reality, it is important to understand the relationship between your expectations and the manifestation process. The more expectations you make of the universe, the fewer opportunities you give the universe to manifest your desires. Let us say that I ask the universe to manifest my dream job. I tell the universe how much money I want to earn, where I want the job to be located, my job title, and what I want my office to look like.

By being so specific in my expectations, I lose out on potentially great job opportunities that may be even a better fit for me. The universe already has all the information that it needs regarding who I am and what I want. I am asking the universe to operate on my limited understanding instead of the bigger picture my life has for me by being so specific in my request.

A better approach would be to know what is most important to me regarding a job offer. For example, I want a job in my industry that pays more and offers me greater responsibility and autonomy in my work. This type of request will more likely result in me getting what I want. The reason for this is that I have told the universe what is most important to me, and I am not overly specific. Because of this, the universe can offer me a wider range of options, or it will come up with a job that I would have never considered, yet it meets my needs.

Rather than giving the universe a shopping list of your expectations, a more effective way to present your request is to think of those most important things and get in touch with the feelings that accompany them. Focus on what is most important to you and how it would feel if these things were your current reality.

By focusing on what is most important to me, and the accompanying emotions, I will be sending a clear message to the universe. That message will be of a vibrational frequency that is a match for what I am asking for. What will make my message the right vibrational frequency is the emotional intensity that I experience when I think about what is most important.

Along with expectations, doubt is another cause of unsuccessful attempts at the Law of Attractions. In a way, doubt is a factor of expectations. If our experience of the Law of Attraction does not meet our expectations, we may experience doubt. The emotion of doubt lowers our vibrational frequency.

You can overcome any doubt in your ability to manifest by practicing with intentions that are inconsequential to you. You will unlikely experience doubt when the outcome is not meaningful to you. As you gain experience in manifesting, you can practice manifesting more meaningful things.

It Is Not Enough To Think About It

You cannot expect to successfully manifest by just thinking about what you want, at least in this dimension. At higher levels of consciousness, manifesting does occur just by thinking about what we want. Further, it occurs instantly. At the lower dimensions of consciousness, it takes more than just thought alone to manifest, which is a good thing. If we could manifest just by thinking about it, our lives would be impossible to manage. At the lower dimensions of consciousness, we need to follow a process that requires us to be intentional, focused, and take action. It could be said that this process is a built-in safety mechanism that was created by the universe!

We just explored what we need to unlearn to reclaim our manifesting abilities. So, how do we unlearn those patterns of thinking and behaving that prevent us from reclaiming our manifestation abilities? The answer to this question is that we adopt new patterns of thinking and behaving that bring us back to alignment with our essential selves. To employ the Law of Attraction, we need to address the following areas:

- We need to know what we want
- Change any limiting beliefs that may be causing resistance for us.
- Create our intention for what we want to happen.
- Raise our vibration through meditation, balancing our chakras, and by other means.
- Visualize or imagine that which we desire to attract into our lives as though it was our current reality
- Visualize or imagine that which we desire to attract into our lives and experience it emotionally.

These six elements of the Law of Attraction overlap, and they do not have to be practiced sequentially. However, they all need to be present for the manifestation process to be successful. The following sections and chapters will address each of these elements. In the next section, we will discuss the concept of resistance.

How to Remove Resistance

Increasing our frequency requires the removal of resistance. The removal of resistance requires raising awareness of the beliefs that are limiting us. There are two major ways of removing resistance: the first way is cultivating love and appreciation. The second way is increasing your awareness of the mental phenomena of your mind.

Love and Appreciation

The frequent references to love as the most powerful force in the universe or that love conquers all go beyond being poetic or spiritual speak; it is a reality! The power of love is that it melts resistance. When we experience love for anything in life, we give up our resistance to it.

To experience love is to experience oneness with our beloved. Because love removes resistance, all blockages are removed from the manifestation process. The challenge for many of us is cultivating a sense of love, especially a love for ourselves. Self-love is the ultimate spiritual achievement. It is the optimal state for manifestation and provides others an opportunity to catch a glimpse of their own divinity.

In many ways, self-love is the equivalent of enlightenment, for to achieve self-love is to cause the darker aspects of our nature to lose their power. When this happens, it releases a tremendous amount of energy that can be used in the manifestation process. When we reach self-love, the Law of Attraction takes on a paradoxical place in our lives. When we have self-love, we become masters of manifesting due to the lack of resistance. However, since we experience self-love, there is little need to manifest anything. There is no longer a sense of wanting. Self-love makes us feel complete or whole. For this reason, the learning of how to effectively use the Law of Attractions should be viewed as being less than a way to get what we desire and more as a stepping stone to learning the truth of who we are. In this manner, the Law of Attraction is ultimately a practice of self-discovery.

Self-Love

One of the challenges of developing self-love is that we associate self-love with selfishness or narcissism. However, there is a big difference between self-love, selfishness, and narcissism.

Selfishness arises from a fear-based belief system. Selfish people do not feel in control of their lives and see the world through the lens of scarcity. For them, there is not enough love, money, or resources to go around.

Because they feel that they are not in control of their lives, selfish people view everyone around them as a threat or a competitor. To give anything up to another is seen as a threat to their security. Narcissistic people are unable to empathize with others and require their admiration.

Self-Love is the polar opposite of selfishness and narcissism. Self-love is based on the understanding that each of us is intimately connected to the universe and interdependent upon each other.

In our personal expansion, we become a mirror for others, reflecting the potential for their own expansion. However, our own personal expansion can only come from honoring ourselves. Self-love is like the lightening of one candle so that it can be used to light all the other candles on a menorah. The following are comments and exercises on generating self-love and appreciation.

Values

When cultivating self-love, it is essential that we learned to live by our values. Anytime we live in a manner inconsistent with our values, we create major resistance in our lives. If your life is not aligned with your values, start the process of making changes in your life so that you can start moving toward greater alignment. If you currently have a job that conflicts with your values, what can you do to create the needed changes in your work? Could you conduct your work differently? Would it require you to take on a different position? Perhaps it means finding a new job. If your relationship does not align with your values, what changes do you need to make? Do you need to transform your relationship or find a new one? Take into account any aspect of your life where you experience a gap between how you live your life and the values you hold.

Whose Life is it?

To be a successful manifestor requires personal integrity. To live with integrity requires that we honor our emotions and how we feel. The emotions that you experience are a direct link to the intelligence of the greater consciousness system. What is important to realize is that your emotions change as your level of consciousness increases. For example, you may become upset with a certain behavior of another. Later on, you may find that this behavior of theirs no longer makes you angry. This does not mean that how you responded earlier was right or wrong. It just means that your increased awareness of this person resulted in you becoming less reactive toward them.

As a link to the greater consciousness system, your emotions are valid at the moment that they are experienced. When you honor your emotions, you honor your connection with the source of all that is. Your emotions are your individualized expression of conscious energy, just as is your experience of life.

Anytime we compromise how we feel to meet the expectations of others, we lose our alignment. To honor our feelings is one of the greatest practices of self-love. Your feelings are your own unique GPS; no one else has the same GPS as you do. The greatest gift you can give to those you love and care about is to become a living example of self-love. By your example, they can learn to love themselves. The following exercise will help you learn how the way that you feel.

For one hour, make a commitment to yourself that you will listen to your feelings and that you will honor them. During that hour, take notice of whenever you go against the way you feel. Anytime you experience uneasiness, it is a sign that you are thinking thoughts or taking actions that go contrary to your feelings. Examples include:

- Agreeing to join others in an activity when you really would prefer to be alone.
- Feeling that you want to do something but rationalizing that you have more important things to do.
- Feeling like you want to just relax and do nothing while telling yourself that doing so would be irresponsible.
- Following the lead of others even though you do not feel right about it. This is what peer pressure is.
- Doing things always the same way just because you were taught or raised to believe that it is the way that it should be done.

When you catch yourself going against the way you feel, stop what you are doing and evaluate the situation. Ask yourself what you could do that would be consistent with the way that you feel. When you successfully do this for an hour, continue this exercise the next day by doing it for four hours.

When you can do this exercise for four hours, keep practicing each day until you can do it for the whole day. When you can do this exercise for a day, it is time for the real test. Schedule a day where you can devote it to yourself. During this day, you will only do only those things that are consistent with how you feel.

Most people have difficulty with this exercise as it goes against how we were raised. If this is the case, you may want to commit to a few hours instead of a whole day. As you feel more comfortable with this exercise, extend the time frame until you can dedicate the whole day to it.

Another challenge people experience with this exercise is that there are things they do not want to do, but they have to do it. This exercise is not about avoiding reality or daily responsibilities; rather, it is about learning to change our perspective. If you encounter a situation where you do not feel like doing something, but it has to be done, do one of the following:

1. Think about the benefits of doing the task and the consequences of not doing it. If the benefits of completing the tasks outweigh the consequences of not doing them, you will feel less resistant to doing the task.
2. Think of how you could change your approach to doing the tasks to make doing them more enjoyable. Example: If you need to do your taxes, put on your favorite music or invite a friend over so that you can do your taxes together.
3. If none of the previous suggestions change the way you feel about the task, postpone doing the task until you come to a point where you can do it with acceptance.

The principle behind the last three suggestions is the eliminating of resistance. In fact, these suggestions having nothing to do with the task; rather, they are ways to modify your perception of it. The key to cultivating self-love, and becoming a conscious manifestor, is to learn how to modify your perceptions to no longer struggle against yourself. Self-love involves living your life based on the way you want to live it, rather than living according to the expectations or judgments of others. The following are exercises for removing resistance and cultivating self-love.

Exercise 1: Discovering the Root Cause of Your Resistance

The following exercise will guide you in identifying your subconscious beliefs. To show you how this exercise works, I will provide you with an example.

1. The first step is to think of an ongoing challenge that you are experiencing in your life. This challenge can be in any aspect of our life. My example will be: I want to be in a relationship, but I have difficulty approaching other people.

2. My next step is to start a line of inquiry using the phrase "What would be so bad if…" So my first question to myself would be, "What would be so bad if I approached someone whom I was interested in?"
3. After reflecting on this, I come up with the response, "I am afraid that I would be rejected."
4. Now that I have an answer, my next step is to drill down further by asking: "What would be so bad about being rejected?"
5. My answer to that question would be, "If I were rejected, I would feel that people saw me as being less, that I am not good enough."
6. I would then use my response and rephrase the question: "What would be so bad if people saw me as being less or not good enough?"
7. My response to that question would be: "It would make me feel that I was undesirable."
8. I would continue to repeat this question by asking: "What would be so bad if I felt like I was undesirable?"
9. My answer to that would be: "It would mean that I am unlovable."
10. Keep going through this line of questioning until you are unable to any further. In this example, the belief "I am unlovable" is as far as I can take the exercise. For this reason, it is my core belief that I hold within my subconscious.

It is important to remember that who you are is not your thoughts or your beliefs. You are just a witness to them. In the example that I just shared with you, my vibratory frequency when I was very young was low due to how I interpreted my experience at that time. My low frequency attracted the belief, "I am unlovable." Additionally, being of low frequency also means that I personalized my thoughts and emotions. So, I allowed my sense of identity to be defined by the belief, "I am unlovable."

Exercise 2: Emotional Diving

An effective technique to uncover subconscious thoughts and reduce your resistance is to immerse yourself in your suppressed feelings. To do this exercise, do the following:

1. Identify a situation that is bothering you. For example: "I do not know if I can make it financially."
2. Next, ask yourself how that situation makes you feel. Example: "I feel worried."

The remaining steps of this exercise require you to focus only on the feelings that you experience rather than thinking about them. For this reason, you want to repeatedly phrase your questions, "How does that feel?" Each time you come up with a response, you will drill down deeper by repeating this question.

3. Continuing with my example, I would ask myself, "How does being worried feel?" I would then focus on the sensations in my body, becoming immersed completely in them. My response might be: "Being worried makes me feel constricted and heavy."

4. I would then continue my questioning by asking: "How does being constricted and heavy feel?" I would then immerse myself in the feelings of constriction and heaviness until a response came to mind, such as: "Feeling constricted and heavy feels like a huge weight is on me."
5. I would continue to drill down on my response by asking myself: "How does a huge weight feel?" I would then immerse myself in the feelings until I got a response, such as: "It feels like I am being dragged to the ground."
6. I would continue my questioning until I started experiencing neutral or positive feelings.
7. When you reach this point, you have transformed your negative emotions.

The next exercise is for cultivating self-love. Cultivating self-love is a powerful way to remove resistance and raise your vibration.

Exercise 3: Loving Yourself

The following exercise is the one that many people find difficult to do. Due to our conditioning, most of us have learned to believe that we are unlovable or somehow flawed. This belief comes from us being socialized to believe that our self-worth is dependent upon the approval of others. The following exercise will allow you to recondition yourself to experience love for yourself. The one who can release resistance toward themselves is the one who can manifest without effort.

1. While before a mirror, look deeply into your eyes and tell yourself out loud, "I love you," using your name.
2. Attempt to feel love for yourself. If you can experience the feelings of love, allow yourself to experience them as fully as possible. If you are unable to experience feelings of love, do not force it. Simply remain aware of any feelings that should arise without judgment.
3. Continue to look into your eyes and say, "I love you" to yourself by name. As you address yourself in this manner, place your focus on any emotions of appreciation, approval, or gratitude that you may experience.
   You can tap into these emotions if you recall what you have done, which you feel good about. Incorporate all of these memories in the way that you address yourself, for example: "I love you (include your name) for the way you did..."
4. Focus on the feelings of love or appreciation you experience as you do this exercise while intensifying the feelings.
5. Try to do this exercise every morning and evening, allowing five minutes per exercise. Do this exercise daily until you begin to experience feelings of love or appreciation for yourself.

The following are additional methods for overcoming resistance:

Journaling

There is a power in writing that allows us to access the subconscious. It is why poets, musicians, and writers can express themselves more fully than just thinking about what they want to say. Most writers will tell you that when they write, they are not the ones that are coming up with the ideas. Rather, they see themselves as being an instrument that is channeling some greater intelligence. Learn to journal daily, writing down whatever comes to mind. Continue writing until you feel satisfied emotionally.

Exercise 4: Visualizations

Visualizing is great for influencing the subconscious; however, aspects of the visualizing process are often misunderstood. The following are some key points to consider when visualizing:

1. There is an abundance of visualizing programs available on the market. They can be useful if you have never visualized them before. However, the most effective visualizations occur when you create your own visualizations. Once you understand the process, learn to trust your imagination and just go with it.
2. Many people feel they cannot visualize, as they cannot develop clear images in their minds. Do not worry about the quality of your images. However you experience your visualizations, trust them. Some people are unable to see images; rather, they experience sensations. With continued practice, your visualizations will become more vivid.
3. Before visualizing, it's helpful to formulate an intention for yourself. Examples of intentions would be:
    a. Visualizing your desires already manifested
    b. Visualizing yourself exploring that which you are resisting.
    c. Visualizing yourself taking on a new challenge as a form of a mental rehearsal.
    d. Visualizing yourself solving a problem.

Affirmations

Affirmations can be useful when manifesting; however, they need to be emotionally based on being effective. Many people make the mistake of simply repeating the affirmation to themselves, which has little power. To be effectively used, affirmations need to be accompanied by emotional intensity. As previously stated, emotions reflect your life state. When you repeat an affirmation to yourself, say it as you mean it!

Repeat it Until You Become It

The exercises that we have just discussed in this chapter are based on conditioning. By associating the emotions of appreciation, love, or acceptance with your thoughts of others and yourself, you will condition your thoughts. A point will be reached when you think about others or yourself; you will experience these emotions.

Reaching that point will require you to repeat these exercises until an association is firmly established for this conditioning to take place. It is for this reason that experiencing your feelings while doing these exercises is so important. The intensity of your feelings will become paired with your thoughts (of others or yourself). This will result in these exercises becoming a part of who you are.

When your conditioning has been established, you will not have to meditate, visualize, or focus on appreciation. Just by entering the proper mental state, you will experience these emotions automatically. Make these exercises part of your daily routine. With time, the high-frequency emotions for attracting your desires will become a part of you. In the next section, we will explore the power of intentions.

Chapter 5: The Power of Intentions

The intentions behind your desires are critical in the process of manifesting, as your intentions determine if you are broadcasting from the ego or from love. As stated earlier, love has the highest frequency, while fear has the lowest. It was also previously stated that we attract into our lives that which matches our life's frequency.

Whenever our intentions for attracting something into our lives are based on self-interest, we have automatically weakened our signal. The reason for this is that intentions of self-interest are fear-based. Conversely, when our intentions are for the well-being of others, our frequency operates from the level of love.

Since love is the higher frequency, we will be more likely to attract that which we desire. For example, my intention may be to attract more money into my life. Suppose my intention for wanting more money is due to the belief that I am inadequate as a person unless I have more money. In that case, I will be operating from fear. Fear will be the dominant frequency, and it will attract the people and situations that reinforce that perspective.

If, on the other hand, my intentions are to attract money because doing so would allow me to take care of my family, then that intention comes from the place of love. As love has the highest frequency, the probability of attracting money will greatly increase.

How Your Intentions Affect Consciousness

What becomes manifested is base on probability. What do I mean by probability? The larger consciousness does not waste energy creating things that are not useful. Everything that is manifested serves a purpose. The purpose of all manifestations is to remind us of our essential nature. The probability of your intentions becoming manifested will be based on how useful the manifestation will contribute to your spiritual growth.

The pleasure and pain brought to us by the manifestations that appear in our lives are intended to get us to look inward. When we see that nothing that enters our lives can give us lasting happiness, we will give up our attachments to the world around us and look inward for an answer.

This can be illustrated by the potential for a traffic accident. The universe holds a certain probability that traffic accidents will occur. However, this probability can be increased or decreased by the intentions held by the individual driver. Suppose a driver is worried about getting in an accident. In that case, that intention will increase the probability of an accident occurring. The reason for this is the driver is focusing on his fears of having an accident. If this same driver felt relaxed, enjoyed the drive, and was driving defensively, the probability of being involved in an accident would drop.

The potential to manifest can also be exemplified by the personality types of the optimist and pessimist. These personality types experience reality differently because their dominant mindset affects whether they are presented with encouraging circumstances or discouraging circumstances. Because of their attitude, the optimist affects the probability of the universe in a way that causes the ratio of encouraging circumstances to be greater than the negative circumstances. In contrast, the pessimist attracts a ratio that is the opposite of the optimist.

Something to Keep in Mind

From the perspective of higher consciousness, the ultimate goal of any spiritual practice is to raise one's vibrational level. In its purest sense, spirituality is less about our beliefs and more about learning to let go of our attachments to them. To release one's attachments to the phenomenal world is to be no longer held prisoner by the illusions of the ego-centered mind. The next chapter will provide instructions on a variety of ways to increase your vibrational frequency.

When doing these exercises, it is important to keep a number of points in mind. First, you are not working toward becoming something different than you already are. Secondly, you are not learning something new. Instead, you are unraveling the layers of societal conditioning to reveal that part of you that you have forgotten about. In the next chapter, we will examine how you can raise your vibration.

Chapter 6: How to Raise Your Energy Levels

This chapter contains a range of exercises intended to expand your awareness of the mind, the body, and the world around you. It is by expanding your awareness that your energetic level rises. We will start with the mind, more specifically, your beliefs.

How to Transform a Limiting Belief

Our beliefs are the lens through which we experience the world. They determine what you focus on and what things mean to you. We all have limiting beliefs, beliefs that prevent us from expressing our greater potential. The beliefs that limit us also lower our vibrational frequency. The following exercise will allow you to identify your limiting beliefs and replace them with empowering ones.

Exercise: Belief Balance Sheet

Our beliefs inform us of perceived potentials for pain or pleasure. If someone distrusts others, it is because they have the belief that people will take advantage of others if they can. If someone is a "people person," they believe that being with other people will result in enjoyable feelings. It is important to emphasize that beliefs inform us of the *perceived potential* of pleasure or pain.

Beliefs do not reflect reality; rather, they are our interpretations of reality. Further, beliefs are often not logical. The person who does not trust others may feel that their belief serves them by protecting them from experiencing emotional pain. Still, they may overlook all the other ways that this same belief creates emotional pain for them. Such is the nature of limiting beliefs. We feel that they serve us even though the cost we incur from having them is conveniently hidden in the subconscious mind. The following exercise will help you gain greater clarity about the cost and benefits of your beliefs.

Materials needed:

- Three sheets of paper
- A writing instrument

Do the following:

1. Get three sheets of paper. Select paper sizes of 8" x 11" or larger.

2. On the first paper, write down as many limiting beliefs that you have. You want to identify those beliefs that prevent you from living the life that you desire.
3. Select the one belief that you believe is impacting you the most.
4. Take the second sheet of paper and fold it in half lengthwise.
5. On top of the paper, write down the belief that you selected.
6. Make a list on the left-hand side of the paper of all the ways this belief has cost you in your life. How has this belief cost you regarding the way you feel about yourself? How has it affected your relationships, your health, or your finances? Think of all the ways that you have experienced emotional pain by holding on to this belief.
7. When writing, keep in mind the following:
    - When writing this list, write down the first thing that comes to your mind, even if it seems irrelevant.
    - Write as fast as you can, and feel the emotions that arise. This is a heartfelt exercise, not a cerebral one.
    - Keep writing until you run out of things to write.
8. By each item you write down, assign an arbitrary point value to how much impact this item has had on you. When selecting the point value, choose the first number that comes to mind.
9. When you have completed assigning the point values, find the total of all the point values and place it at the bottom of the page.
10. For the right side of the page, repeat Steps 6-8, except this time, you will write down all the ways that this belief has benefited you.

When you have completed step 10, think of a new alternative belief that empowers you. For example, if your original belief was, "Things never go my way," your new belief maybe, "When I raise my vibration, my life will get better."

On the third paper, repeat steps 4-10, using your new belief, with the following exceptions: Reverse Steps 6 and 10 by writing down all the ways that you believe that you would benefit from this new belief for Step 6. When doing step 10, write down all the ways you believe it will cost you.

When you have completed the two sheets, do the following:

1. Immediately review your lists, allowing yourself to experience any emotions that arise fully.
2. Review your lists every day, once in the morning and once before you go to bed. Do this until you become fully associated with the emotions that you experience.

When you become fully associated with the costs of holding on to your old belief with the benefits of adopting your new belief, your mind will become reprogrammed with your new belief.

Balancing your Chakras

As discussed earlier, chakras are the body's energy centers. They are the interfaces between universal energy and the localized energy fields that we know as our bodies. Our attachments to thoughts, the denial of emotions, and not eating a natural diet are all factors that can lead to unbalanced chakras. Fortunately, there are numerous ways that chakra balance can be regained. The following are suggestions and exercises for balancing our chakras.

Affirmations for Balancing Chakras

Affirmations are empowering statements that we make to ourselves with a sense of conviction. By repeating affirmations, one creates a new focal point for attention. The increased attention leads to the affirmation becoming established in one's belief system.

The following are affirmations for the seven chakras. These affirmations have the power to balance them. When using affirmations, it is important to say them with a sense of emotion and certainty. It can also be helpful to say them while looking into a mirror.

Crown Chakra

- I trust the wisdom of the universe.
- I accept the present moment.
- The power of the universe flows through me.

Third-Eye Chakra

- My wisdom is growing.
- I am learning to trust my intuition.
- I am developing greater clarity in my understanding of life.

Throat Chakra

- I speak my truth.
- I am direct and respectful in my communication.
- I speak from the heart.

Heart Chakra

- I am learning to love and appreciate myself.

- My compassion for others is growing.
- Life's eternal love flows through me.

Solar Plexus Chakra

- I have complete acceptance for my strengths and my weaknesses.
- I am determined to make a difference in life.
- I trust my life and the direction that it is taking me.

Sacral Chakra

- I adapt to whatever life brings my way.
- Life's creativity flows through me.
- I embrace my sexuality.

Root Chakra

- I am feeling balanced and secure in my life.
- I remain stable as my emotions drift by like the clouds.
- I am secure in knowing that life will provide me with what I need.

Chanting and Mantras

I am confident in assuming that you have experienced the power of music to change the way you feel. How music affects us varies greatly from individual to individual. A soft and mellow tune can make one person feel relaxed, while another will need to hear heavy metal to feel the same way.

Scientific research has shown a connection between listening to music and the release of certain neurotransmitters such as dopamine, cortisol, endorphins, and oxytocin. Further, music therapy has proven to enhance both emotional empowerment and healing.

From a spiritual perspective, the power of music should be no surprise. The vibrational frequency of music will depend on the kind of music being that is being played. Our vibrational frequency is elevated as the vibrational frequency of the music is increased. Conversely, music with a lower vibrational frequency can lower ours.

With this understanding of how music's vibrational quality can affect us, it is easy to understand how chanting can do the same. There is a reason why chanting has been practiced since ancient times and by different cultures worldwide.

Chanting the sounds of the seven chakras provides a wide range of benefits. These benefits include improved breath control, getting in touch with each chakra's elements, thinking about others, and reflecting on our lives. Each chakra carries with it meaning and symbolism. Because of this, chanting offers a powerful way to rewire our minds by overriding our limiting beliefs with the richness that each chakra holds. The following are suggestions if you are chanting for the first time:

- As you would with mediation, find a place where you would be comfortable chanting.
- When chanting, use your natural tone of voice. You do not want to strain yourself by using a pitch that is not natural for you.
- While chanting, let the sounds flow out slowly throughout your breath.
- As you exhale, give each syllable equal time to your breath and feel their resonance.
- You can also rapidly repeat each sound if reciting a one-word mantra.
- When chanting the name of chakras, you can:
    - Start with the crown chakra and work downwards
    - Start with the root chakra and move upward
    - Chant the name of a single chakra repeatedly.

When chanting, what is most important is to be mindful by focusing on your body and the sounds you are chanting. The following are the sounds of each of the seven chakras. For correct pronunciation, the letter "a" in these sounds is pronounced "ah," and sometimes as "uh." Example: The sound of the root chakra is "Lam." Phonetically, the "a" is pronounced "Lahm."

The Chakra Sounds

Root chakra (Muladhara): "Lam." Phonetically: "Laahm."
Sacral chakra (Svadisthana): "Vam." Phonetically: "Vaahm."
Solar plexus chakra (Manipura): "Ram." Phonetically: "Raahm."
Heart chakra (Anahata): "Yam." Phonetically: "Yaahm."
Throat chakra (Vishuddha): "Ham." Phonetically: "Haahm."
Third eye chakra (Ajna): "Aum." Phonetically: "Ohmm."
The crown chakra (Sahasrara): The crown chakra is different in that no sound is made. For the crown chakra, one remains silent and is reflective.

Chanting balances chakras by restoring their vibrational frequency. Sometimes we hear someone say something that deeply resonates with us. The profound impact has less to do with the words spoken than the sound of the voice delivering the words. The quality of their voice is what opened us up and raised our energy level. We are doing the same thing when we chant the chakra sounds; we express the sounds that open up the chakras and raise our vibration.

Observing Chakra Energy

Meditation is a powerful way to balance your chakras and raise your vibration. The topic of mediation will be covered in another section, but for now, here is a beginner's mediation for balancing your chakras.

1. First, find a quiet and comfortable to mediate. You can do this meditation sitting on the floor or in a chair.
2. Close your eyes, take a deep breath, and slowly let it out.
3. Now breathe normally. As you breathe, place your attention on the sensations that you experience as you inhale and exhale. Follow the flow of your breath.
4. Accept everything that you experience without judgment. If you become distracted by thoughts, accept that this has occurred and return your attention to your breath. Do this as often as needed.
5. Feel the tension in your muscles being released. Notice the sensations that you are experiencing as tension is being released.
6. Place your attention on the root chakra by focusing on the area of your tail bone.
7. Now imagine a glowing red light spinning in the area of your tail bone.
8. Next, place your attention on the area just beneath your navel, the area of your sacral chakra. Imagine an orange light spinning in this area. Imagine that this orange light is pulsing in time with the flow of your breath.
9. Shift your attention to the area just above your navel, the area of your solar plexus chakra. Imagine a yellow light spinning in this area.
10. Place your attention on the center of your chest, the area of your heart chakra. Imagine a glowing green light spinning in the area of your heart chakra. You can enhance your experience by placing your hand in this area and feel the sensations as you breathe.
11. Shift your attention to the hollow of your throat, the area of the throat chakra. Imagine a blue light turning as you breathe.
12. Now place your attention on the area between your eyebrows, the area of your third eye chakra. Imagine an indigo-colored light spinning in this area. Imagine the light getting brighter as it spins.
13. Finally, place your attention on the area located on the top of your head, the area of the crown chakra. Imagine a purple light shining from this area. Imagine this light connecting you with the energy of the universe.

You can also focus on one chakra per meditation session if you feel that is all you need or running short on time.

Super Foods for Chakra Balance

Some foods work toward balancing the body's chakras; they are known as superfoods. By knowing which chakra needs balancing, you can select the right diet. You can also incorporate all of these superfoods into your diet and address all of your chakras.

- For balancing your root chakra, eat tomatoes, elderberries, raspberries, and strawberries.
- For balancing your sacral chakra, try oranges, bell peppers, and parsley.
- For balancing your solar plexus chakra, consume lemons, bananas, and chamomile.
- For balancing your heart chakra, eat green vegetables, green apples, and lemon balm.
- For balancing the throat chakra, have blueberries, black currants, and sage.
- For balancing the third eye chakra, try indigo vegetables and spruce.
- For balancing the crown chakra, eat thyme, red grapes, and eggplant.

Additional Ways to Raise Your Vibrational Level

There are numerous other ways to raise your vibrational frequency, and they all work in the same way. They all enhance awareness of the body's energy while removing obstructions that impede its flow.

- **Yoga**: The word "yoga" is derived from Sanskrit and means to "unite" or "join." The primary objective of practicing yoga is to achieve Samadhi, which is to rest in pure awareness. It is accomplished by learning to harmonize bodily movements, breathing, and attention to work in unison.
- **Qigong:** A century-old Chinese method for balancing the life energy known as Qi or Chi. Qigong involves combing bodily moments, breathing, and meditation to increase the flow of energy. Increased energy flow raises spiritual awareness, promotes positive health, and enhances martial arts training.
- **Tai Chi:** Tai Chi is also an ancient Chinese practice for increasing energy flow. It is also a form of martial art. The practice of Tai Chi and its benefits closely mirror that of Qigong.
- **Being in Nature:** If you ever felt a change in how you felt when spending time in nature, it should be no surprise. The natural world is pure and has a high vibrational frequency because of it. Conversely, that which is created by humans has lower energy levels. As a society, we have developed a lifestyle that has us spending most of our time indoors with our electronic devices. By committing each day to spend time in nature, you will take an important step in raising your vibration. Spending time in nature can be as simple as going to a park or a garden.
- **Healthy Eating:** Whole foods are foods that have not been processed, nor do they come pre-packaged. Fruits, vegetables, grains, nuts, and fish are examples of whole

foods, and their consumption will raise your vibrational level. Process foods, on the other hand, lower energy levels.

In the next chapter, we will explore one of the most powerful ways to increase your manifestation powers, which is the practice of meditation.

Chapter 7: Meditation

The purpose of meditation is to redirect your attention from the outer world and place it on your inner world. Our outer world is a projection of our inner world; only when you understand your inner world can you move beyond the illusions of the mind. When meditating, we shine the light of awareness on the mental phenomena that create our experience of reality, which brings about a harmonious mind.

When you can get clarity of your inner world, you will use the Law of Attraction with greater precision. Meditation is about becoming aware of the present moment. It means that everything that we experience while meditating is valid. When performing these exercises, allow all thoughts to appear, but do not hold onto them.

Guidelines for Practicing Meditation

Before we launch into the first meditation, I want to share some helpful guidelines to make your meditation experience more enjoyable. The first guideline is to throw out all the rules! I am talking about the rules or expectations you have for yourself, your expectations for what you want to experience, and your beliefs of what should or should not be happening.

Whatever enters your awareness during the exercises, allow it to happen. Do not try to resist, change, control, or modify anything that is experienced. The best meditative experiences occur when one gives up all effort to make things happen. Your only job is to witness what you are experiencing as you dive down into the deeper realms of consciousness. The practice of meditation is not about becoming something different; instead, it is about remembering the truth of who you are.

The following mindfulness exercises are staggered according to their level of difficulty. It is important to be comfortable with each exercise before progressing to the next one. When performing these exercises, approach them with an attitude of openness, non-judgment, patience, and persistence.

The meditations are divided into two categories. Category 1 is basic, while category 2 is advanced. The basic meditations are intended to increase awareness of the mental phenomena known as thought, emotion, and bodily sensation. The advanced category is intended to transform sensations, cultivate super emotions, improve decision-making, and experience the oneness of consciousness. **Note:** The sequence of the following meditations is intentional. Each meditation provides the foundation for the next one. It is recommended that you not advance to the next mediation until you are comfortable with the prior one.

Category 1 Meditations – 10 Minutes

Meditation 1: Clear Seeing

The purpose of this meditation is to learn how to experience life without projecting your thoughts on it. The more that you can do this, the more you will raise your vibration.

1. Sit down, make yourself comfortable, and relax.
2. Close your eyes and focus on your breath. As you do so, become more and more relaxed.
3. Now, open your eyes and look around at your surroundings. What is the quality of your experience as you view your environment? You may wish to rate your experience from 1-10, with ten being the highest.
4. Now close your eyes and allow yourself to relax. I want you to imagine that you are an alien from another planet and that you have been sent down to Earth to observe what it is like here. You do not know anything about this planet, and you have no words to describe your experience. All that you have in your immediate and direct experience.
5. Keeping all of this in mind, open your eyes and observe your surroundings again. You can scan your environment, focus on a particular object that you find interesting, or you can do both. Take your time and observe.
6. When you are ready, rate your experience of observing again.
7. Now compare the quality of your experience during the second observation with that of the first one. Did you notice a difference? What were those differences? Was there freshness to your second observation that was missing in the first?
8. If you could not detect a difference, that is okay. Continue to practice this technique until you can detect a difference in the quality of your experience when observing.

For many of us, there is a lack of awareness of our inner world. It is because we spend most of our waking hours focusing on the world outside of ourselves. For the same reasons, we often lack an awareness of our bodies. We may be unaware of its subtle sensations and feelings. The body is the interface that allows consciousness to experience the physical world. In fact, the physical body plays a vital role in allowing us to develop spirituality.

Meditation 2: Perceiving Sensation

The purpose of this meditation is to increase your awareness of the sensations of the body. The more aware you become of the body's sensations, the more you will raise your vibrational level without personalizing them.

1. Close your eyes and allow yourself to follow your breath during inhalation and exhalation. Place your attention on your breath. Feel it as it courses through your body.
2. Now place your attention on the sensations of the body. Place your attention on any sensation of the body that appears in your awareness.
3. Do you feel a tingling in your hands or feet? Do you feel the tension in your back, shoulders, or face? Do you feel the weight of your body? Or, do you feel the pressure on your buttocks from the chair or ground you are sitting on?
4. Allow yourself to experience the body's sensations without judging any of them, even the ones that may feel unpleasant. Sensations are not good or bad. Good and bad are value judgments that exist solely in the mind.
5. Are the sensations that you experience stable? Are they always the same, or do they change? Are they always there, or do they come and go?
6. Just stay in the awareness of your body's sensations; allow yourself to experience them for as long as you desire.
7. This is the end of this meditation. Please feel free to allow yourself to continue to meditate on the body for as long as you wish

Meditation 3: Perceiving Emotion

In Meditation 2, the purpose was to increase your awareness of bodily sensations. In Meditation 3, you will do this same thing but with emotions instead of sensations.

1. Sit down in a comfortable position and close your eyes.
2. Follow your breath during inhalation and exhalation. Place your attention on your breath. Feel it as it courses through your body.
3. Take on an attitude of complete allowing that you will have complete acceptance of whatever arises in this meditation.
4. Observe the perceptions, thoughts, sensations, and emotions that arise within you. Allow them to come and go on their own accord. All you need to do is be the observer of them.
5. Now pay attention to any emotion that arises; become an observer of it. What happens when your focus is placed on emotion?
6. Do not place any meaning on the emotion that you experience; do not think of it as being positive or negative. Words such as "positive," "negative," "pleasant," or "unpleasant" are products of the mind
7. There is no intrinsic meaning to anything in life. All meaning is derived from the mind. Emotions have no power of their own; they derive all their power from us personalizing them.
8. When observing emotions, do so with complete allowing. Do not try to change anything about it.

9. As you observe your emotions, do you notice a change in how you experience them? Do they change in intensity? Do they become stronger or milder? Can you locate where the emotions come from? Can you observe where they go?
10. As you observe emotions, ask yourself, "Am I my emotions, or am I the one that is aware of them?" If emotion is experienced as being unpleasant, does awareness feel unpleasant? If emotion is experienced as being pleasant, does awareness feel pleasant?
11. Awareness does not experience anything; awareness can only know of experience. Awareness is like a beam of light shining on a snow-covered field. The light does not feel the cold of the snow; it only illuminates it. As you observe emotions, be as the beam of light.
12. This is the end of this meditation. Feel free to remain in meditation for as long as you wish.

Meditation 4: Perceiving Thought

This meditation continues from the previous three meditations by guiding you in increasing your awareness of your inner realm. You did meditations on increasing awareness of your bodily sensations and emotions. In this meditation, you will increase your awareness of thought.

1. Sit down in a comfortable position and close your eyes.
2. Follow your breath during inhalation and exhalation. Place your attention on your breath. Feel it as it courses through your body.
3. Take on an attitude of complete allowing that whatever arises in this meditation, you will fully accept it.
4. Observe the perceptions, thoughts, sensations, and emotions that arise within you. Allow them to come and go on their own accord. All you need to do is to be the observer of them.
5. Now place your attention on your thoughts. Observe your thoughts as they appear and fade in the space of your awareness. Remain as the observer. Do not judge, evaluate, or analyze your thoughts; allow them to be just as they are. Simply be aware of them.
6. You may find yourself experience racing thoughts. Just acknowledge that your thoughts are racing.
7. Do not judge your experience should you experience disturbing thoughts. Your thoughts have no power other than that which you give them. Let your thoughts move about your consciousness freely. Stay as the observer; nothing else is needed.
8. Now follow a thought from the time it arises to the time it fades away. Through your observation, can you find the place where thoughts arise from? This question is not to be thought about; its answer needs to be observed and experienced by you.
9. Where do thoughts go when they disappear from awareness? Can you observe this?
10. Notice that after a thought fades, there is a space or emptiness before the next thought appears. Place your attention on this space. Should you become distracted, simply

return your attention to this space between your thoughts. Do not exert any effort in this observation; do not try to locate this space. Let this space come to you. Simply allow yourself to be the observer.

11. Can you know a thought before it appears in your awareness?
12. If you can observe your thoughts, can you be your thoughts?
13. This is the end of this meditation. Feel free to remain silent and still for as long as your desire.

Category 2 Meditations – 10 minutes

Meditation 5: Transforming Sensation

The purpose of this meditation is to use your increased awareness of bodily sensations to target areas of low vibration and raise them.

1. Sit down and make yourself comfortable; if you like, you can close your eyes.
2. Place your attention on your breath as it travels in and out of your body. Allow your awareness to wash over your body and experience the sensations of the body.
3. Now scan your body with your awareness for a relaxed, calm, or pleasant sensation. When you find such a sensation, place your focus on it.
4. As you observe this sensation, I want you to ask yourself the following question: "What color is this sensation?" Accept the first response that comes to mind.
5. Now ask, "What size is this sensation?" Again, go with the first answer that comes to mind.
6. Now ask yourself, "Does this sensation have a texture to it? Is it smooth, rough, soft, or hard?"
7. Now search the body for a sensation that feels unpleasant. Perhaps it has tension, pressure, heaviness, or hardness to it.
8. Just as with the pleasant sensation, ask yourself, "What is the color, size, and texture of this sensation?"
9. Using your awareness, allow yourself to imagine that the qualities of the unpleasant sensation are taking on the qualities of the pleasant sensation. If the pleasant sensation had a green color, imagine the color of the unpleasant sensation turning green. If the texture of the pleasant sensation was soft, imagine the unpleasant sensation growing soft, and so on.
10. Take your time and transfer the qualities of the pleasant sensation to the unpleasant sensation.
11. Now observe the unpleasant sensation. Has the sensation changed? Has this sensation developed a more pleasant quality to it? If not, continue to practice this meditation.
12. This is the end of this meditation.

Meditation 6: Cultivating Super Emotions

Super emotions included gratitude, appreciation, and compassion. They are called super emotions because of their high vibrational frequency. The following meditations are for cultivating these emotions.

Gratitude

1. Sit down in a chair or on a pillow, whichever is more comfortable for you.
2. Close your eyes and place your attention on your breath as you breathe normally.
3. Place your awareness on the sensations that you experience as your breath enters your body during inhalation and leaves it during exhalation.
4. Allow yourself to experience everything that arises in your awareness without any form of judgment or resistance. Greet every experience with complete acceptance.
5. Anytime you find yourself becoming distracted, gently return your awareness to your breath.
6. Everything that you experience is an opportunity to express gratitude:
    - You can experience gratitude for a person, a pet, or for nature.
    - You can express gratitude for the challenges you have experience and what you gained from them.
    - You can express gratitude for being alive.
7. Allow yourself to witness every experience that arises in your awareness without judging it, identifying it, or analyzing it. Can you find gratitude for the thoughts, emotions, or sensations that you experience? Whatever appears before you, allow it to manifest in your awareness without any interference by you.
8. Should you find yourself reacting to any of your experiences, allow yourself to be a witness to your reactions without any form of judgment.
9. When you find yourself experiencing gratitude, try to intensify that feeling. Place your awareness on the feeling of gratitude. What happens when you focus on the emotion of gratitude? You can use this technique to intensify any emotion or feeling that you experience.
10. Allow yourself to experience the emotion of appreciation as deeply as possible.
11. If you have trouble with this exercise, keep practicing it until you experience the level of appreciation that you desire.

Appreciation

1. Sit down in a comfortable position and close your eyes.
2. Now breathe deeply, hold your breath briefly, and then exhale.
3. Feel the relaxation in your body.
4. Feel yourself becoming more and more relaxed.
5. Follow your breath during inhalation and exhalation. Place your attention on your breath. Feel it as it courses through your body.
6. Think of someone or something that you love. As you think of your subject, think of all the ways that you appreciate them.
7. Fully experience your feelings.
8. As you experience these energies, intensify them by employing your other senses, such as touch, hearing, smelling, and taste. To do this, add these other sensory dimensions to your mind's representation of your subject.

Example: If I am thinking of my spouse, I would also imagine her touching me, hearing her voice, smell her perfume, and tasting her kiss.

9. By engaging your other senses, the feelings of appreciation will be experienced more deeply.
10. We are now going to switch gears. For this exercise, think of a person for who you have neutral feelings. For example, it could be the store clerk where you do your shopping or the person who delivers your mail.
11. Think about what you can appreciate about this person.
12. As before, fully experience the feelings that you are having and try to intensify them.
13. Now, think of someone who irritates you.
14. Think about what you can appreciate about them.
15. Fully experience the feelings that you are having and try to intensify them.
16. Now think of someone who you hate.
17. What can you appreciate about them?
18. Fully experience the feelings that you are having and try to intensify them.
19. Now think about yourself. What can you appreciate about yourself?
20. Fully experience the feelings that you are having and try to intensify them.
21. The level of your appreciation has less to do with the world around you than it does with your ability to take charge of your energy level. Emotional mastery is the ability to generate appreciation for any experience that you may have.
22. This is the end of this exercise.

Compassion

The following is an exercise for expanding your compassion. This exercise is really a series of sub exercises, with each one creating the foundation for the following exercise.

Step 1:

I want you to think of a person or animal that you love. When you have identified the subject of this reflection, I want you to think of all the hardships and challenges that they have experienced. Think of the sufferings that they have experienced and make their suffering your own. When you have connected with their sufferings, express your love to them, and wish them happiness.

Step 2:

In this next exercise, you will repeat what you did in the first exercise; however, you will choose a subject with neutral feelings for this time. For example, your subject could be the clerk at the register where you do your shopping or the mailperson.

Even though you may not know anything about this person, I want you to imagine the sufferings that they may have experienced in their life. Use your intuition or your imagination but make their suffering as real as you can. Allow yourself to experience their sufferings as your own. When you have connected with their sufferings, wish them happiness.

Step 3:

In this third exercise, you will repeat what you did in the last two exercises using another subject. In this exercise, your subject will be someone you dislike, avoid, or do not get along with. I want you to think of the sufferings that they have experienced in their life. As in the previous exercise, you can use your intuition or imagination if you do not know this person's background. Allow yourself to experience their sufferings as your own. When you have connected with their sufferings, wish them happiness.

Step 4:

This exercise differs from the previous three exercises because you will not be identifying your subject ahead of time. Instead, you will perform this compassion exercise as you go about your day. I want you to notice the people around you as you conduct your daily business. Take time to imagine the potential sufferings of the people that you see. Allow yourself to experience their sufferings as your own. When you have connected with their sufferings, wish them happiness.

Step 5:

This is the final exercise, and for many people, the most difficult one. In this exercise, you will be the subject of your meditation. I want you to reflect on the sufferings that you have experienced in your life. Allow yourself to experience your sufferings fully; do not minimize anything. Get in touch with the pains that you have experienced. When you have connected with your sufferings, wish yourself happiness.

The exercise that you just completed was an exercise in experiencing compassion. The subject of your compassion began with the ones that are the easiest for us to experience compassion for, those we love. Each succeeding exercise became more difficult because the subject of your compassion became further removed from you emotionally.

Most people have trouble showing compassion for themselves, which is why you were the subject in the final meditation. The power of your compassion for others is dependent on your ability to have compassion for yourself.

When we lack compassion for others, we lack compassion for ourselves; we project our lack of compassion for ourselves on those around us. Conversely, when you develop compassion for yourself, you can truly have compassion for others. The power of compassion is also vital if you are to become an intentional manifestor because compassion increases your vibration to a higher level.

Meditation 7: Self-Love

The previous exercises provided guidance for cultivating super emotions. This mediation for cultivating self-love will draw from these exercises.

1. While looking into a mirror, look deeply into your eyes and tell yourself out loud, "I love you," using your name.
2. Attempt to feel love for yourself. If you can experience feelings of love, allow yourself to experience them as fully as possible. If you are unable to experience loving feelings, do not force it. Simply remain aware of any feelings that should arise without judgment.
3. Continue to look into your eyes while telling yourself, "I love you," using your name.
4. As you address yourself in this manner, place your focus on any emotions of appreciation, compassion, or gratitude that you may experience.
5. You can tap into these emotions if you recall things that you have done that you feel good about. Incorporate all these memories in the way that you address yourself, for example: "I love you (include your name) for the way you did..."
6. Focus on the feelings of love or appreciation that you experience as you do this exercise. As you do so, try to intensify these feelings.
7. Try to do this exercise every morning and evening, allowing five minutes per exercise. Do this exercise daily until you begin to experience feelings of love for yourself.

Meditation 9: The Body's Energy and Decision Making

The meditative exercises in Section One were provided to develop greater awareness of perception, emotion, and bodily sensation. In this exercise, you will use your awareness of the body's sensations to make decisions based on the profound wisdom of life's energy.

1. Sit down in a comfortable position and close your eyes.
2. Follow your breath during inhalation and exhalation. Place your attention on your breath. Feel it as it courses through your body. Allow yourself to relax.

3. I want you now to think of a decision that you need to make. If you currently do not have a decision to make, create one that is relevant to you.
4. Next, think of all the choices that are available to you when making your decision.
5. Now think of the potential costs and benefits for each choice option. For example, if I had to decide on whether to buy a new car, I would consider the costs and benefits for each choice option that I am considering. Example: If I decide to buy the car, I would have a new car, but I would use up all my savings.
6. Now think of the potential costs and benefits for each of your choice options. When doing this part of the meditation, do not over-analyze the situation; just go by whatever answer comes to you. This is not intended to be an intellectual meditation.
7. Now return your attention to your breath and allow yourself to relax. Do not engage with any of your thoughts; allow yourself to become relaxed and still within.
8. Now, while remaining in your peacefulness, I want you to review your potential choice options, one by one. Consider each choice separately, giving it your full attention.
9. As you review the choice option, ask yourself, "Should I say 'yes' to this decision?" When you do this, pay attention to the sensations that you experience in your body.
10. When you think of this choice option, do you feel constricted or relaxed? Is your breathing relaxed or shallow? Does your chest feel hard or soft? Does your body feel stiff or tingly? Notice the body's sensations and the quality of your breathing as you reflect on each choice option.
11. Without exception, you were intended to be happy in this life. Happiness is your birthright. Which option brings you the greatest sense of peacefulness in your body? Which choice option brings about the greatest ease in your breathing? Regardless of what your mind or conventional wisdom may, that is the choice option that is right for you.
12. As before, if you had difficulty experiencing the body's sensations as you considered your choices, please practice this meditation until you can do so. Do not continue to the next meditation until you do.
13. This is the end of this meditation.

Meditation 10: Contemplating Awareness

Throughout this book, some themes appeared repeatedly. These include consciousness as the foundation for all of existence. Any sense of being separate from the world around you is just an illusion. This final mediation provides guidance for bringing forth the realization of these deeper truths.

Note: You will be asking yourself some questions when performing this exercise. Answer these questions based solely on your direct experience at that moment. Do not go by what you know intellectually. Also, the words "consciousness" and "awareness" can be used interchangeably.

1. Sit down and allow yourself to relax.
2. Breathing naturally, place your attention on the flow of your breath as you inhale and exhale, notice the sensations that you experience.
3. When you feel relaxed, select an object for observing.
4. Observe the object for a few seconds, allowing your eyes to be relaxed. Do not strain them.
5. As you observe the object, determine whether the act of seeing is separate from the object being seen. In other words, does seeing stop at a certain point, at which point the object begins, or does the act of seeing and the object being seen flow into each other?
6. Now determine if the act of seeing begins from within you or occurs from the outside of the body.
7. Next, ask yourself if you are aware of seeing? In other words, how do you know that seeing is taking place? Note: The question is regarding the process of seeing, not that which is being seen. How do you know the process of seeing is occurring? Are you aware that "seeing" is taking place? As indicated before, do not think of the correct answer to this question; only go by your direct experience at this moment.
8. Confirm to yourself that seeing and the object being seen are not separate, that they indeed flow into each other as one.
9. Confirm to yourself that seeing occurs from within the body, not outside of it.
10. Confirm to yourself that there is the awareness of seeing that there is a knowing that seeing is taking place at some level of your being.

If you can confirm all of these points, we are left with the following conclusions:

1. The process of seeing and the object being seen are inseparable; they are one.
2. Seeing originates from within you. From this, we can logically conclude that you, the process of seeing and the object being seen, are inseparable.
3. There must be an awareness that seeing is taking place; otherwise, how else would we know that seeing is occurring? Hence, the awareness of seeing and the act of seeing are inseparable.
4. Because the awareness of seeing and the act of seeing are inseparable, and the act of seeing and the object being seen are inseparable, all these things are occurring within awareness.
5. You are aware of your existence.
6. You, the process of seeing, and the object being seen are inseparable; they are one and the same.
7. You are awareness itself.

This exercise may seem esoteric or philosophical but do not be fooled. If you can directly experience these conclusions for yourself, you will be light years away from most of humanity, which believes that they are a separate object. All problems arise from seeing ourselves as being separate.

As long as we see ourselves as being separate from those around us, we will always experience limitations, lack, frustration, or the need to persuade others to see our point of view. The previous exercise can be repeated with the remaining sensory modalities as well:

Sensation or touch

1. Close your eyes and touch an object.
2. Confirm to yourself that the sensation of the object being touched is indistinguishable from the object being touched.
3. Confirm to yourself that sensation arises from within the body, not from outside of it.
4. Confirm to yourself that there is an awareness of the sensation that there is a knowing that sensation is taking place at some level of your being.
5. If you can confirm all of these points, we are left with the following conclusions:

- When touching (with closed eyes), we cannot distinguish between the sensation and the object being touched.
- Sensations originate from within you. From this understanding, we can logically conclude that you, the process of touching, and the object being touched are indivisible.
- There must be an awareness that sensation is taking place; otherwise, how else would you know that the sensation is being experienced?
- The sensation of the object and the object being touched occurs within awareness.
- You are aware of your existence.
- You, the sensation, and the object being touched are inseparable; they are one and the same.
- You are awareness itself.

Hearing

1. Confirm to yourself that hearing and the sound being heard are not separate, that they indeed flow into each other as one.
2. Confirm to yourself that hearing occurs from within the body, not outside of it.
3. Confirm to yourself that there is a knowing that hearing is taking place at some level of your being.

If you can confirm all of these points, we are left with the following conclusions:

1. The process of hearing and the sound being heard are inseparable; they are one.
2. Hearing originates from within you. From this, we can logically conclude that both the hearing process and the sound being heard are found within you.
3. There must be an awareness that hearing is taking place; otherwise, how else would you know that hearing is being experienced?

4. The process of hearing and the sound being heard occurs within awareness.
5. You are aware of your existence.
6. You, the process of hearing, and the sound being heard are inseparable; they are one and the same.
7. You are awareness itself.

In the previous chapters, we explored the dynamics and mechanics of the Law of Attraction. In the remaining chapters, we will examine how you can apply the Law of Attraction to the major areas of your life. We will begin with relationships, which is the topic of the next chapter.

Chapter 8: Using the Law of Attraction in Relationships

We have covered a lot of information so far. In this chapter, you will learn how to apply this information to your current and future relationships. There are three simple steps to applying the Law of Attraction:

1. Identify what you want your outcome to be.
2. Identify what has prevented you from achieving your outcome in the past.
3. Raise your vibration

You can think of your relationship outcomes as your intentions. When you identify the limiting beliefs that have prevented you from achieving your relationship outcomes in the past, you can change them by adopting new empowering beliefs. Doing this will raise your vibration and increase the probability of you manifesting your intentions.

By raising your vibration, maintaining it, and releasing your intention, you will intentionally manifest your relationship outcome. Here are some examples of how you can apply the Law of Attraction in Relationships:

- Attracting a compatible partner: Think about the qualities that you want your partner to have. Which of these are most important to you? When thinking about these qualities, consider all the life areas, including physically, emotionally, mentally, spiritually, and financially. When you have identified these qualities, make them the focus of your intention.
- Improving the quality of an existing relationship: To improve an existing relationship, you must first start off by asking yourself some questions about you! Ask questions like:
    - Would I want to be in a relationship with someone who was just like me?
    - How have I contributed to the challenges that we are currently experiencing in our relationship?
    - What beliefs do I hold about myself and the other person that are creating challenges for the relationship?
    - How have I contributed to the unhappiness of my partner?
    - How have my own beliefs contributed to my own unhappiness?

After acknowledging your role in creating relationship challenges, you can create the intention to bring happiness for both you and your partner. It is important in relationship challenges that your intentions be pure and unconditional. This means that your intentions for your partner's happiness are independent of your own needs.

In fact, when releasing your intentions, do not even consider the relationship; consider the happiness of the individual. To make your intentions even more powerful, let your intentions be how you can contribute to the other person's happiness. Likewise, you can create intentions for your own happiness, using the same methods just described but with you as the focus.

It is important, however, that I make the following qualifier. If you are in an abusive relationship, emotionally or physically, do not employ the Law of Attraction in an attempt to save the relationship. As I stated before, everything starts with us. We attract into our lives that which is a match for our vibration. Before you can change anything, you must change yourself first and change yourself to change your vibration. You cannot do this if you are in an unsafe situation. Take care of yourself first, and the universe will accommodate the changes that you make.

You may be wondering why you should focus on creating happiness for your partner, as most self-help books teach that it is your own happiness that you should focus on. In the next section, you will discover why.

The Mirror of Relationships

There is a purpose as to why we have appeared in manifested form. That purpose is to wake up from the dream that is created by our minds. The dream that I speak of is the one that leads us to believe that we are just physical bodies with a mind. We can return to wholeness and the oneness of being through our manifested form. The mirror that is our relationships can make this possible.

The return to wholeness and oneness does not require us to dismiss the physicality of our bodies or the physical realm that we find ourselves in. It does not require that we die and merge with some spiritual realm. It does not mean we have to abandon our current lifestyle and become monks or adopt spiritual practices. The return to wholeness and oneness is an inner journey where we gain the courage to challenge our deep-seated beliefs and learn to let go of them.

The greater consciousness, or God, is the ultimate manifestor because it lacks any sense of identity or beliefs about itself; it is simply pure awareness. At this level, just an intention manifests into existence instantly. As manifested beings of the greater consciousness, we too can manifest; however, our manifestations do not instantly occur as lag time is involved. This lag time is due to the restrictions imposed by the physical realm and because of the ego.

Our beliefs about ourselves and others create resistance, which creates lag time for our manifestations to appear. The more that we overcome our inner resistance, the more effective we will become in manifesting. Fortunately, the universe has offered us the ultimate mirror for recognizing resistance; that mirror is our relationships.

The people who enter our lives did so because they were a vibrational match to us. Since the vibrational match may have come from subconscious beliefs, identifying our subconscious beliefs is necessary. Regardless of whether our beliefs are conscious or subconscious, we project them on others, which then becomes our image of them. In truth, we can never know another person.

From the perspective of higher consciousness, we never have a relationship with another person; rather, we have a relationship with our interpretation of them. For this reason, the people in our lives serve as a mirror to our inner realm. When we realize this, we can understand why relationships are complicated and why misunderstandings occur. We project our inner lives on the people around us, which then becomes our image of them. When they do not meet our expectations, we become hurt or frustrated; we hold them responsible for our unhappiness.

The world's collective consciousness has only recently (evolutionary speaking) begun to rise toward higher levels. Our history has been to view relationships not as mirrors but as objects through which we hoped to experience fulfillment and wholeness. From fairy tales to Hollywood, we have been taught to look for Mr. or Miss Right to deliver us from our sense of separation from the world and make us feel loved, desired, and whole.

Such a recipe for finding happiness is doomed for failure. No person or object outside of you can ever give you want you are looking for. To do so is no different than asking your mirror at home to provide you with love and fulfillment.

Everything you will ever experience is a projection of yourself that becomes superimposed on the objects of your experience. Ultimately, everything that you experience is an aspect of yourself. Ultimately, you are the source of all that you experience, and you are found within all that you experience

Everything that you could ever desire already exists within the realm of consciousness because consciousness is the source of all that exists. The Law of Attraction is just a conceptual model for how consciousness operates. The only thing that prevents us from being intentional creators is the limiting concepts we identify with due to our attachment to our manifested form.

Ultimately freedom lies in transcending all beliefs, including spiritual beliefs, and opening up to all of experience with complete acceptance and abandon. Finding your true love or the relationship of your dream requires that you stop searching for it and investigate the timeless and boundless realm that exists within you and is you. The most effective way to experience that realm is meditation.

Law of Attraction Exercises for Relationships

The following exercises will benefit you by identifying your limiting beliefs, changing your limiting beliefs, lowering your resistance, developing greater awareness of the nature of your mental phenomena, becoming aware of your projections, and enhancing your ability to experience love and compassion for yourself and others.

There is no specific way to approach these exercises. You can pick the ones that resonate with you, or you can do all of them. For best results, I recommend that you do all of the exercises and that you do them in the order that they are sequenced. I have staggered these exercises from simplest to the most difficult, especially for the meditation exercises.

Exercises for Beliefs

Uncovering Deep Seated Beliefs

Previously in this book, we discussed subconscious beliefs and how they impact the manifestation process. The following are two exercises for uncovering your subconscious beliefs:

Exercise 1

To show you how this exercise works, I will provide you with an example.

1. The first step is to think of an ongoing challenge that you are experiencing in your life. My example will be: I am afraid of being rejected by others.
2. My next step is to start a line of inquiry using the phrase "What would be so bad if…" So my first question would be, "What would be so bad about being rejected?"
3. My answer to that question would be, "I would feel that people saw me as being less, that I am not good enough.
4. I would then use my response and rephrase the question: "What would be so bad if people saw me as being less or not good enough?"
5. My response to that would be, "It would make me feel like I am worthless."
6. I would continue to repeat this question by asking: "What would be so bad if I felt like I am worthless?"
7. My answer to that would be, "I would feel like I am unlovable."
8. Keep going through this line of questioning until you are unable to go any further. When you have reached this point, you will have identified your subconscious belief. I am aware of the fear of being rejected; however, the core belief behind this belief is "I feel like I am unlovable."

Exercise 2:

This next exercise can be used to identify the subconscious beliefs causing you to want things; in this case, your relationship wants. For this exercise, I will use the example: "I want to get married."

1. What would becoming married give me?
2. It would give me someone to spend my life with.
3. What would having someone to spend my life with give me?
4. It would give me a sense of security.
5. What would a sense of security give me?
6. It would give me a sense of peace.
7. My subconscious belief is that I want a sense of peace, but my conscious belief is that I want to get married.

Habitual Patterns

1. Start becoming more aware of your daily thinking and actions.
2. When you catch yourself thinking a habitual thought or behaving in a habitual way, ask yourself the following questions:
    a. Do I have a choice of thinking or behaving differently?
    b. Is there a payoff for me thinking or behaving in this habitual way?
    c. How would I like to think as opposed to my current habitual thinking?
    d. How would I like to behave as opposed to my current habitual behavior?
    e. Would these new ways of thinking or behaving retain the payoff that my current thinking or behaving offers?
    f. Would these new ways of thinking or behaving bring me greater happiness?

3. If you said yes to the last two questions, start incorporating your new way of thinking or behaving in your daily life.
4. Whenever you catch yourself repeating your old thinking or behaving, remind yourself that you are now dedicated to your new ways of being.

Changing a Belief

In the previous exercises, you identified a limiting belief that is causing you relationship challenges. In this exercise, you will trade that belief for an empowering one.

1. Get two sheets of paper. Select paper sizes of 8" x 11" or larger.
2. Take the first sheet of paper and fold it in half lengthwise.
3. On the top of the paper, write down your belief.
4. Make a list on the left-hand side of the paper of all the ways this belief has cost you in your life. When doing this part of the exercise, think about how this belief has affected you in your life areas. Ask yourself how this belief has affected you in the following areas:
   - Your self-esteem.
   - Your emotional health.
   - Your relationships.
   - Your physical health.
   - Your work.
   - Your finances.

   When writing, keep in mind the following:
   - When writing this list, write down the first thing that comes to your mind, even if it seems irrelevant.
   - Write as fast as you can and feel the emotions that arise. This is a heartfelt exercise, not a thinking one.
   - Keep writing until you run out of things to write.
5. By each item you write down, assign an arbitrary point value to how much impact this item has had on you. When selecting the point value, choose the first number that comes to mind.
6. When you have completed assigning the point values, find the total of all the point values and place it at the bottom of the page.
7. For the right side of the page, repeat Steps 6-7, except this time, you will write down all the ways that this belief has benefited you.

When you have completed step 8, think of a new alternative belief that empowers you. For example, if the original belief was "No one will ever love me," my new belief maybe, "The only love that I can depend on is the love that I give to myself."

On the second paper, repeat steps 1-8, using your new belief, with the following exceptions: Reverse Steps 6 and 8 by writing down all the ways that you believe that you would benefit from this new belief for Step 6. When doing step 8, write down all the ways you believe it will cost you.

When you have completed the two sheets, do the following:

1. Immediately review your lists, allowing yourself to fully experience any emotions that arise.
2. Review your lists every day, once in the morning and once before you go to bed. Do so until you become fully associated with the emotions that you experience.

When you become fully associated with the costs of holding on to your old belief with the benefits of adopting your new belief, your mind will become re-programmed with your new belief.

The following is an alternative to the last exercise for changing your beliefs and involves meditation:

1. On the piece of paper, write down a belief that you have that limits you in your relationships.
2. When you have written down the belief, sit down in a comfortable position and close your eyes.
3. Allow yourself to follow your breath during inhalation and exhalation. Place your attention on your breath. Feel it as it courses through your body. Relax.
4. Think about how having this belief has cost you in your life. As you think about the costs you paid for having this belief, get in touch with the feelings that come up.
5. What has been the cost to your happiness for holding on to this belief? Can you think of specific instances? What price did you pay in your relationships? Who is no longer in your life because of this belief? Get in touch with the feelings that come up.
6. Has this belief cost you money? Did this belief lead you to engage in risky behavior with your money or health? What about your sense of self? Get in touch with the feelings that come up.
7. How has this belief affected your self-confidence or self-esteem? Take the time to feel the pain that this belief has created for your life.
8. Allow yourself to experience it fully and experience the emotions and feelings surrounding this belief.
9. How will this belief affect your future if you continue to hold on to it? Imagine how your life will be a year from now, five years from now, 15 years from now? What consequences will you experience if you continue to maintain this belief?
10. As mentioned before, thoughts and beliefs do not have any power other than the power we give them. Unto themselves, our thoughts and beliefs lack any power. Our beliefs are not true or untrue; they just exist. It is us who grant them power over our lives.

11. Now open your eyes and get your writing instrument. This negative belief you just meditated on exists because you believe it provides a benefit.
12. Write down all the ways that having this belief benefited you, even if it does not sound rationale. For example, if you have a belief that you cannot depend on or trust other people, the benefit of this belief may be that it protected you from getting hurt.
13. Now think of a belief that will offer the same benefit but will not create limitations for you. If your old belief was people cannot be trusted, a new belief could be, "I can trust others because I am learning to trust myself." Write down your new belief.
14. When you have written down the belief, sit down in a comfortable position and close your eyes.
15. Allow yourself to follow your breath during inhalation and exhalation. Place your attention on your breath. Feel it as it courses through your body. Relax.
16. I want you to think of the new belief that you wrote down. Think about what your life would be like if you operated from this new belief from this moment on.
17. How would living with this new belief make you feel about yourself? How would it impact those that you care about? What would your life be like? Think about your life like one year from now if you started to live by this new belief today. What do you think it would be like five years from now?
18. As you think about what your life would be like, allow yourself to experience the emotions and feelings that you experience. Allow yourself to sink into these emotions and feelings. You may want to visualize yourself acting from this new belief.
19. Practice this meditation every day for three weeks, which is how long it normally takes to create a habit. The mind cannot tell the difference between visualization and actual doing. By meditating, you can reprogram your subconscious, leading you to take the appropriate action.
20. Start becoming more aware of your daily thinking and actions.
21. When you catch yourself thinking a habitual thought or behaving in a habitual way, ask yourself the following questions:
    a. Do I have a choice of thinking or behaving differently?
    b. Is there a payoff for me thinking or behaving in this habitual way?
    c. How would I like to think as opposed to my current habitual thinking?
    d. How would I like to behave as opposed to my current habitual behavior?
    e. Would these new ways of thinking or behaving retain the payoff that my current thinking or behaving offers?
    f. Would these new ways of thinking or behaving bring me greater happiness?
22. If you said yes to the last two questions, start incorporating your new way of thinking or behaving in your daily life.
23. Whenever you catch yourself repeating your old thinking or behaving, remind yourself that you are now dedicated to your new ways of being.

Exercises for Emotions

Diving Deep into Emotions

We discussed earlier that emotions are a mirror to our thoughts. We also discussed how our subconscious beliefs can override our intentions to manifest. This exercise aims to guide you in transforming your emotions at their deepest level; thus, changing them at the subconscious level.

1. Identify a concern that you are experiencing in your relationships. I will use the following concern as an example: I am frustrated with my child being irresponsible.
2. Now that I have identified my concern, the next thing would be to identify how I feel about the situation, which I have done already.
3. Upon identifying how I feel about the situation, the next thing to do is to get into a relaxed state. Using the basic mediation that was presented earlier in this book is ideal for this.
4. When you are relaxed, ask yourself, "What does being frustrated feel like?" Notice: You want to describe what the emotion feels like, not what you think about it. To avoid falling into this trap, phrase your response as "It feels like_________?
   Here are some examples:
   - "It feels hard and edgy."
   - "I feel like I want to cry."
   - "It feels heavy."
5. My response to this question would be that feeling frustrated feels heavy, like I am being pulled down."
6. I would then follow up by asking, "What does heavy or being pulled down feel like?"
7. I would then respond with, "It feels like I am stuck."
8. I would continue my questioning by asking, "What does being stuck feel like?"
9. My response: "Feeling stuck makes me feel like I want to go to sleep or escape."
10. I would follow up by asking, "What does going to sleep or escaping feel like?"
11. My response would be, "It feels like I am freeing myself."
12. My last response, "It feels like I am freeing myself," has a whole different feeling than my initial feeling, which was feeling frustrated. When your line of questioning leads you to feel a neutral or positive emotion, you have transformed your original emotion at its deepest level.
13. When doing this exercise, it is important to mention that there is no way that you can do it wrong or come up with the wrong answer. As long as you respond at the feeling level, your response will be valid for this exercise.

Exercises for Improving Your Relationships

Projections

From the perspective of higher levels of consciousness, there is no distinction between your inner world and the world around you. All relationship problems occur when we experience others as being separate from ourselves and mistakenly believe that which we project on them originates from them. The following is a meditation for reclaiming your projections.

Exercise 1: Projections

1. Sit down in a comfortable position, close your eyes, and relax.
2. Follow your breath during inhalation and exhalation.
3. When you feel calm, I want you to think of someone you believe has treated you unfairly. When you have identified this person, I want you to recreate in your mind the specific situation where this person mistreated you.
4. Where did the situation take place?
5. Imagine the surroundings of this location.
6. Where was this person when the situation happened? What were they doing at the time? See it in your mind; visualize it with as much detail as possible.
7. What did they say or do to you that caused you to be angry or hurt?
8. How did you feel when the situation happened? What did it feel like? What did you tell yourself?
9. Now I want you to recreate this same situation in your mind with one difference. I want you to relieve the situation without any form of judgment or analysis.
10. As you run through the situation a second time in your mind, focus on the other person you believe hurt you. Can you say that you are absolutely sure that this person intended to hurt you? Is it possible that you were projecting your own beliefs on this person's intent?
11. If, while reliving the situation, you experiencing hurt or anger, from where do these feelings arise? Did this person impose these feelings on you, or were these feelings generated from within you?
12. The hurt that you believe that this person caused you, whether it was intended or not, are you not committing the same offense against yourself at this moment by holding on to these feelings? How long will you continue to carry this hurt?

Exercise 2: Projections

1. Think of a person in your life whose qualities bother you or push your buttons.
2. When you have identified the qualities, write them down on a piece of paper. I recommend that you use one piece of paper for each quality that you identify.

3. For each quality, write out all the reasons why this quality bothers you. For example, if the quality is that the other person is insensitive, you could write something like this: "By being insensitive, you make the world colder. It can lead to others feeling hurt, and it prevents you from experiencing the emotions and feelings of others. Being insensitive is like living in a barren desert. "

4. Remember that how you experience the outer world around is a reflection of your inner world. That which bothers you in others is also found to some degree within you as well. If you are disturbed by the insensitivity of others, it is because there is a part of you that is insensitive. Further, you associated emotional pain with being insensitive.
5. Now reflect on how you may benefit if you had the same quality, if not to a lesser degree. Using the previous example, a benefit of having a degree of insensitivity in you would be that it would keep you from being bothered by what other people think of you. Maybe you would be less reactive, or it would give you a greater degree of freedom to do what you want to do without worrying about what other people might think.
6. By acknowledging the nobility of your subconscious aspects, that which you are keeping suppressed, you relinquish your resistance to it. Doing this will lose its potency as a counterforce when using your conscious mind to attract what you desire.

Relationships are the most powerful tool for learning how to raise your vibration and becoming successful in using the Law of Attraction. The people who have entered your life did so because you attracted them; there are no accidents or mistakes in this universe. Just as a magnet draws iron filings, you have drawn people toward you; your relationships are the mirror that allows you to view your subconscious.

For this reason, we often hear of the story of the person who leaves a relationship because they are unhappy, only to find themselves in the same situation upon entering a new relationship. Until we learn to use our relationships as a mirror to the shadows of ourselves, we will continue to perpetuate our experience of life.

Before exploring the dynamics of how relationships serve as a mirror, it is important to repeat a statement made earlier in this book. All of our experiences are projections of our own minds. Your relationships, as is will all of life, are a mirror of your inner world. However, as long as we base our life experience on intellectual or rational thinking, we will attribute our problems to the people, situations, circumstances, and events "outside" ourselves.

As a child, Jane always felt that her father did not love her. Unlike her siblings, who he seemed to enjoy being with, he seemed distant to her. She was a curious child and wanted to explore the world around her. Her parents, who came from a traditional upbringing, would try to suppress her curiosity, believing that little girls should be quiet and reserved.

From the time we are infants, we learn that we need to depend on our parents to meet our needs. If we won our parents' approval, we were more likely to get what we wanted. If we did not meet their expectations, it might have led to punishment or disapproval. In our efforts to meet the expectations of our parents, we suppressed aspects of ourselves while adopting new aspects that met our parent's expectations. Jane learned that being curious and explorative was not rewarded while being quiet and reserved was. Further, she developed the belief that the reason for her father being distant was because she was unlovable.

Through continued exposure to her parents, Jane learned to suppress her desire for curiosity and exploration until they become part of her subconscious; these qualities become unrecognizable. As she grew older, she saw herself as being a person who was quiet and reserved. Jane also became judgmental or critical of those she saw as curious and adventurous, especially those who were strong in these traits. She felt this way toward them because, at a subconscious level, they reminded her of the pain that she experienced by being that way herself. She also recreated the relationship that she had with her father. She did so by attracting men who were also distant from her. Her subconscious beliefs were a vibrational match for these kinds of men.

Jane's story is our story, as we all have learned to suppress natural aspects of who we are to be accepted. Though we may not be conscious of these suppressed aspects, they attract the people and situations into our lives that are consistent with their frequency. This is why many people have problems getting the result they want from life. They are unaware that they are broadcasting a signal to the universe that contradicts what they consciously desire. Remember, the Law of Attraction is always working, whether we believe in it or not. The only question is we are aware of what we are broadcasting to the universe, both consciously and unconsciously.

No thought or emotion is inherently negative or positive. It is us that assign meaning to our thoughts and emotions. All of our sufferings and unhappiness result from judging our thoughts and emotions and developing resistance toward them. When we can give up our resistance toward any aspects of ourselves, we free up energy and quiet the mental noise that absorbs our focus. From the perspective of higher awareness, there is nothing in this universe inherently good or bad. Even those aspects of ourselves that we attempt to suppress or battle with have noble aspects about them, aspects that serve us. When we give up our resistance to anything in life, it will work on our behalf.

Your desire to find that perfect person arises from the belief that you will feel whole by doing so that you are incomplete until then. Your sense of wholeness can only come about when you can find peace within yourself. You need to allow those who enter your life to mirror back your projections without judgment. Use the exercise in this chapter to learn what the other person is revealing about you. At the higher awareness level, the ideal relationship is not about making each other happy; it is about supporting each other as each person discovers their own truth and happiness.

Every person that has ever entered your life did so because you attracted them. Not only did you attract them, but they also entered your life as a guide or mirror for your next expansion. For this reason, your search for Mr. or Ms. Right is just a fairy tale. In truth, every person who has ever entered your life was the perfect person for you at that time.

Exercise 4: Entering the Perspective of Another

Ultimately, the key to creating a fulfilling relationship lies in understanding another person's perspective and honoring it. This leads us to a discussion of the Law of Attraction that is usually not elucidated. The Law of Attraction is often discussed from the perspective of attracting relationships, money, or other physical items into our lives; however, a discussion of attracting insights is often absent. To better understand this, it is first necessary to develop an understanding of the nature of thought.

As indicated throughout this book, we identify with our minds and bodies, creating a sense that each of us is a physical being separate from other living beings and physical objects. This sense of separateness extends to the mental phenomena that we experience, which includes thought. We believe that our thoughts are created by us, that our thoughts are exclusively our own minds.

Further, we experience our thoughts as being reality, which then leads to the creation of expectations. Nowhere are our expectations more evident than in our relationships.

All arguments and struggles within our relationships result from other people not meeting the expectations that we hold in our heads. Suppose we are firmly attached to our thoughts and expectations. In that case, there can be no space or flexibility to accommodate alternate perspectives. We can reveal our greater potential for creating extraordinary relationships with a deeper understanding of the nature of thought and the Law of Attraction.

By learning to calm our minds through meditation, we can use the Law of Attraction to gain access to the perspective of the people that we have relationships. All arguments and misunderstandings with others result from us not moving beyond our own perceptions, making it impossible for us to understand the perceptions of others. It is just like a person who only speaks English trying to understand someone who speaks only Spanish. We can enter another person's perspective by holding a sincere intention to do so and then creating the space to receive this information.

The following is an exercise for doing so. However, it is important to note that success in this technique requires practice, the ability to enter a meditative state, and the ability to remain open. Do the following:

1. Before entering your mediation, think about the person whose perspective you want to enter.
2. When thinking about this person, think of their frustrations and concerns that they have and the reasons for it. You do not have to understand or even agree with their perspective; your job is to just acknowledge their frustrations.
3. Announce to yourself your intention to enter this person's perspective.
4. Enter your meditation, reminding yourself again of your intention.
5. When you reach a calm mental state, repeat the intention one last time. From this point on, do make any attempts to influence your experience or hold any expectations. Simply remain open and allow whatever you experience to present itself.
6. Practice by repeating this exercise until you experience the perception of the other person.

This next meditation can be used to manifest the relationship that you desire.

1. Sit down in a comfortable position, close your eyes, and breathe normally.
2. Place your attention on your breath by focusing on the sensations of it traveling through your body.
3. As your focus on your breath, you will experience the appearance of thoughts. When they appear, simply ignore them and return your attention back to your breath.
4. If you keep your focus on your breath, there will come the point when you can maintain your awareness of it without any effort. When you reach this stage, do the following:
    a. Imagine how you would feel if you had the relationship that you desire? Experience these emotions as fully as possible.
    b. Imagine what you would see if you had the relationship that you desired.
    c. Imagine what you would touch if you had the relationship that you desired.
    d. Imagine what you would hear if you had the relationship that you desired.
    e. Make these experiences as real as possible and then intensify the feelings.
    f. When you are ready, awake from your meditation

In these exercises, you are directing your awareness toward detecting the available information within consciousness for improving your relationships with others. However, this exploration for information is just the first step. When you have received information from the universe, your next step is to validate this information.

Talk to the person you want to improve your relationship with and see if they agree with your findings. If they disagree, it could mean that the information you gathered was contained in your own projections. Either way, you can use the feedback you get to take action to support your relationship with that person. When you do this, your vibrational frequency, and that of your relationship, will be raised. When this happens, you will attract more situations and events to build upon what you have started.

Chapter 9: The Law of Attraction and Work

What is your purpose for working? Is it to earn money so that you can support yourself? Is it because it fulfills you? Is it because you are passionate about the field that you work in? Regardless of your answer, you work because you believe it offers you something. If you want to live from a higher level of awareness and making the biggest impact through your work, you may want to view work differently. Rather than just viewing work as a means to get money or a certain feeling, what if we viewed work as a means to express love?

As long as we do things to get something out of it, we are operating from a place of scarcity. Your essential nature is that of absolute abundance and is devoid of need. In fact, you, as your essential nature, do not need to do anything as you are beyond need. What if we changed our purpose for working from gaining something to giving something?

At the most basic level, all work involves providing a product or service for the customer; however, inherent in that is the belief that we need to do x to get y. If I sell cars, I may believe that I need to work hard and meet my quotas to be successful. Based on this model, I need to make a concerted effort to sell cars if I am to earn money. What if we adopted a new paradigm and identified our talents, skills, and passions, and made love our service or product? Your talent and skills are love manifested in a way that is uniquely your own. What you do for work is just the context for expressing love, which is your actual product or service.

Rose was a clerk at a busy convenience store; however, being a clerk is just a job title. Her real job is to give love to every customer that enters the store. Most customers who come into the store do so because of how Rose makes them feel; what they buy is secondary. She is quick to greet them and ask them how they are doing. While most people who work at the store see it just as a job, Rose uses her position to give love.

Because her focus is on creating love and value for her customers, Rose does not experience her job as "work." For her, the convenience store is her second home, and her customers are her family. Because of her attitude, she cannot help but positively impact her job, and management definitely notices. She has received several promotions and enjoys the favor of her employer. Rose's love is expressed in everything she does in her job. Every person who is fortunate to come in contact with her is benefited. Rose is the darling of her management team, and they support her any way they can.

The most powerful force for attraction is love, and it is also the most powerful creative force. Those who love what they do may seem to work hard, but it does not feel like work. Whenever we do what we love, our actions seem to flow effortlessly, and we lose track of time. Not only do our actions flow effortlessly, but we also come up with our best ideas. What has just been described is the state of flow or being in the zone. Being the zone is the same thing as living the Law of Attraction.

The state of flow comes when we allow our essential self to take precedence over our ego-based minds. To be in the flow state is to be in love. Most people think that we need to be doing a certain activity to be in flow. While it is true that the flow state is most often achieved when we are doing things that we enjoy doing, this is just an illusion that we have bought into. You are the creator of your experiences, and you are the one that provides meaning to your experiences. The activity or work that you are doing is just a prop.

Everything you feel or think is projected onto experience; experience cannot make you feel anything. The difference between someone who loves their job and hates their job has nothing to do with the job. The difference between these two people is what they are projecting on to the job.

As long as we feel our experience is the determining factor of how we feel, we will reactively live our lives toward our experience. When we realize that we create our experience and its meaning, then we have the power to get into the flow state and be love, regardless of the situation. Reaching this state of existence takes time, patience, and committed meditation practice or other reflective practice.

Regardless of your job, ultimate success comes when your primary product or service is love, and you take ownership of it. It is not what you do but how you do it. When every aspect of your work life is based on love, you will be successful. How do you base your work or business on love? You treat what you do as if you owned it, and you expect only the highest quality from yourself.

Make everything that you do a sacred act, a gift to your beloved. This type of attention needs to flow through every aspect of your work. It means becoming fully aware of how you interact with your team members, customers, vendors, processes, and systems. Your focus needs to be on how you can provide the greatest care in all that you do. True prosperity comes to those who create the greatest value for those they serve, and who you serve is is all of life. The following are characteristics of love based work:

1. Taking a sense of ownership for all aspects of the workplace or organization.
2. Considering the organization's problems as your problem.
3. Constantly look for ways to improve things and share them with the decision-makers.
4. Conduct your work as though the final product or service is for your beloved.
5. Take action to support others who are experiencing challenges in the workplace.
6. Extend your sense of responsibility from your assigned work to the organization as a whole.
7. Find ways to improve the customer's experience.

If you have your own business and are self-employed, the characteristics of a love-based business are:

1. Continuously looking for ways to improve your systems and processes.
2. Conducting your business as though the final product or service is for your beloved.
3. Treating your team members, your customers, and your vendors as your most important resource.
4. Finding ways to conduct business that minimize impact to the planet and is sustainable.
5. Eliminating processes that result in social injustice.

No work can be truly successful long-term or create true value as long as the focus is on just making money. True success only comes when our endeavors create lasting value for the planet as a whole. Whether it is the destruction of the environment or the exploitation of people, eventually, the costs to the world will not be able to be ignored. When we work through love, we will personally benefit, as will the world. It will happen because we will be attracting into our lives the very best that the universe can offer.

Exercise 1: Knowing What You Were Meant To Do

Reflect on the past and try to remember when you were the happiest. When you remember a time, think about what you were doing and how you were doing it. For example, if you were happiest when you were being creative, what was the context in which you were creative? Where were you? Were you alone, or were there others around you? Be sure to write down all of this information and be as detailed as possible. When you can get the details of the memory, repeat this exercise again by choosing another memory. Complete this process until you run out of memories.

Now think of your skills and talents. Make a list of all those things that you are good at. Your skills and talents should be those things that come naturally for you; you do them without any effort. Examples include:

- Being compassionate
- Being a good listener
- Having a sense of humor
- Being creative
- Being good with numbers
- Computer skills
- Speaking skills
- Analytical abilities
- Athletic ability

When you have completed your list, review them and allow yourself to experience the feelings that arise when you read your lists.

After you have reviewed your list, mediate. As you go deeper into your meditation, ask the universe for guidance. Ask how you could use your talents and skills in a way that will create value and happiness for yourself and others. As you meditate, allow yourself to experience the feelings you would have if you were already working in your dream job.

Spend as much time as you can to immerse yourself in that feeling. Continue this meditation each day until you receive the guidance that you need for manifesting your desire. When this happens, continue this meditation until your dream job is fully manifested.

Exercise 2: Meditating on your Dream Job

1. Sit down in a comfortable position, close your eyes, and breathe normally.
2. Place your attention on your breath by focusing on the sensations of it traveling through your body.
3. As your focus on your breath, you will experience the appearance of thoughts. When they appear, simply ignore them and return your attention back to your breath.
4. If you keep your focus on your breath, there will come the point when you can maintain your awareness of it without any effort. When you reach this stage, think about how you would feel if you had the work that you desired? Experience these emotions as fully as possible.

5. Imagine what you would see if you had the work that you desired.
6. Imagine what you would touch if you had the work that you desired.
7. Imagine what you would hear if you had the work that you desired.
8. Make these experiences as real as possible, making them more intense whenever possible, and then let them go.
9. When you are ready, awake from your meditation.

By doing these exercises and intentionally working from love, you will fully employ the Law of Attraction. You will elevate your frequency and attract the opportunities and circumstances to align with your desires and passions.

Chapter 10: Law of Attraction and Money

Of all the areas in our lives, few affect us as profoundly as our finances. Whether it is an abundance of it or a lack of it, money can have a powerful emotional impact on us. Whether rich or poor, money plays a dominant role in the consciousness of most people. Because of this, we have developed strong beliefs and attitudes about money. Here are just a few examples of the more common ones:

- Money is the root of all evil.
- Money does not grow on tree
- The desire for money is not spiritual.
- Most rich people got that way by taking advantage of others.
- It is selfish to ask for things that we cannot afford.
- I cannot become financially successful because I have too many things stacked against me.
- It takes money to make money.

All these beliefs point to a misunderstanding of money. Each of these beliefs implies that money has an inherent power or value. They also imply that money causes us to behave in a certain way.

Let us begin by debunking these beliefs and explore a more empowering perspective of money.

Money is just a means to measure the exchange of value. If I pay a vendor $50 for a new pair of shoes, both the vendor and I have agreed that the shoes are worth $50. The worth of money is purely subjective as our government assigns value to money.

The value of money used to be based on the gold standard. As we are no longer on the gold standard, the value of money is purely subjective. The price of the shoes that I bought was also subjective. Supply and demand will result in the price of the shoes fluctuating.

Many people make a mistake because they focus on making money, which has no inherent value, instead of focusing on the value they have to offer, which creates money. Money is made when we find a way to create value for others, and they are willing to compensate us for it.

Some people have generated millions of dollars and have lost it all, only to rebuild their wealth again. Some people can only dream of becoming rich and live out their lives in scarcity. There is only one thing that separates these two groups, and that is their beliefs.

The person born rich, or created their own fortune, has a mindset that provides them with a sense of certainty that they can attract money. For these people, making money just comes naturally. Those who have never experienced financial richness have developed a mindset of scarcity. That sense of scarcity is only reinforced by their family's history, the neighborhood they live in, or the stereotypes they have bought into through socialization.

If our dominant belief is that we can create wealth, then that will appear in our lives, given that we apply ourselves and find a way to create value for others. Conversely, if our belief is that we are impoverished, that we were born disadvantaged, that we cannot get a break, then that is what we will attract.

The difference between wealth and poverty has less to do with money and opportunity than it has to do with mindset. Henry Ford, Steve Jobs, Oprah Winfrey, and J.K. Rowling, and Chris Gardner are examples of people who came from very modest beginnings only to generate fortunes as adults.

Regardless of your story, the formula for generating money is not as difficult as it may seem, especially when you consciously employ the Law of Attraction. The following sequence of exercises will point you in the right direction to address your conscious and subconscious mind.

Exercise 1: Belief Balance Sheet

Materials needed:

- Two sheets of paper
- A writing instrument

Do the following:

1. Get three sheets of paper. Select paper sizes of 8" x 11" or larger.
2. Write out a list of all your beliefs about money. If needed, refer back to the examples in the earlier part of this chapter. When you write your list, do not make it an intellectual exercise. Instead, write whatever comes to mind.

3. Select the one limiting belief that you believe is impacting you the most.
4. Take the second sheet of paper and fold it in half lengthwise.
5. On top of the paper, write down the belief that you selected.
6. Make a list on the left-hand side of the paper of all the ways this belief has cost you in your life. How has this belief cost you regarding the way you feel about yourself? How has it affected your relationships, your health, or your finances? Think of all the ways that you have experienced emotional pain by holding on to this belief.
7. When writing, keep in mind the following:
   - When writing this list, write down the first thing that comes to your mind, even if it seems irrelevant.
   - Write as fast as you can, and feel the emotions that arise. This is a heartfelt exercise, not a cerebral one.
   - Keep writing until you run out of things to write.
8. By each item you write down, assign an arbitrary point value to how much impact this item has had on you. When selecting the point value, choose the first number that comes to mind.
9. When you have completed assigning the point values, find the total of all the point values and place it at the bottom of the page.
10. For the right side of the page, repeat Steps 6-8, except this time, you will write down all the ways that this belief has benefited you.

When you have completed step 10, think of a new alternative belief that empowers you. **Example:**

Old Belief: Money does not grow on trees.

New Belief: Money grows to form the ideas that I foster and pursue.

On the third paper, repeat steps 4-10, using your new belief, with the following exceptions: Reverse Steps 6 and 10 by writing down all the ways that you believe that you would benefit from this new belief for Step 6. When doing step 10, write down all the ways you believe it will cost you.

When you have completed the two sheets, do the following:

3. Immediately review your lists, allowing yourself to experience any emotions that arise fully.
4. Review your lists every day, once in the morning and once before you go to bed. Do this until you become fully associated with the emotions that you experience.

When you become fully associated with the costs of holding on to your old belief with the benefits of adopting your new belief, your mind will become reprogrammed with your new belief.

Exercise 2: Know Yourself

Money is created when we create value for others by addressing an unmet need. When the value that you provide also happens to align with your passions and joys while providing a solution to the needs of others, then you have a winning formula.

Take time to reflect on what you enjoy doing. Think about what makes you happy or passionate. If there is something that you enjoy doing, then odds are you are also good at it. Make a list of all the things that you can think of. They could be as simple as enjoying talking to being as complex as repairing computers.

Exercise 3: Identify Your Qualifications

Make a list of all your skills and talents. Skills are considered those abilities that you have that you had to learn. Example:

- Accounting
- Repairing cars
- Scuba Diving

Talents are those abilities that come naturally to you; they did not require any learning. Examples:

- Being compassionate
- Having a sense of humor
- Being persuasive
- Being athletic

Exercise 4: Identifying Needs

This exercise involves identifying an unmet need. This need can be local, national, or global. Think of needs as problems, which can vary in magnitude. Problems can be as minor as forgetting where you left your keys or glasses to be as relevant as water conservation or energy shortages. As you go through your daily life, remain alert to the needs of others and if they are being met.

The last four exercises in this five-step process serve the following purposes:

- Changing any disempowering beliefs about money can get you motivated.

- Creating financial success requires persistence and determination, which is why doing what you love will greatly improve your chances for success. If you love what you are doing, you will more likely stick with it despite the bumps in the road.
- Knowing your qualifications will provide a support structure for doing what you love.
- Identifying unmet needs will make what you have to offer relevant to others.

The last two exercises are for coming up with an idea and attracting money using the Law of Attraction.

Exercise 5: Coming Up with a Winning Idea and the Law of Attraction

Take time to reflect on the information that you gleaned from these exercises. Can you come up with the idea that fuses all these components together? Coming up with a winning idea can take time and research. If you find yourself unable to come up with an idea, you can also use the Law of Attraction.

The Law of Attraction can be used to find an idea and attract people and circumstances that can help you manifest a money-making enterprise. However, you must do the first three exercises before turning to the Law of Attraction. The information you gain from these exercises will clarify your intentions. To utilize the Law of Attraction, do the following:

1. Review your lists from the exercises in this chapter. You may also want to incorporate the lists from Chapter 11 on work.
2. After reviewing the list, create an intention. Example:
    a. I will find an idea that addresses a need and creates happiness for all involved.
    b. I will find a way to align my joys and strengths with service to others.
    c. I will attract the people and circumstances to successfully serve others.
3. Enter your meditation. When you reach a calm state, release your intention to the universe. Upon releasing your intention, give up all attachment to it.
4. Repeat this meditation until your request is manifested.

Exercise 6: Attracting Money using the Law of Attraction

1. Sit down in a comfortable position, close your eyes, and breathe normally.
2. Place your attention on your breath by focusing on the sensations of it traveling through your body.
3. As your focus on your breath, you will experience the appearance of thoughts. When they appear, simply ignore them and return your attention back to your breath.
4. If you keep your focus on your breath, there will come the point when you can maintain your awareness of it without any effort. When you reach this stage, think about how you would feel if you had the money that you desired? Experience these emotions as fully as possible.

5. Imagine what you would see if you had the money that you desired.
6. Imagine what you would touch if you had the money that you desired.
7. Imagine what you would hear if you had the money that you desired.
8. Make these experiences as real as possible, making them more intense whenever possible, and then let them go.
9. When you are ready, awake from your meditation.

The key to using the Law of Attraction is to raise your vibration, have a clear intention, experience your intention at the emotional level, and practice detachment. Do not cling to your intention or hold any expectations. Trust that the universe will respond to your intentions when the time is right. In the next chapter, we will explore the area of health.

Chapter 11: The Law of Attraction and Health

As everything in this universe is made of energy, the Law of Attractions affects every aspect of our life, and our bodies are no exception. Our thoughts about our bodies and our health will manifest as our experience of them. From a universal perspective, both our bodies and health are the manifestation of thought.

Our thoughts are so powerful that they can even override our genetics, which should be no surprise. While genetics may hold the body's blueprint, that blueprint first had to be created. What created the blueprint was consciousness. In fact, the power of consciousness over our health and bodies can be witnessed in our daily lives.

While no one has an accurate estimate, the human body cells can range from 50-70 trillion cells. Each of these cells is replaced after days or months, depending on the cell. Further, each cell carries out numerous functions while coordinating its functions with all the other cells. What is it that orchestrates all this cellular activity seamlessly across the countless generations of cells?

As we go through the various stages of life, we undergo numerous changes. Our knowledge and understanding change, our experiences change, and our bodies change. Despite all these changes, there is an aspect of us that is changeless. That which is changeless is our awareness. Regardless of all the transformations that we undergo, that which is aware of change remains unchanged. As consciousness, we are eternal and unchanging; however, our physical bodies undergo continuous change by the second.

Why do some patients experience spontaneous remissions of cancer? Why does the placebo effect occur? How can one person take a sugar pill, believing it to be a new experimental drug, and show therapeutic benefits comparable to another patient who received the actual medication? Questions like these continue to elude both scientists and researchers because they focus on the human body being a mechanical and physical structure rather than the expression of a unifying intelligence and wisdom.

The beliefs that we have about our health and bodies result in the Law of Attraction manifesting the conditions that reinforce our beliefs. When we express any resistance toward our bodies, the

Law of Attraction will manifest in our bodies that which we focus on. If we fear that we are succumbing to illness, that focus can manifest as an actual illness. Suppose we focus on our dissatisfaction with our weight. In that case, our bodies will manifest the conditions that make our weight loss attempts unsuccessful or nonsustainable.

If we focus on how we are getting older, the Law of Attraction will manifest those conditions that lead to the acceleration of the aging process. Suppose we focus on our fear upon receiving a diagnosis of a life-threatening disease. In that case, our chance of survival will automatically be reduced. Similarly, suppose we focus on our desire to live our life fully, despite the diagnosis. In that case, our chances for recovery will be enhanced.

If we have a positive outlook toward life, feel love and appreciation, are forgiving, and pursue life with a sense of excitement, our mindset can negate the effects of the disease. Most of us have heard of the stories of how one individual can engage in unhealthy activities and live a long healthy life. In contrast, another individual, who lives a life free of such activities, passed away early.

The guiding principle behind all the examples just described is that of emotion. Our emotional health determines the frequency of our bodies. High-frequency emotions will be reflected in the body's frequency, just as low-frequency emotions will reflect in the body. Self-love manifests as physical health, just as resistance toward our body manifests as health issues.

Where you are today with the health of your body is most likely due to your dominant beliefs. Our physiology is heavily influenced by our emotional health. An experiment was conducted where two subjects rode a roller coaster. Before riding the roller coaster, the subjects were tested to determine their physiological markers such as blood pressure, hormone levels, and other physiological factors.

The first testing of the subjects was for establishing a baseline. The subjects then rode the roller coaster. The first subject loved the ride and could not wait to go back on. The second subject found the ride scary and could not wait for it to end. Upon the conclusion of the ride, the subjects were retested. The subject who enjoyed the ride had the physiological levels of a person experiencing wellbeing. The subject who found the ride to be a threatening experience expressed that in their physiology. Their stress hormones were elevated, while other physiological markers reflected a body experiencing stress. Both subjects experienced the same ride; the only difference was their beliefs about their experience.

Any time we experience anything other than sincere acceptance or love for our bodies, we are engaged in war with our bodies. Instead of trying to lose weight, it would be more productive to focus on self-love and enjoying a healthy lifestyle. Instead of quitting smoking, try focusing on living a life where you focus on experiencing greater meaning and fulfillment every day. Instead of succumbing to the belief that aging means a decline in your ability to enjoy life, start meditating to discover the truth of who you are, which is beyond beliefs.

Everything that we believe to be true about our health and our physical bodies is based on our blind acceptance of what we were told. We have learned to accept what societal attitudes, statistics, and research have told us about health, the aging process, and the human lifespan as facts. However, all of this information is based on beliefs.

Like the placebo effect, if we believe what society says or what statistics and research reveal, our minds and bodies will comply. As with any other aspect of life, our health experience is based on what our minds tell us. When we do this, our understanding is based on the limitations of the intellect. When we transcend the intellect, our understanding is based on the infinite potential of the greater consciousness.

To transcend our intellect, all that is required from us is to provide our intentions; the universe will take care of everything else. The health of our bodies is the physical expression of the health of our thoughts. Just as we should strive to remove resistance toward our mental phenomena, we would be wise to eliminate any resistance that we have for our bodies. Fortunately, by addressing our minds, we will simultaneously address the body. The most powerful way to do this is by cultivating self-love.

If you intend to use the Law of Attraction to improve your health, I urge you to do the self-love meditation described in Chapter 6. When you have completed this exercise, do the following exercise:

Exercise 1: Meditation on Health

1. Sit down in a comfortable position, close your eyes, and breathe normally.
2. Place your attention on your breath by focusing on the sensations of it traveling through your body.
3. As your focus on your breath, you will experience the appearance of thoughts. When they appear, simply ignore them and return your attention back to your breath.

4. If you keep your focus on your breath, there will come the point when you can maintain your awareness of it without any effort. When you reach this stage, think about how you would feel if you had the health that you desired? Experience these emotions as fully as possible.
5. Imagine what you would see if you had the health that you desired.
6. Imagine what you would touch if you had the health that you desired.
7. Imagine what you would hear if you had the health that you desired.
8. Make these experiences as real as possible, making them more intense whenever possible, and then let them go.
9. When you are ready, awake from your meditation.

It should be noted that how this book was formatted does not reflect how consciousness works. This book dedicated a chapter to each of the major life areas. In truth, everything is one. When you do exercises in any of the life areas, all life areas will benefit. By outlining each life area in a separate chapter, this book allows you to focus your attention on one life area at a time.

Conclusion

This book took a deep dive into the Law of Attraction; however, it is not necessary to understand everything in this book to effectively employ the Law of Attraction. You can become a more effective manifestor by just remembering the word "integrity." When we live with integrity, we become true to ourselves while earning the trust of others. To live with integrity also involves valuing ourselves and believing in our self-worth. Instead of focusing on developing your manifestation abilities, focus on developing an appreciation for yourself and the world around you. Use what you learned from this book to enhance your understanding of these matters. When this occurs, you will witness your dreams becoming a reality.

Meditations on Attraction and Abundance:

Table of contents:

Part One

Introduction

Meditation is a practical tool to still the mind and to experience consciousness. Consciousness is the deepest layer of ones ability to understand, grasp and attract.

When the eternal lake of consciousness is quiet and still, Meditation can help with that, then one becomes aware of one's true nature.

Daily Meditation keeps a quiet mind, and resources the still lake of consciousness for a higher and eternal purpose.

'All purposes which are fulfilled by the ocean can also be fulfilled by a small well.'

Sit still, properly and attentive. The spine is upright, flat on the ground or a mat.

These meditations can be practised while sitting, or laying in an awake state, for best results find yourself facing North.

Be comfortable and have a meditative space around you, with the least distraction. Only when nature is still, attraction and abundance can be tapped into.

Meditating with Supreme Abundance

From the natural periphery, we start our meditative journey to the personal nature.

This nature is essentially eternal and full of abundance.

This abundance comes in energy and with quality. It has character as well as form and personality.

Be aware of this present situation and breathe. Gently in and out again, equal and aware, every breath is likewise streaming into the nose, and out again. Loosen the muscles on the shoulders, and neck, and open up the chest with a straight posture.

The life air is flowing into the nostrils and reaching the heart. Here, all attraction happens.

The heart is the spiritual abode of personality and bliss, everlasting wisdom and eternity.

Be aware of the breath touching the heart and notice it streaming out again. This process of conscious breathing keeps the focus on the subject matter.

The subject of personality is connected to a sense of self, or ego, which naturally expresses a desire. One is just aware of this thought, whatever it may be.

This is the matter of the mind, and the senses, knowing very well that there is coming and going of the breath.

Notice the duality of in-and-out of the breathing. Are both equal?
Inhale one... two... three... four, exhale one... two... three... four. Pause for a moment. Repeat. Inhale one... two... three... four, exhale one... two... three... four.

Imagine sitting on a still lake of consciousness. The moon is shining in full and the light is reflected very authentically on the lake. This still lake receives the light of the moon very nicely, and hence the lake is still, the light can shine through the surface onto the ground of the lake.
The light is both reflected by the still lake of consciousness and touched deeply to the ground of the unconscious. Both are reached and pervaded by crystal clear moonlight.

Clearing stage

This purity shall help us to be aware of past attractions, therefore the meditations are dedicated to clean the mirror of the heart-mind, which is full of material dust.

Through conscious breathing, the mirror can be cleansed and one can see the truth within. Natural desires and thoughts are arising and passing, equally as the breathing arises and passes.

Everything, like ebb and flood, comes and goes, but what we have attracted is still present with us. Therefore, we use a special technique of meditation to reduce the mind-clutter and to make space for pure attraction.

Pure attraction comes in form of a person to you. The Person is the Highest Person, and Absolute Truth. Situated in the temple of the heart lingering on the lake of consciousness. This Absolute Truth is sitting on a nice patio, with a beautiful seat made of the softest cushion grass. The Supreme Person is clothed in silk and finest wool, decorated with abundant jewels, amulets, golden bangles and a beautiful flower garland.

This highest Supreme Person is the source of all abundance and attraction. The name of this person is Krishna, which means the all-attractive one. All-attractive. So whatever you can imagine, whatever you have ever dreamed of, whatever is possible and impossible is granted through the permission of this Highest Person.

The Supreme Personality sits within the heart of every living being, and one can address this spiritual state as follows:

'O, Supreme Attractor, please grant me access to the realm of consciousness where all is possible. I am hungry for attraction and abundance. Please allow me a bite of this transcendental joy and bliss. May all beings be happy.'

Contemplate, and breathe. Sit comfortably and stay in this consciousness for a moment. Become aware of the stillness of the lake, and just notice the mind focusing its intention on the longing for attraction.
Breathe, and just accept this moment as it is, the Supreme Personality is hearing and listening.

For a moment, come to ease and listen to the matter of the breathing, how it is still present, knowing to be alive.

Give thanks and gratitude to the present moment, in mind, word and action. Fold your palms together, in front of the chest and be aware of the subtle energetic currents flowing from the palms and along the arms, shoulders, neck, head and heart.

A natural hunger or lusty desire is attracting whatever one is open to receive. However, before we can accept any outer circumstance, one has to accept the inner circumstance. Therefore, by approaching the Supreme reservoir of all attraction one has direct access to unlimited resources within. This resource comes in form of conscious waves of energy.

Prepare and be aware, whatever you like to attract is just a connection. Not so far away, but the more precious and kindly we ask, the better one can receive.

Open the hands and palms facing upwards. This gesture helps to let go of unwanted and unnecessary clutter in mind and energy. Just surrender and let your palms face to the sky. Breathe equally, and relax. Everything is fine, we are just about to clean the mirror of the heart and mind with simple sounds.

Simple sound Bath meditation

Sit peacefully, relaxed and in a meditative space of tranquillity. Be prepared for sound, so find a comfortable seat or lay down flat. In both ways, when meditating face North and open the palms to the sky.

This hand gesture means 'openness', or
'ready to receive'.

Now use breath to calm down the mind and continue with equal breathing for a few deep moments. Let the inhale and exhale be equal and focus on the heart.
Notice the constant stream of air flowing along the nose tip, in and out it goes. Very equally and rhythmic. Body, spine, emotions and mind are in alignment and balance.

Feel the ground, either on the buttocks or with the whole body. Be aware of the whole body as a unit. This wholeness starts within the heart. Focus here and breathe equally, with an equanimous mind.

Whatever thoughts arise, be aware and let them pass. Don't worry, like ebb and flood, thoughts arise and fade naturally. Just observe this phenomenon and keep balance.

Balance is everything. In a Space, to create balance, one can utter the syllable AUM. This word (□) or Omkara is the whole manifestation of the All-attractive Supreme Personality.

When we utter this sound, the whole body vibrates in a natural frequency. Simultaneously, it is a greeting to address the Supreme Reservoir of all things and worlds.

This divine sound is very simple, yet ultimately profound. One can hear this resonance everywhere in nature, for example in the rivers or even within the breath. Be aware of the sound of the breath and just listen for some equal breaths.

Breath, equally in and equally out again. Be aware of the sound and let it sink into the heart space.

Here is the centre of Attraction and one can witness how the whole body is maintained from here. Let the sound of the breath evenly sink into the belly and to the feet.

Be aware of the sensations and remain in balance.

Now, one can utter the sound. The mouth is fully open to start uttering the Aaaahh, as long as possible. This sound A vibrates within the abdomen or more specifically within the area of the navel. This is the sound of creation.
Now, you can utter the sound U, nice and long. Keep it, maintain and feel it. This sound vibrates within the heart space, straight up the spine, and it is the manifestation of Unity and connection.
Now, you can utter the sound Mmm. The mouth is completely closed and it vibrates in the area of the throat. Keep it inside and let it sound, even up to the crown of your head. The whole jaw, skull, neck and shoulders are addressed with this sound of purity.
So, A-U-M are three individual sounds, in a connected flow of sound. This is pure, creative energy which addresses the Supreme reservoir of all Attraction.

Sound and Tone: AaaaUuuuMmm. Feel it, vibrate with it and let it free naturally.

Practice makes perfect. Repeat and rehearse. This sound is to create space and purify existence. It addresses also the lake of consciousness just on the feet of the Supreme Attractor whose eyes are like the sun and moon.

So let's speak to the heart's content, addressing the Supreme Attractor in person, one can utter this sacred sound which acts as a spiritual key for tuning in and saying Hello.

Of course, the Supreme Personality is always very nice to devotees who are thus addressing his abode and Reservoir of all pleasure:

Om (A-U-M), O highest person, please accept my humble request, I am here to learn how to attract...
May this meditation lead to Your Reservoir of abundance, pleasantness and attraction.
Thus, the highest person who sits within our hearts knows what is our desire and can listen.

When, in meditation, one shall know what to attract: Let's say, ‚One wants to attract... a pure and healthy life', or ',...a good way to learn for my exam. 'one can easily say it. From the heart, everything is accepted. Just be humble and utter your wishes internally, externally, or write it down.

We shall for now envision internally, but we will come back to external, and contemplative methods like writing.

Just imagine why you came here. What is the purpose of your visit?

Like a messenger comes to the King and reports news or proposes an inquiry, one can be inquisitive and ask for anything. The Supreme Reservoir in person understands and is always open to granting a conversation or even permission.

Good things, prescribed in scriptures, like purity or the search for the absolute Truth are always welcome.

This Truth is essentially within everyone's heart and thus one carries it around everywhere.

Meditation means also internal contemplation. Therefore, help yourself with enough time and space. Five-minute meditations fill a gap or can be integrated before a meal, proper sit, breathe and meditate. Meditation can thus make every life circumstance a conscious effort for attraction and well-being. Meditation creates space, like with a Mantra (Om), and within this space, one can attract anything. Be patient and listen. Enough space for meditation is necessary to feel attraction and abundance holistically.

Pure Sunshine Meditation

Just sit, together with the Supreme Person who is very beautiful and renounced on the lake of consciousness. It is almost sunrise, and the sky is glowing very beautifully. See the stars and planets on the firmament, these are like all the persons, forefathers, masters, saints and heavenly beings in innumerable numbers. Knowing the sun comes up, the Supreme reservoir of light unfolds.

The rays of this sunlight spread internally and externally, from within the solar-plexus translucent light is emanating around the heart, shoulders, arms, hands, hips, legs, feet and head. The bliss and energy of the sunshine spreads around the whole being and warmth is present.

The horizon now gives a sense of smile. Golden and brilliant, the effulgence of the sun purifies all the senses and equips one with happiness and comfort.

Consciously breathe and equally feel the breath. Rhythmically in and out again. Very equal, and with an equanimous mind. The light of the sunshine makes one smile, and happiness and joy are attracted, like flowers of a tree blossom when touching the sunlight. Smile, be happy and content. All the joy, happiness and love is surrounding you.

Light Mantra Meditation

There is a Mantra, an affirmation, on how to still the mind, and create good vibrations. It goes like this:

I am the Light of the World,
I am the Light of the World,
I am, I am, I am the Light of the World.

You are the Light of the world,
You are the Light of the World,
You are, You are, You are the Light of the World.

We are the Light of the World,
We are the Light of the World,
We are, We are, We are the Light of the World.

Light is life. Light is love.
Light is everything around.

With every light, one can blink and address the eyes, the receivers of light.

Blink and let the eyes shine. Smile and give thanks for the light.
With steady practice of this Mantra, one can still the mind and attract light in dark times.
Light can be interchanged with everything that makes life liveable, like:

I am the Love of the World,
You are the Love of the World,
We are the Love of the World.

I am the Peace of the World,
You are the Peace of the World,
We are the Peace of the World.

I am the Unity of the World,
You are the Unity of the World,
We are the Unity of the World.

Or speak an affirmation of goodness, purity and blessing.

I am attracting Goodness now and forever,
You are attracting Goodness within time,
We are attracting Goodness evermore.

Let purity bring Me closer to myself,
Let purity bring Us closer together,
Let purity bring Them closer to themselves

May all beings be blessed,
May the world, time and circumstance be blessed.

Affirmation work effectively through devotion and repetition, therefore repeat these phrases in perfect alignment. Feel the purpose and need for the affirmation knowing that words attract, whatever we say.

In regards to sacred Mantras like AUM and Affirmation, it is most common to create a mood of prayer including honesty and compassion.

Thank you for this light, thank you to shine bright
Thanks for all the love from the sky above.
Thankfulness, Truth and Compassionate Love.

Sitting upright and align to sky and earth, being grounded and free to speak is the basis of every good meditation.

To create a meditative place one can speak the following formulas, to purify a meditation room:
May this space be clean and free of envy, anger and other things,
May this place serve for meditation and affirmation.
May I find a comfortable seat.

To speak honestly means also to speak in full understanding of the purpose. Why Am I here? To meditate, ok. Let the room know, light a candle or incense and find your own space of tranquillity.

Create an oasis of abundance within the heart, as well as within the living space. Practically, every space can be transformed into a meditative space.

Everybody is a temple and everyone is living in their temple.

One who knows about the sanctity of a space can still the lake of consciousness easily. Thus, wishes and desires are reflected perfectly and the ground can be visible.

From the ground sometimes unconscious or stored attractions are coming to the surface. Like a habit, a thought pattern, or a simple word. These can be fetched, transformed and used with the matter of the breath and consciousness. Everything in life has a reason, a ground to exist.

This concludes the clearing stage, part one.

Part Two

The source within the Heart

Breathe and be aware of the heart space. Here, in the heart, all energies meet and create balance. Balance is key for Meditation.

One can have balance through an equanimous sitting position, and according to the matter of the breath.

Balance is like a mountain. Very firm and steady.
Just be a mountain, and whatever comes, thoughts, distractions, itching, trembling, pain, just be steady and keep the meditation very equally and peacefully.

Just inhale and be aware of the little pause between the in-and out-breath. Be aware of the subtle sensation of the breath moving into the nostrils and moving out again. Just simply be steady and aware, that the breath is connecting us to all the life. In consciousness, there is no difference between gold, stone, wood, water, and other things. They are all-natural matter. Even sensations like tickling, itching, vibrating, warmth, cold, are all the same, rising and passing.

Like a wind sweeps over the land and makes many trees dance, but the mountain remains steady. Be that mountain. A mountain is a steady magnet. Just attract goodness, by being a magnet for pure goodness. Uttering sacred syllables and affirmations help to get through the storm, yet one has to focus and face any difficulty. Easily, then one attract beauty, wealth, fame, wisdom and so on.

Just breathe equally and hold the key balance. Sit on the feet of the Supreme Balance in Person and be aware of the heart. Here, within the heart wonders are happening. By breathing consciousness travels along the channels of energy from the outside to the inside. Within, in the heart, the air can unfold and circulate. Here, balance finds its expression. Notice the little pause even so after the exhale. Stillness takes care of the necessary space within the heart and the flowers of the garden of the heart can blossom to attract nectar-hunting honey bees.

Just be aware of the inhale, equal, and the exhale, equal. Find yourself in this wonderful space where the grass is very soft and lush, there are colourful cows grazing peacefully on the field and one can see the juicy green fields along the garden where nice desire trees are cultivated.

A gardener takes good care of all the plants by removing the weeds of ignorance. By conscious breathing one can, little by little, remove these weeds to get rid of fatigue, greed, pride, envy, and lust. This garden is a sacred space to meditate and there is even so the everlasting lake of consciousness just in near sight. A sunny morning provides wonderful and auspicious perspectives of the sunlight reflecting the whole spectrum of colours.

Notice the lake of consciousness and be aware of its state. Is it still? Is it fickle? How is this pure lake behaving? Slowly lean towards the lake and see your reflection within the waters. How are you seeing yourself?

Reflect and contemplate, lean back and relax within the meditative garden of your heart. Here, one can also plant the seed of good fortune. By addressing the divine feminine, the aspect of you that sets free fertility and purity.

Be aware of the subtle sound of the breathing and just remain like the steady mountain beyond the fields and meadows. The garden is waiting for a special seed, a desire-seed.

So, whatever you desire, you can cultivate. It takes time to plant, but at the right moment, one can implement a good seed in good soil.

Whatever you wish for, be clear about it, check it and nurture this wish like your little child. Be aware of this phenomenon that brings life to sprout. Whatever it may be, hold your hands together and think about a seed that likes to grow.

One can plant abundance, happiness and wealth, by giving all these to the Supreme Balance offering it with love.

'Please, let this desire-seed sprout into wealth, abundance and happiness.'
Then, one can put it into the ground of the hearts garden.

Just envision how a simple seed can grow into a full blossom tree, full of lively blossoms and an abundance of fruits. Just see the shapes, colours and luminescence emanating from that growing tree. However, it needs time to ripe, the desire can sprout very wonderfully.

Breathe and be equipoised just knowing that everything is already in place. Similar to a tree, one needs to find deep roots in meditation to attract fruitful results.

Love Attraction: Offering and Receiving Love

If it would be sold in a shop everyone would buy it. Love. It comes from the heart and is the essential force that connects us humans, person to person. Its divine quality is bliss and truthfulness.

So, just sit under that desire tree and imagine yourself to be very nicely situated in a peaceful. mode of observance. Seeing the cows grazing on the field, listening to the birds in the sky and being aware of the subtle sensation of the life air streaming into the nostrils and out again.

Equally, breathe, and feel the touch of the roots. The lower back, buttocks or whole body may be equally touching the ground. Envision an energetic connection with the ground and also with the heart. From the heart, light illuminates the sight and one can see the spring in the garden of one's heart. The tree is giving a nice shelter before the morning sunshine.

By breathing one can consciously access this garden of hearts, where even friends and family can take a rest. Just call out to someone and see the connection to this person. A loved one might be just waiting to be invited. Love is all you need, just connect to your loved one and let the force act. Love is intelligent, natural life force. Just be a channel for this energy and submit. Smile and be happy, because your loved one is just appearing at the entrance of the garden.

Wonderful as it seems, but your friends have no shoes on! Where there is a beautiful lush garden with soft grass, ain't no one needs shoes. Greetings and a warm welcome, there is enough space under the tree. Just feel free and breathe.

It's okay to dream away, however one may be aware of the breath. Whenever there is doubt, fall, or fear, just breathe. Breathing brings balance. 'Here you are invited to wish for a nice fruit', says the desire-tree. Just speak or think it out, what would you like. The desire-tree is providing you and your friend. Cheesecake? No problem, the desire-tree is a wish-fulfilling desire-tree and no desire remains open. It can read your mind.

Speaking of the mind. The mind is like a well that can provide the necessary contact for abundance. If you have a full mind-well, well, that's good, because then one can fetch from the mind-well and give away the awareness. Awareness is the potency from a mindful reservoir. When the mind is empty, well, then it is easy to fill up. Is the mind full, well then, one can fetch awareness from this well. Awareness of attention is the attraction towards the sense objects. While. meditating, one can notice these sense objects and senses to attach, and detach. Once there comes a subtle stream of air, it touches the skin, one can feel, but then it fades just like the breeze fades. Same with sound, taste, smell and sight. Of all the senses and sense objects form, shape and colour are the most attractive, especially to the eyes.

This is why one can envision a garden of wonderful trees or one can determinedly stare at the nose-tip. Both has an effect and keeps the mind busy and attached. To detach the mind, one can use the hands, clapping once or twice. This sound is very powerful and overpowers the attached senses easily.

Just consciously attach your mind and focus towards an object of desire, maybe an apple or a banana, or a cheesecake. Put all the energy of attention into the process and remain still, for a moment, let go. Smile, and offer the desired object to your dear friend or loved one. Leave the breathing natural and see.

Mindfulness can be a process of loving transmission. One can even give love to others just by thought. Further, when the mind is engaged in loving transmission connecting to a higher wish or desire, the senses become fixed. Focusing the mind on the nice form of the Supreme Personality, the origin of all abundance, the. All the senses are automatically engaged in the service of the mind. Then, smelling can be very inspiring, hearing a wonderful experience, seeing a miraculous occasion, touching a blissful act, and tasting a joyful endeavour.
Mindfulness can lead to abundance by steady application and determination, as well as faith.
In meditation, one can access these realms of subtle energies, like the lake of consciousness.
Here, many seeds of desire are stored, and these seeds again act as potential outcomes.

Offer a Smile

Just sit mindfully with your loved one under that tree within the garden of your heart and breathe. Consciously, rhythmically and equal. Find a smile and also offer this to your friend. Love attracts, and the more attention we give, the more on can reciprocate. Just see your friend from the bottom of the sole, to the tippy toes, along the ankles, calves, knees, thighs, and the upper body. How is this loved one dressed, and what special features can you make out? See the upper body and chest, the arms, hands and fingers. Finally, see the neck, chin, jaw and eyes. See the eyes and forehead. Smile gently, and see your loved one as a meditative companion who has always been within the garden of your heart.

This is even how to attract associates, ad loving relationships. We can desire nice friendships and good relations, and of course one can meditate upon these. One who has a spiritual teacher knows, it is best to see from the feet to the head.

Give thanks and appreciate the community. Be aware of this eternal moment within the garden of the heart, underneath that desire tree. Watch the lake of consciousness be very nice and still. The sunshine of the midday is reflecting within the waters stillness and here swans and cranes are playing in the rear.

Beyond the beautiful lake of consciousness, there are mountains of steadiness and determination, and even upon the peaks, one can see a little reflection of the sunshine. Within the trees, there are plenty of flower blossoms and fruits. Many beautiful leaves are dancing within the wind and the sound of birds is most enchanting. The subtle breeze charms with a sweet aroma of forest fruits.

You and your friend are in meditative harmony, just breathing and enjoying. There is nothing to do, there is no must, no stress, just endless happiness. Blissfully dreams come true, and a slight bluish hue reflects from the lake of consciousness.
A meditative dream bird lands nearby within a forest grove. It is a very colourful bird, with black, purple, silver and blue feathers. Can you guess what kind of bird is this?

Attracting Peace: Padala meditation

Find a comfortable seat. Breathe equally in and out, find your ground and balance as you erect your spine. Gently look upwards, open the throat area and relax the shoulders.
Bring both palms together and chant a Mantra for Peace:
Om Shanti Shanti Shanti x3
Close your eyes, open your hands upwards, create a smile and find yourself watching the life air. See the breath moving into the nostrils and out again. See yourself sitting in a nice and lush forest close to a spring. A wonderful soothing sound sparkles next to you and calms your mind. (Play watery sounds) Listen and find ease.
While we sit in this forest we can hear the sounds of birds (play sounds of birds) and there comes a beautiful peacock, gracefully stepping out of the forest.
A shimmering blue feather cloak opens and we see the full splendid form. We hold the image, all feathers spread widely shining in silver, purple and white. The top of the crown-like wings hosts a beautiful eye. Innumerable eyes are wide-spread around the peacock, who greets us:
'Hello, peace be with you. Welcome to our blissful paradise. I am Padala.'
We smile. Smile and give thanks to the moment and Padala, the Peacock.
Padala says, 'come and explore the wide land on my back.'
We hop on and start our journey. Breathe and feel the lightness come with every breathing, in and out. With every breath we feel lighter and lighter, lifting up the sky above. 10 meters off the ground, 20 meters of the ground, 40 meters of the ground. We lift higher and higher with every breath we take. 100 meters of the ground, we can see the crowns of the trees, the peaks of the mountains and in the far, the endless horizon.
We fly in one direction and fly intensely. Breathe and breathe intensely. We are safe with Padala, so start to watch your breath again equally going in and out.
'I will bring you to my master, he lives in the paradise valley.'
We come to fly and see there is a vast green valley with a sacred stream and many abundant flowers and fruits. We come closer and closer, 100 meters, 80 meters, 40 meters, we breathe through and slowly get a feel of this paradise valley. A Lush and plentiful scent of the land makes us feel peaceful. 20, 10, 1 meter off the ground, we slowly descent with Padala down to the green valley field.
We sigh of relief and gasp for fresh air. The land smells nicely and we find the beautiful Padala walking us to a small little hut, where a shimmering light protects the entrance. Only you can come here with your companion and guide Padala. We open the door and in this little hut there sits a person, so familiar and wise, the face shines in a transcendental glow of joy and happiness. We recognize this face and observe a warm welcoming smile. We smile back and give thanks for the invite to the masters home.

'You have come a long way, take rest and come to ease. We will have tea soon.' The masters long white robe shimmers of purity and wisdom. We will hold the stillness and peace for a while so one can ask any question to the wise master.
(Holding silence)
We breathe and come out of the silence for another smile.
, Here', the master says, 'take this favourite feather and you will be welcome everywhere you go, just open it for the host to see.'
The master gives us a feather.
'This feather is a sign of peacefulness and lightness, keep it dear to your heart.'
We accept and bow in reverence.
We leave and come back to The Valley. We breathe and come back to our body, we sigh and come back to the room. Chant Om Shanti, Shanti, Shanti.
Frieden, Peace, Shalom.
Close your palms together, give thanks to the peacock Padala, the master and all living beings alike.

Attracting Happiness Meditation

Be aware of the breathing. Moment to Moment one can notice how the breathing is equally streaming in and out. The breath is very subtle yet profound, streaming into the nostrils and flowing to the heart. From here the whole life air is distributed all over the body. The body is charged with life energy and happiness.

Happiness can come in many ways, but the easiest is light. Light is always present and can be transformed into anything one likes to attract. The human body is like a magnet with two poles, and like light, it has a dual character. When there is balance in the body through meditation. Happiness can ignite a fire of freedom and bliss.

So, breathe equally and mindfully. The mind is sometimes compared to a flickering lamp, but one who is steady in meditation can easily still the flickering of the lamp. This is the purpose of meditation.

See this lamp, or candle within your vision and know that from one candle one can ignite many more candles, easily this can be done from a simple hand.

Sit equally and in a comfortable position. Put one hand on the area of the navel and breathe equally. Feel, how the belly rises and sinks with every breath. With inhalation, the belly rises, and with exhalation, the belly sinks to normal.

Just be aware of the balance between inhalation and exhalation. Let it be the basis for a steady and happy meditation.

An endless source of happiness is found within the heart, therefore, let’s focus on the heart and its beat. This beat is the rhythm of one's life. Now, put one hand onto the chest and feel the heartbeat.

Be aware and notice its character, what does the heart say? What is within the heart's desire? Is the rhythm equal and in harmony?

Just notice the beats and sit straight. Now, use your hand to move in a clockwise circle around the chest area and belly. Let it be a flowing movement, connecting both heart and belly.

Breathe, and smile.

Now, use the hands to swipe the other parts of the body. Just swipe. Eventually, one can do this sweeping with the awareness, cleansing the whole body, energy and mind.

Now, come back to the heart and happiness. Smile, again. Breathe equally in and out. Let the smile sink into the heart and remember a moment of happiness within your life. Maybe just very recently, what did make you considerably happy?

Let it be a simple thing, like a smile, and continue seeing this memory to be present and within the heart. Let the memory pass, and breathe equally.

Be aware of your whole body. Now, remember a person that makes you especially happy. See this person in form and character, with full heart and within the inner vision. Be aware of the moment with the person, right here within the heart. Breathe and let it sink into the garden of the heart. Welcome to the lake of consciousness, where everybody is fully in balance, peace and happiness.

The Supreme Abundance greets also from this place of the heart. Breathe equally and come to ease. Sweet birds are flying around the sacred trees, making the atmosphere very wonderful and serene. Can you see the lake of consciousness? Is it still? Are you aware of the little sensations that are going on, maybe warmth or cold, tickling, throbbing, vibrating. Just focus on the heart and the garden of a happy heart.

All together with the Supreme Abundance who sits very comfortably on a cushioned throne overlooking the lake of consciousness, garlanded and scented very nicely, Supreme Abundance is smiling and inviting to have a comfortable position to see the sunset.

Happiness can be so simple, like watching a sunset together. The lake of consciousness is very nicely reflecting the effulgent rays of the sun, turning the whole atmosphere into a joyful place. As the golden globe enchants and enlights everything with a tranquil glow of happiness one can witness the sweet songs of the birds. A natural symphony creates balance within the system and here, in this heartful land, there is no lack of happiness.

One can be grateful and appreciative to be here, and now. Breathing equally in and out, in respect to nature and heaven. One can give thanks to the light, especially of the sun who provides blissful light to everyone.

By folding the hands together, and holding the palms on the chest, and in front of the heart one can speak the following affirmations:

Thanks Giving to the Light,
May all beings be happy,

Shine bright into the night,
May all beings be happy.

Even in the darkness,
There is happiness,
Love and Lightness,
always in bliss.

In every heart, and every breath.
In and out, equally breathe and relax.
Let the sunlight give healing and happy light to the core and notice that even the sunshine shines from within. A simple smile makes a perfect sun,
glowing and igniting the spark of happiness in everyone.

Now one can affirm happiness and prosperity in one's life:

May I attract happiness and love,
May all beings be happy and loved.
May love and happiness surround all.

Happiness shall fill my life,
My life and every life.
Happiness shall speak to me,
May all beings happy and free.

May prosperity be present,
May I see health and happiness.
Abundance for the world and I.
May all beings be happy and free.

Sit in a comfortable position and open the palms to the sky. Just receive. Be content and satisfied, happily awaiting the bliss.
It is already there, you see? Breathe and be happy.
Within endless energy of heart and soul, one can fetch the happiest of all: Life. From life comes love and from love comes life. Life is already filled with happiness, one just needs to be open, trusting and receptive.

Trust in your ability to trust and be patient, breath by breath a conscious relationship with the abundant heart takes place. This is the best way. Breathing equally, and remaining in balance. In and out, rhythmically, with great attention to the sensations. From the nose-tip to the heart, and from the heart to the belly. Happiness has taste and a wonderful feeling. Be aware of the emotional sensations and continue, giving attention to the heartbeat.

Envision a brilliant light pervading the matter of the body, flowing from the heart like a pure river of consciousness into the energy channels of the body. From the belly, the whole body is nurtured, likewise with energy. Therefore be aware of the light around the abdomen and let the awareness spread around the hips, legs, knees, ankles and feet. Let the light of awareness rise into the upper body parts again, streaming from the feet to the ankles, knees, thighs and lower body, to the upper body, chest, back, shoulders, arms and hands. Let the light of awareness now find the head. The neck, shoulders, jaw, chin and ears are all surrounded by beautiful, conscious light. Around the eyes, and on the crown of the head the light finds expression and blossoms into a sweet golden lotus flower.

See every petal of the lotus flower as a unique and magnificent creation. See it shining, embrace it and be aware that the lotus flower cannot be polluted, or contaminated. It has a protective layer that holds away all impurities. Embrace this pure golden lotus flower, and let it grow in the lake of consciousness.
Offer this lotus flower to the Supreme Abundance and hold the beauty and golden splendour of the sun within the heart. Breathe, equally in and out. Be aware of the sensations around the heart, body and mind.

Rest in this position and consciously focus on the nose-tip. By breathing in, one can connect a thought to the breath. By breathing out, one can let go of a thought. Be aware, and inhale with the thought of pure light. Exhale with the thought of letting go.
Inhale with the thought of golden happiness, exhale with the thought of letting go. Inhale with the thought of protection and peace, exhale and let go of fear, anxiety and pain.

With every breath, there is an exchange of energy and transformation happening. One can transform the subtle energy of the breath into life force, and thus attracting the life one desires. Through the permission of the Supreme Personality, one can receive all the protection, abundance and prosperity, health, happiness and freedom.

Attracting Protection Meditation

Just sit comfortably and witness the breathing coming in and out, be aware of the subtle sensations of the life air which is transferred to the heart. Here it is transformed into life force or prana, the subtle current of energy that makes the universe move.

By controlled breathing or pranayama, one can attract consciousness, through focus and determination one can deliberately open the gates of consciousness to set forth a river of energy. This source of this river and lake of emerging conscious energy or prana is the Supreme Origin, the source of all attraction.

See the Supreme Abundance sitting with very beautiful garlands and silks sitting on the patio, along with many servants and playmates. Some musicians recite beautiful verses and there is one who is constantly fanning the Supreme Person who sits comfortably on a throne of finest gold and jewels.

Within the moment the Supreme Personality is fully satisfied and so shall we be. Be aware, and happy to be alive. It is a blessing and a gift to live and have control over one's actions. Be aware of little sensations. Sit very comfortably and notice the body, full of awareness and in balance. The breathing goes in and out, equally, inhale and exhale hold a little gap in-between. Just notice the length of the inhale, be aware of the gap, then exhale and notice the length of the exhalation. Start all over and balance in and exhale, so they are of equal strength and length.

Don't force, let every breath flow naturally and consciously. Let the spine be erect and the chest wide and in harmony with the upper and lower body. Proper sitting is the means of perfect meditation. Cross-legged in the lotus posture is the prime of all Meditation positions, but meditation can work everywhere and with everyone.

Just sit comfortably and notice the buttocks on the ground, feel the spine erecting and straightening up, until one reaches the head where skull, jaw and neck are in alignment. The shoulders are relaxed. The muscles around the eyes are soft, if not, and this happens in daily life, one can massage the skin and muscles around the eyes. Rotate the eyes clockwise and shift your gaze from left to right, up and down. Circle again. This serves as a calibration of the gaze which is highly important.

This gaze shall be straight with an equanimous mind. Leave the eyes half open and half closed, be aware of the gaze naturally shifting towards the inner eye, the space between the eyebrows. Naturally, one can perceive an inner vision of the Supreme Balance, the origin of all consciousness. Here, one might also see a lake that is still and pure, that is the lake of consciousness. From this lake, all energies flow into life, and whatever gate, or doorway we open, the energy flows into this channel. This is how attraction finds a path of expression. This is how conscious energy becomes manifest.

One has to know what gate or doorway to open.

For now, be guided and aware of the gates of protection opening. The gatekeeper, a servant of the Supreme Balance, unlocks the power of will and sets free a stream of energy into the channel of protection. Protection is a simple and effective energy that surrounds us since time immemorial. Humans have sought shelter and protection wherever in history, and now we can imagine a great forest grove of ancient sequoia trees, the giant mammoth trees of the World, spanning a life of over 2500 years.

Hereunder such a tree, one can find an imaginative shelter and protection. The tree is very humble and wise to give shelter and so it has been the mercy of the forest grove to shelter us for this moment.

Breathe equally in and out, and be aware of the subtle nature of the forest. Strong and mighty these trees give confidence and patience, protection and peace. Just reciprocate and receive the eternal service of nature here on earth. With great trunks and huge energetic branches, the balance is upheld and energy can flow easily in these channels.

Be conscious and know that the Supreme Origin is also the source and seed of all energies, trees, forest and winds.
Be aware of the life air, fresh and serene flowing from the forest groves into the heart. The heartbeat is noticeably slower and finer, the air cleanses the energy channels and the purity of the forest gives protection to all impurities.

Honour and respect this magnificent place, and strength, protection and peace shall be present immediately.

Trees have been sheltering humans forever and still give presence, balance and protection. Whenever there is no way out, in daily life or meditation, just think about the forest and take (an imaginative) stroll around the groves of ancient forests. Be aware of the sounds, smells and presently, be aware of the heartbeat. Feel the tranquillity and shelter.

Trees are the great guardians of this earth and we have been guest for long enough to know that the elements are our friends. Likewise, the waters, which are gently flowing along the groves to nurture the land and animals. This beautiful place also holds flowers and herbs which are aromatic and lushly spread across the grove.

Breathe, and be aware that finding shelter is necessary, one can submit and see that life is always depending. The trees are creating the oxygen we need, and the other way around, the trees are absorbing the carbon dioxide of our lungs to transform it into oxygen. Naturally, the trees have been feeding us with oxygen, since life existed, and one can be eternally thankful.

Give thanks and appreciation to the forest grove, where a beautiful river flows, and where birds are singing a sweet song.

Part Three

Natural Attraction Meditation Story

Just be humble and steady as a tree and life will flower.

Once upon a time, there lived the oldest and wisest trees in the world. These trees were so rooted, that no one could shake them, as these trees were holding onto the ground, no one could ever rip them out, no giant, no dragon, no king, nor queen, but they all know, the wonderful humbleness of a tree.
So humble and kind, the tree doesn't care, about all this, the tree is not winning any prize, but the honour and respect of all humankind. Even the wind, sometimes tries, but hardly comes to terms with this forest kingdom, where the trees hold onto their roots.

So find a comfortable position and imagine your spine. You see the spine, vertebrae for vertebrae and there is also a root, imagine, the root coming from the lowest bottom of the spine and spreading throughout the soil, into the layers of the ground. That ground then is the fundament for our balance.
So we breathe and breathe in the balance. Equally in and out, Balanced breath, equally in and out.

All in harmony and balance, the breathing flows naturally and the body is aligned with all the elements. As the spine is straight, we are relaxing our jaw and head. We can let go of any tension, to relax and ease, into a smile.

Breathe and smile, gently.
Breathe and be in balance.
Like the roots of a tree, we find steadiness in the ground.
And we can also tone a sound, that helps us to relax.

Let's open our mouth, wide and full, on AHHH, hold the sound as long as possible.
AHHHH
Now breathe again and find the balance and harmony, in the ground, and of course, we can tone another sound.

This time for our heart, the Sound goes UHHHH, very mild and long, we can tone this once more, UUHHHH and there you connect to your heart and now let's embrace the smile, let's connect to our head with HUMMMM, long and gently, sound HUMMMMM.
These three sounds, AHHH, UHHH, HUMMM are the essential building blocks of life.

Like a tree has a seed, that's the AAH, it also has a stem, that's the UHH, and of course, it has a crown and that's the HUMMM. All together these three sounds AUM give the primal sound, a wonderful attraction.

Sometimes, a lot of flowers are coming from a tree, sometimes, the tree dances in the wind to find expression, and sometimes the fruits of a tree are growing from just a little seed.

One seed has all the information a tree needs to live on for thousands of years, and even in the nights, the trees are growing upwards and downwards, isn't that interesting?
As all the beings, like the trees, are part of this world, we are also growing in the night, yet, we have to be sure, that we are relaxed and ready for the upcoming night. Therefore the trees prepared a nice soothing song for the upcoming good night.
It is again, around that time, where everything sets, from the shine, of the sun, to the son, of a kingdom divine. Please, enjoy the moment, and breathe, like we are here together to live.

Enjoy the moment and breathe, The air comes in and out, there is so much doubt,
But leave it all behind,
Be sure and one shall find,
That there is more to the dark,
That there is always a spark,
That ignites the wisdom of life.
Even though we respect the light,
We know, it must be night, Whenever we are in sight,
we arrange to be alright,
With a song, that goes all night long.
Sing it and feel it in the breath.
Sing it and feel it in the air,
Breathe and be enjoying the now. Everything is in care, just trust, just trust. There is no more, do‘s or must.

Just relax and keep the breath, Feel the peace and the ease.

Root yourself to the ground,
And hear the beautiful sound.
It is the air, in the space,
Now imagine a face,
Let it be kind and smile,
Hold it on for a while,
Enjoy the sight,

attracting the night

A moment we listen to the trees, we are also listening to our selves, conscious and wise, we are all rooted on the same earth.
Be kind and bring your friends, to this wonderful kingdom of peace and harmony. Enjoy every bit of it.

Attracting Trust Meditation

Find a comfortable seat, bringing your whole body into balance between earth and sky. You can sit or lay on the ground in a comfortable place. Watch your breath coming equally in and out. Working with the breath is the one fundamental trust, as we live, we breathe.

Come to terms with your body, come to ease, settle, there is nothing to fear, relax, with a voice that is guiding you into meditation.

Just trust the breathing as it is coming and going, gently notice the breath and be aware of the sensation of the breath entering the nostrils and leaving them again.

Equally in and out again, breathe and be aware of how it comes into your nose tip, into your body and your heart.

Here in the heart, the breath is home. The beloved invites the lover and everything comes home. One can notice there is awareness in the breath which is bringing us home into the body and the heart.

We notice every part of the body, from the heart to the belly, to the spine, to the shoulders and head, and even to the tippy toes. Feel how the heart is opening and the chest is widening. Here in the heart is where the eternal spark of light resides.

Breathe out all you are letting go of and receive all you breathe in. One can make up a thought, we are letting go, and we can make up a thought that we receive, therefore we can inhale I Am Trust, and exhale all that we are not. Breathe, in I am Trust and breathe out again. Continue and know that the thought and words travel with the breath, into your heart.

Find peace and relax the body, coming to a state of trust and harmony.

With every single breath, one is becoming lighter and lighter. I am Light travels with the breath and comes into every cell of the body. The whole body is now very light and even so light it starts to float and lifting of the ground, just with the help of the breath.

The body is so light and trusting the body floats into the space of Trust, the whole body is now fully in a space of trust and peace. Feel the ease, the small breeze from the air entering the nose and coming to the heart.

In our imagination we can see a nice tender space where we can land again for good care, like in a flower field, full of moss and soft ground, landing there it feels like we are home in a space of trust and balance.

Feel the balance of the breath, equally inhaling and exhaling, as the thoughts arise we can just notice them like we notice the leaves dancing in the wind.

See the beautiful wind playing with the trees, also these trees are giving us shelter and equanimity, just trust and find a nice space close to that tree.

The trees are holding up the earth and likewise, we can hold trust within us, just steady and always growing up towards the sky.

Embrace nature and feel the rhythm of the breath, find the heart and maybe there is a friend who likes to join us.
Do you have a friend you like to play with? Invite this friend with a smile into the garden within the heart.

This friend is appearing with also a smile greeting us dearly and giving us a glance of gratitude and compassion. Trust is our friend and we have the happy community of someone who knows the way.
Let's sit and listen to the spring source that is coming down the stream, the subtle element makes us clear and the friend smiles again.

To trust means to have full faith in goodness.

Whatever will be, everything turns out just for a reason. Therefore always be thankful and happy for all the little things. Even watch the flowers who are so happily growing on the field providing nectar for the bees, and see the trees?
Do they ever complain? Still and steady they hold on for days and days on end, especially when there is a good friend. Walking along the small stream, the water is crystal clear and there is a fish or two within the river that flows into the lake of consciousness.
One can sit on the lake and watch the eagle birds glide and hover for good. Effortless the wind is holding them in space and every face is enjoying the fresh breeze, nothing better than this.

The eagle glides in a circular motion upwards without any flaps and the beauty of the moment seems to last forever, light and kind, the trust is in the air, who else should care? There is the lovely friend, the family, or maybe the brother or sister and when everyone you know comes together, then it is time for a nice festivity.
On the lake, there is much to see, as some great mountains are erected on the vast horizon giving us a glimpse of majesty, the royal throne of the earth's surface, and up above there thrones the sun within the space.
All elements give a nice picture and the community plays music, or just enjoys the peaceful, trusting moment of harmony and whenever there is a light there can be equanimity.
Finding a reflection in the lake, one can see a mirror face of the wonderful surface, within this endless space.
Holding the moment of trust, even when there is no doubt, no lack and desire to be somewhere else, that is balance and trust.

Giving a hand to someone, and see there is a smile that illuminates the world, that is trust. Even together or just being alone, that is trust. Know to be content even when there is a surprising event, like a dancing tree.
Without any fault, everything finds a place on this earthly surface, even the rain. All come the same, yet we trust and have everything we need. A shelter is right there. But behold, there is a light within the hut, there might be someone in there. All in care, just trust and see, everything is in divine harmony.
'Knock, knock someone there? 'The door opens and it is our favourite teacher, simply waving with a hand, smiling and inviting into his land. A shelter of hope and peace, just trust and feel the ease.
Warm and cosy it shall be, yes there is a certain equanimity. A stove heats the water for tea and the smell of wood is right with thee. How come we are also all living this dream collectively?
Life is miraculous and wonderful as sometimes unexplainably we just trust and see the magic unfold within the matter of the now, breathing and opening our hearts for the chance of goodness, one shall receive the mercy of the light.

' I have no fright, as I know it is forever and alright. Life as it is, the spirit shall go on and on.'
The tea boils and one can maybe feel a little of that spirit of life, being timeless and eternal, forever lasting like the connecting of the friends and family. Whatever shall be, shall be.
In the future we trust in Peace, Love and Unity, knowing everything is in divine harmony. Breathe equally.
Notice the subtle sensation of the thoughts and the breath coming to terms with the light, knowing everything shall be alright. The perfect harmony is here, within the heart of everyone.
The flowers and the trees, the friends and families all together like to live in harmonies. All are the same in their goal to come back home.
Where the heart is there is bliss, and all longing to never miss a chance of meeting someone new, just trust and what we will do? Smile and breathe, greet as a friend always and forever one to be.
Then, all shall be happy.

Within the whole body, there is now the light of trust spreading and we can know that all living entities are seeking the same light of trust, and trust is everywhere and there and within the heart. Like there is air within the space there is love for all in the face of a smiling heart.
We are all a part of this world. Even when the sun sets for a goodbye it shall still shine, let's embrace the stillness of the lake one more time and see the setting suns face shining for a good night over the hills and within the heart, all we are a part.

This space is here and now for us to feel, from the tippy-toes to the head, to the chest and all around the nose, with the jaw and around the neck, the arms, shoulders and hands are relaxed, as well as the fingertips and the lips, the jaw and the neck.
The whole body is filled with lightness and trust, as we breathe there is no must, but we can do, whatever there is to do! We can also trust! Where there is no must, just let be, and feel free to also renounce and come back home to the premises of the body where the soul finds its heart.
There, everything is a start and we begin to breathe.

Be aware of the breath and let it flow naturally, just be aware of the body and relax from the head to the toes. The sunshine is now all gone, yet one can see the reflection within the sky, that is coming in beautiful colours and o 'wonder why we deserve to be blessed. Of course, because we trust.
Let's adjust the body to find a comfortable way, of trusting our close ones every day, maybe invite them for a dream with the heart-full space of trust, giving oneself to the best.
Give thanks and appreciation to the best ones close by, and be grateful for every single breath, as it comes naturally, we give thanks to nature accordingly.
All the appreciation to the world family.
May all beings be happy and live in equanimity.
Now, close the eyes and see yourself, just sitting in a nice tranquil state of equilibrium. This beautiful light of love surrounds you, and here you can take shelter, with all the joy and gratitude.
Maybe now, you can see yourself from head to toe, from toe to head, and again from head to toe. Nice light surrounds you and helps you to grow.

As the sun shines we all need light to grow, for a moment we can see our friends and family within this world. With light and growth. Smile and greet all the known faces.
Be aware again of the heart and be aware of the breath. This is your shelter, and only you know the truth within your heart, so does every person know the truth within their hearts.
Let the truth shine, and just relax, as a smooth chant can help purify and prepare for the night.

I am the Light of the World,
I am the Light of the World,
I am, I am, I am the Light of the World.
You are the Light of the World,
You are the Light of the World,
You are, you are, you are the Light of the World.
We are the Light of the World,
We are the Light of the World,
We are, we are, we are the Light of the World.

Be happy and smile

Imagine there is a light, a beautiful light, that shines from within
your heart. It is so bright and beautiful, it's around your whole body.
Breathe and feel the lightness throughout the whole body. See that light expanding with every breath. In and out, the breathing is equal and natural, the light expands and surrounds even the aura around you.
From within your heart there shines the source of this light and with every breath, we illuminate our whole body, from the head, one can see the head glowing in a beautiful protective light, to the feet. With every breath, the light travels throughout the body.
We start from the crown of our head, there is a light slowly sinking into the face. We breathe and with every breath, the light sinks lower and lower into the area of the eyes. Our eyes and all the muscles around the eyes are illuminated with protective, healing light.

Just focus on the breathing and let the light sink into the ears, the cheeks and the jaw. All the little tissues and membranes are equally illuminated, around the nose, on the jaw, and inside of the head, where the nose meets the mouth. We focus on this point, where the nose meets the mouth and sense our breathing. We can even hear the breath coming in and going out again. It is a constant stream of energy that comes with the air, and the sound is clear and soothing.
One can find comfort in the sound of the breath and know there is a light, a life protection from within and around us.
The Life Breath is everyone's mandatory need and we can connect with this friend our whole life. It is always there for us. Let's breathe again and feel how mandatory and friendly the life air is.

See the focus where the nose and mouth meet. and sense the air coming into the nostrils and going out again. It is a constant Hello, Breath. Goodbye Breath. Always and ever coming and going. We are just witnessing this process, this endless stream and ensure everything is smooth and equal.
Equally in and out again, the protective light shines within our whole head and a feeling of peace and protection spreads around the face. We can smile and ease into the breath. Maybe sigh or yawn, whatever feels now fine with you.
Also note any sensation, whatever it is, warmth, cold, vibrating, tickling, throbbing, pulsing, any sensation is possible, and whatever comes, we keep on breathing.
We see the breath travelling into our nostrils and down the throat into the lungs. From our head and our heart the protective light also illuminates the throat and neck area.

Along the spine, the protective light shines in every cell from the head, to the throat, to the middle of the body.

Here the light sinks further down with the breath and we include as many parts as possible, like the shoulders and arms, elbows, wrists and hands.

All are surrounded by protective light. We can open our hands to the sky and see how the light illuminates now every cell, even the fingertips.

Let's put our hands into our middle, onto the belly and feel into the body. Protective light is spreading from the hands and the heart into the belly and around the whole lower body.

The healing light of protection expands and brings peace and ease.
We breathe and with every breath, the light sinks further down the spine, from the belly to the hips, into the root of the spine.

Here we relax and find that the healing light of protection is welcome to also illuminate our thighs, knees, legs, ankles and feet. The healing light of protection even shines into the smallest parts of the tippy toes and brings peace and relaxation.

From the tippy toes we can come upwards, according to our breath we can travel with the awareness, the light of protection up the legs, to the bottom of the spine and again, slowly up the spine to the heart. Here, in the heart, we hold this healing light of protection and let it blossom like a flower.

With every breath, each pedal of this wonderful flower of light expands from the heart and shines throughout the whole body.

The whole flower of light is now really beautiful and blossoming. We can imagine we are meeting a friend, and we can bring this flower as a present to the heart of this friend. Let’s smile and innerly say: Here, this is the light of my heart, may it protect and bring you peace.

You can repeat this prayer and see your friend kindly accepting it.
Here, this is the flower of my heart, may it protect and bring you peace.
Here, this is the flower of my heart, may it protect and bring you peace.

Here, this is the flower of my heart, may it protect and bring you peace.

By saying this we give meaning to the flower and the light, therefore one knows what this light intends to do.

Protection and Peace is now upon us and we can see the whole body of ours and our friend be illuminated.
By breathing we uphold the light, by breathing we maintain the luminosity.

Whenever we are in a hurry, we can also call this protective light and ask for a healing light of protection. Please Light, Protect me, and give me shelter of Peace.
The healing light is like the breathing always with us, when we are aware of it, it comes into presence.

In our imagination let's wander around our home and in the garden to maintain this healing light. Just breathe and feel the connection to the sunlight.
See how the light of protection and the sunlight are the same.
See the trees and the grass, and know all this is grown from the sunlight, one with the light of protection.

See the sky and the endless horizon and know, your inner voice can always call for the light of protection.

May All beings be in protection and Peace, May All find relaxation and ease.

May All have a life of light and love. May All live in Peace and Harmony, May All join the Unity.

This attractive light can bring us from the unsafe shores of darkness to the beautiful shores of the light kingdom.
Find yourself comfortable and relaxed, you are now safe and in protection.

Self-Confidence Meditation Story

There is a space within the universe where we are all safe and sound. It is the heart of the Absolute Truth, the well-wisher of all beings, as it is the location of the Highest Truth, the one living there is the creator of this universe, with many names and faces, this person gives us shelter in form of a forest flower.

This forest flower is the protection that sits within everyone's heart.
This story my Father always told me, the son Samatura says, smiling and having a glance into the sky, but where is security in the outside world? When I feel insecure, what can I do?

Samatura is now not a little child anymore, he can think and be aware, of certainty and uncertainty. Like us, he knows, there are dangers in the world, but he is brave enough to live a life.
He breathes through and follows the river into the forest where his teacher is situated. 'Sandapa will know, he is a wise man and contributes to the wellbeing of all his disciples and students, but he is more encouraged to share his message of self-aware and peaceful living in this world.

The question of Samatura still roams in his head, where there is confidence in me, there also must be confidence within everyone.
Let's prepare to meet Sandapa, who usually sits under a tree in the forest and writes his scriptures and ancient texts. He is living in the forest for his whole life and never had any fight. Living in security and peace he teaches this message for
everyone, especially for the Son of the Kingdom who one day will remain in a position to lead the kingdom to many more generations.

Sandapa awaits the young disciple and son of the Kingdom with a smile. He is very lean and tall, with bright eyes and tender cheeks, his hair is white and he sits under a tree.
I see you are walking alone from the kingdom, do you think you are free? Bring a friend to come along with you, therefore security will come true. Sandapa grins and knows all the questions by his disciple. Yet, he invites him to sit for a meditation and we all can join.
Let's find a comfortable position, where we are aligning with the ground and with the sky.
Come to ease in that position and gently close your eyes. Let it be like a window opening for the holy altar.
There, on this altar, you see many beautiful deities and pictures of saints, like great masters and mystical beings.

See yourself sitting in this holy place and find ease, watching the candle lights and smelling attractive flowers, so fragrant and nice, the whole room is filled with joy and happiness. It is secure and safe, therefore we don't have to worry about anything. Just breathe, equally in and out, see the air flowing in regularly, and constant, and see it flowing out, regular and constant.

One is safe, to be breathing means to be in the security of life. Here in the body, we are safe, here in the sacred room we are safe, here with a guide and teacher we are safe. Feel the shelter and open your heart, like a lotus flower. Let this lotus flower bloom and see every petal of this lotus flower adjust to the light.

The light shines from your heart and illuminates the room, the petals of the lotus flower open and one is surrounded by this lotus flower light.
Did you know, that lotus flowers even grow in the deepest swamps, where there is hardly pure water and light? Yet, the lotus flower remains unspoiled and graceful in-midst this nature.

Let's go for a soothing and mild walk down the forest lane to find a swamp with many lotuses. There we see the trees opening up a way for Us, the alley leads straight to a little muddy swamp, where we find a wooden floor. Let's wait here and see the flowers in the distance.
With shimmering silver and purple, the petals of the lotuses surround the yellow golden middle, the stigma. It is a splendid wonder to look at, but how can the lotus flower feel safe in this swamp, so dark and moist?

It is a wonderful question, let's explore the answer and ask the Lotus flower, Sandapa smiles and plugs a lotus flower, which he will offer to the sacred altar in the room. He knows the answer already but he promises us to bring this lotus flower into a safe place, where he gives it to the other offerings like fruits and milk to the deities.
While we return, the Lotus flower starts to speak and gives us many interesting answers to our questions.

In a subtle and clear voice the purple-golden Lotus says:
'I am all attractive, beautiful and kind, as the sunlight comes, I open up. I trust, the sunlight is my benefactor bringing grace and growth.'

As the Lotus explains the ways to come to a place of security we share a human place of security we call home, this home is the place where we find community and joy in the things we do,
together with our loved ones, we live here, work, study and find attraction naturally.

Samatura is obliged and puts this beautiful lotus flower on his head, ‘I will bring this back to my father, so I can tell him everything about attraction, what I learnt today with you. Thank you, kindly accept my humble obeisances.’ Samatura bows in reverence and walks on with a lotus flower on his head.

In a beautiful kingdom, that longed to be at peace,
We can explore and walk around the forest at ease. There also is a teacher and when we kindly ask, please.
Give us an answer to our questions, bring us release,
The teacher may illuminate the darkness into light.
As long as there is no fight, we are alright.
Let’s enjoy this little bit of life, feel and shine bright.
Even, when we have to say goodbye the day and hello to the night.

As always the day ends, in every wonderful kingdom, and eventually, there comes the night. In this Kingdom, it is a tradition to have a safe and sound ceremony, with oil lamps, and a concert. Beautiful and serene at the same time, the students of Sandapa, as well as the Son of the King, Samatura, are joining the good night ceremony with lights and chants. Samatura chants:
May all beings be at peace, May all beings find their ease, Shall all live in harmony, Peace, Love and Unity.

The trees are watching the stars, the birds are tweeting their songs, together with the stars that illuminate the night, today there shines a special light, it is a full moon show, with special honour to all the Mothers and Teachers.

There, Mother Nature becomes a special thanks and appreciation, there also all the teachers are handed wonderful flower garlands and presents for their service.
All fits together under the beautiful night sky, the mild wind blows into the trees and makes the leaves start to dance.
There is a chance we see Mataja making a sacred fire, one can sit and see the sacred procession of incense and milk, with flowers and oil lamps, we can also see the holy rivers and streams, that are being honoured and everyone from the kingdom joins together in harmony.
We feel safe and sound on this night.

We can breathe balance and attraction. With every inhale there comes balance and with every exhale we let go of the uncertainty. We inhale attraction and let go of uncertainty with the exhale. Breathe and feel the balance coming to you, and the uncertainty leaving you, more and more we relax and find space to smile.

Let's be happy and celebrate life as it is. Even on this night, there is certainty, tomorrow the sun will rise, as always, we give thanks to our Mothers and Teachers that help us on our path and we thank Mother Earth for Life.

This Lotus flower shines in the most wonderful colours and protects us. The light reaches every part of the body, every cell and we see ourselves in this light, engulfed and surrounded with a healing light of attraction.

Put your palms together and feel the harmony and attraction. Feel good and let the breathing be natural. Like a lotus flower, you can now open your hands and bring them to your lotus eyes. Surround your eyes with the healing energy of the hands and let your eyes bathe in the palms of your hands.

Breathe, equally in and out. Breathe, just naturally.
Maybe sigh, or massage your head, around the eyes and your jaw to feel fine. All is now safe and sound, with a smile we are ready for a good, good night.

Attracting Joy and Satisfaction Meditation

Start again. Breathe in and Breathe out. Watch the Flow and Feel the Sensation of the natural breath. If you cannot feel, slightly hard breathe intentionally and let it flow again. Watch the flow and feel satisfaction. One is Alive with the Breath. No breath, no life. Breathe and be at ease. Gently smile. Every Breath is another try for a good life. Make every breath count and be aware of the sensations.

Whatever comes, goes. All we fail, all the misery may come and go.

All the goodwill may come and go.

We are not perfect, we are still learning. Remind yourself of great dissatisfaction and remember to forgive yourself. Forgive and Receive the power to try again. Now Breathe in, Breathe out. Breathe satisfaction and forgiveness. Repeat for a while. Feel content and start again, try with a new insight and resolution. Dissolve with forgiveness, nurture with joy. Breathe joy, let go and forgive. Breathe in satisfaction and breathe out forgiveness. Now, remember yourself, with a second chance, to better, to come out of misery and failure, with goodwill. We are not perfect, but we can try our best.

Just see yourself as you are. See yourself as you are. Breathe in and out, equally in and equally out. Just feel. Bring your palms together and bow.

Observing joy in the world

Start to observe. The whole world in your breath. All the life that breathes is alive. Even the small pieces and parcels, even the plants and trees, even the bees and butterflies, even the animals, humans, all beings alike. All breathing, all alive. Just breathe, be with joy, breathe out. Let it flow. See yourself in a joyful glow of shining golden light. With every breathing expanding. Expand your light from the inside out, from the core to the universe. Breathe. Joy travels with the breath, so see all the beings with this golden light of joy, even in the smallest particle, see the light boundlessly expanding into the world, into the universe. Meet the sun, joyfully shining the light onto the world. See all the world connected to that light and observe yourself in this joyful light. Breathe into this light and be aware of every sensation. Be aware of the natural flow of the breathing. In and out. Every breath connects us to the world, to every being. All the joy is with us, glowing in a beautiful golden light. See the sun, see the joy, observe yourself and be aware of the balanced breath. In and out, observe, equally in and out. See your family, watch them happily be. Set yourself free and smile. With all the joy, all the happiness. May all the joy and happiness surround me.

Breathe. Enjoy.

May all the Joy surround me.

Palms together, in front of the chest, let the thumbs touch the heart. May all the joy surround me.

Bow.

Cultivating joy

Be aware of your natural flow of respiration. The natural breath. Life. Coming in and going out. Whatever comes, it goes. Even love and joy, come and go. Breathe all the joy, let it flow out into the world. See all the beings within a golden light of joy. Let this golden stream be and find the joy inside. What is making me joyful now? What brings me lasting joy? Finding the core, finding the peace and harmony. First we still the mind by breathing. Joy, with the matter of happiness and lightness coming from that source. Stillness. Awareness. Happiness. Breathing in, stillness comes, breathing out, restlessness goes. Ease in and naturally breathe. Let it flow. Let all the joy come and let it go. Thoughts may come, thoughts may go. Keep a balanced mind and find joy within this equanimity. Find peace and harmony from the ease of breathing. Life is there. Breath opens the gates to joy. See it open and observe the joy as it is. Observe and be aware of the natural flow. Feel it sinking in, into the heart, into the root. Now breathe deeply into the root, into the ground, to cultivate to nature the soil of joy. Breathe with all the attention and love. See your breathing moving to the root, feel the bottom of the belly and be aware of the heart. Silence yourself. Rest.

Cultivating satisfaction

Connecting with the feeling of fulfilment and contentment that does exist within you Breathe through. Like a big sigh, a relief, a liberation. A sigh of freedom. Imagine yourself on the peak of a mountain, totally liberated and free. Breathe the fresh air of fulfilment and be. Content you sit there and just breathe. See yourself just right there on the top, breathing and satisfied. Nothing to do, endless possibility. Just be and feel. Content and fulfilled. At peace. Just breathe. Bring your awareness to the natural flow of respiration and breathe every moment full of satisfaction. See yourself grow a smile of contentment and feel a sensation of peace. Breathe. Equally in and out. By breathing a feeling we cultivate the feeling. Within every cell of the body, feel the contentment and satisfaction. All the body is at peace. From the head to the feet. From feet to head.

Breathe and let the satisfaction wander along the body. From the head along the spine to the bottom, below to the feet. Let the feeling of contentment wander from the feet to the thighs to the buttocks. Along the spine up to the chest area, to the shoulders and neck. All fulfilled, all satisfied, flowing to the very peak of the head and the face. We breathe and create space. With every breathing satisfaction comes and goes. We keep the natural flow. Balance yourself. Relax

Joyful affirmations

This is a mantra meditation. The joyful affirmations can be repeated silently in your head or spoken out loud. Try to connect with the meaning behind the words.

May All the Joy be with All
May all the love be with all
May all the happiness be with all Love, Peace & Harmony
May all the Joy be with Us
May all the love be with Us
May all the happiness be with us. Love, Peace & Harmony
May all the Joy be with You
May all the Love be with you
May all the happiness be with you Love, Peace & Harmony
May all the Joy be with me
May all the love be with me
May all the happiness be with me Love, Peace & Harmony
I am the Joy of the World
I am the joy of the world
I am I am the joy of the world
You are the joy of the world You are the joy of the world

You are, you are, you are the joy of the world
We are the joy of the world
We are the joy of the world
We are, we are, we are, the joy of the world.
Love, Joy and Harmony Peace in Unity Satisfaction
Love Attraction
Joy and Harmony, Peace in Unity Satisfaction

<u>Affirmations to attract life satisfaction</u>

This meditation takes the form of a mantra. You can repeat the affirmations silently inside your mind or out loud if you prefer. Allow yourself to really feel the words and let them resonate.
Repeat each fresh phrase like a Kirtan, call and response.
I am satisfied with all there is, Nothing more, nothing less, Balance in equanimity,
Feel Peace and Harmony.
I am satisfied with you, Content and true, Here and Now,
I take a bow
Silence in my mind, Love in my heart,
We are all a part
Of a wonder world, From the breath, From east to the west, I Live to try the best.
I affirm to be content Here and Now,
With All there is
On the way to bliss,
I bow, Balance is now

Silence in my mind, Love in my heart,
We are all a part,
Of this moment world, A Moment to Moment, Breathe and feel, Peace, Love and Unity I affirm Harmony Within all there is,
I am bliss,
I am Balance,
I am equanimity,
Peace, love and unity.
I meditate upon the Wholeness,
Balance for everyone,
Peace for everyone,
Love for everyone,
Unity for everyone,
Harmony for everyone,
Bliss for everyone

I meditate upon the Highest Absolute, May you be merciful with Us,
May we serve for the highest good of all, May we All live in Peace and Harmony. Love and Unity,
Here and Now,
I bow.
Namaste

Meditation for Abundance

Be in balance. Body and mind, breathe in and out. Equally in, equally out. Let there be space with every breath. Let there be freedom with every in & exhalation. Let it flow, like the abundant river we know. The source comes from within. Endlessly, tirelessly. Springing from the Self-fulfilment comes naturally. Peace, Love & Harmony all come naturally from within. Breathe. Equally in and out. See and observe your whole body.
From the core, a beautiful golden light fulfils your inner space. From the very core to the inner dimension and layers of all you are. Layer by layer every part of your body is flooded with shining golden light. From the core spreading to the skin, from the head to the toes. The whole body is illuminated with a beautiful golden glow fulfilling all there is. Now, Peace, Love and Harmony is with you. Now joy flows through every vein. Now satisfaction may be with you, too. Flowing through every part of your body. From Toe to Head and along the spine. Including your Back, including the heart, back to the head, to the face and the nostrils. Focus on the part below the nostrils, and observe the natural flow coming and going. Be aware of the natural breath. The natural flow of respiration. Observe that stream and see it coming in and going out. Equally in an equally out. Balance yourself and feel equanimity. Relax and rest.

Abundant Contentment

Just breathe. Observe and watch the natural breath as it is. Be aware of every sensation and know the balance within you. Feel the balance and equanimity within. Breathe equally in, equally out.

We see ourselves sitting in peace, right here, right now. See yourself in every situation that hosts contentment. May it be on a walk through your favourite part of the world. May it be a nice conversation with a loved one. May it be a chance to be in absolute serenity. Whatever it is, see yourself content, fulfilled and at peace. Rest in that image for a while and observe your breathing. Be aware of the sensation of the breath moving in and out, be aware of the image of yourself in contentment. Find yourself in total peace and reflect upon this image. May it be always there with you, whenever you come out of balance, come back to your natural breath and come back to that image of contentment. See yourself, observe yourself, rest in that peacefulness. See yourself within the moment of absolute peace and feel the peace. Just sitting there and breathing. Just being content and at peace.

Bring this image into your daily life, into the natural flow of your day. Include this image of yourself into the rhythm of your way. See how you nurture your inner peace and internal contentment. See yourself within daily life and see yourself content. Simply breathe. Equally in an equally out. Balance yourself and know the natural flow of life as it is. Relax and rest.

Part Four

How to write your own meditations

It is the best practice, writing and manifesting a piece of selflessness. Just pick out a pen, or notepad and write.

Whatever it is, as soon as you let go, it becomes meditative. Stilling the mind comes from the heart, and through writing one expresses the heart, along the arm to the fingertips onto the paper.

Give it a try and benefit from it, a whole life long this practice can bring long lasting attraction, of all the hearts desires.

CPSIA information can be obtained
at www.ICGtesting.com
Printed in the USA
LVHW062037151221
706301LV00008B/195

9 781801 348652